The Music of Counterculture Cinema

ALSO BY MATHEW J. BARTKOWIAK
AND YUYA KIUCHI

Packaging Baseball: How Marketing Embellishes the Cultural Experience (McFarland, 2012)

ALSO OF INTEREST

Soccer Culture in America: Essays on the World's Sport in Red, White and Blue, by Yuya Kiuchi (McFarland, 2014)

Sounds of the Future: Essays on Music in Science Fiction Film, edited by Mathew J. Bartkowiak (McFarland, 2010)

The MC5 and Social Change: A Study in Rock and Revolution, by Mathew J. Bartkowiak (McFarland, 2009)

The Music of Counterculture Cinema
A Critical Study of 1960s and 1970s Soundtracks

MATHEW J. BARTKOWIAK
and
YUYA KIUCHI

McFarland & Company, Inc., Publishers
Jefferson, North Carolina

LIBRARY OF CONGRESS CATALOGUING-IN-PUBLICATION DATA

Bartkowiak, Mathew J., author.
　　The music of counterculture cinema : a critical study of 1960s and 1970s soundtracks / Mathew J. Bartkowiak and Yuya Kiuchi.
　　　p.　cm.
　　Includes bibliographical references and index.

ISBN 978-0-7864-7542-1 (softcover : acid free paper) ∞
ISBN 978-1-4766-2051-0 (ebook)

　　1. Motion picture music—United States—History and criticism 2. Counterculture—United States—History—20th century. 3. United States—History—20th century. I. Kiuchi, Yuya, author. II. Title.

ML2075.B35　2015
781.5'42097309046—dc23　　　　　　　　　　　　　2015018614

BRITISH LIBRARY CATALOGUING DATA ARE AVAILABLE

© 2015 Mathew J. Bartkowiak and Yuya Kiuchi. All rights reserved

No part of this book may be reproduced or transmitted in any form or by any means, electronic or mechanical, including photocopying or recording, or by any information storage and retrieval system, without permission in writing from the publisher.

On the cover: (left to right) Dennis Hopper, Peter Fonda and Luke Askew from the 1969 film *Easy Rider* (Columbia Pictures/Photofest)

Printed in the United States of America

McFarland & Company, Inc., Publishers
　Box 611, Jefferson, North Carolina 28640
　　www.mcfarlandpub.com

To Sara, Ella, and Porter
—Mat

To Nicki
—Yuya

Acknowledgments

Our sincere thanks to the following folks: Country Joe McDonald, Robert Greenwald, Shelia Whitely, Jerry Goldberg, Ruth Elderbrook, Thomas M. Kitts, Lori Petri, Patricia Stuhr, The Marshfield and Lake DuBay Nelsons, Gary Hoppenstand, Ann Larabee, Peter Rollins, Jerry Lippert, Cynthia Miller, the great people at the Margaret Herrick Library, Barb and Dale Bartkowiak, Noriko and Tsuneo Kiuchi, Anna Komanecki, the ENG 277s, the Kruegers, Dr. Obie, and Rod at the Peanut Barrel. And finally, a hearty thanks to the good folks at Bell's, Lagunitas, O'so, ThumbCoast, Ommegang, Blue Heron, Capital, Sam Adams, Anchor, New Glarus, Big Lake Brewing, New Holland, Goose Island, and the Point Brewery for end-of-the-day respites from some heavy days studying ultra-violence, generational discord, and oppression.

Table of Contents

Acknowledgments vi

Introduction 1

1. Framing Utopia: *Monterey Pop* and the Heart of the Counterculture — 7
2. Creating the Downfall: *Gimme Shelter* and the "End" of the Counterculture — 20
3. Searching for the *Real* Times, Baby: *Head* and the Unmaking of the Monkees — 34
4. Love in Counterculture Film: Music's Diplomatic Role in *Harold and Maude* — 47
5. Space Is the Place: *Barbarella* and Hearing the Future — 58
6. Did the Soundtrack Also Blow It?: Using Rock to Capture Counterculture Generational Identity — 71
7. Setting the Escapist Scene with Music: Sex and Comedy in an Exotic World — 83
8. Generational Genocide: Selling Youth Rebellion in Roger Corman's *Gas-s-s-s* — 95
9. African American Artists in Hollywood: Isaac Hayes' Contribution to *Shaft* — 107
10. I'm Watching It for Its Music: *Deep Throat* and Its Soundtrack — 118
11. Challenging Normativity and Pushing Boundaries: *Midnight Cowboy* and Cultural Resistance — 133
12. Ambiguous Meaning of Music: Combining Technology and Music in the Dystopian World of *A Clockwork Orange* — 145

13. Understanding Country Ways: A Talk with Country
    Joe McDonald About Counterculture Film 166
14. Bringing the 1960s to Life: An Interview with Director
    Robert Greenwald 182

Coda 190
Works Cited 193
Index 203

Introduction

The term "counterculture" is a tough one to wrestle with in many ways, even when ascribed to a specific time and place. Defining the 1960s and early 1970s, counterculture in the United States represents a struggle over legacy and meaning in itself. From those seeing a mass amalgamation of interests, perspectives, and goals to those seeing definitive lines of division between factions of this population, the ability to pinpoint and hence study the counterculture can be a consuming one. From these umbrella concerns to smaller concerns of whether to go with "counter-culture" or "counterculture" in referencing the phenomenon, there is much to discuss.

The following chapters will not attempt to corner an absolute definition and a definitive prognosis on legacy. Instead, the book will focus on a myriad of themes connected to the counterculture and its legacy, through a specific lens, an intersection of the debate. There are many arenas in which to measure this time period and a counterculture powerful enough, that it may, in some eyes, appropriate or own the very term itself: on the political stage, out in the streets, within student organizations, in radical groups, on television, at a music festival, on the news, at the end of a joint, at the end of a gun, etc. Here, the focus will be on the intersection of music and film, and its powerful, commercially viable, and *popular* potency in the time period itself and as a cultural, political, and social text since.

Films produced during the 1960s and early 1970s as well as films focusing on those times continue to influence ideological, historical, political, and cultural conceptions of the time and the lasting influences of the countercultural in everyday life. An important part of how those texts have created a narrative of the time and of the counterculture is through their uses of music to tell the story. Though films associated with the "New Hollywood" movement in film, did remain traditional in many senses when it came to scores and soundtracks, many featured more progressive uses of music, including the incorporation of popular music and experimental forms. Music, in documentary and narrative forms, became the focus of the camera's eye itself. It also became a key player or character within the films themselves. One can hardly imagine *Harold and Maude* lacking the voice and direction given by Cat Stevens nor picture Wyatt and Billy the Kid searching for the American Dream without being propelled by the voice of Roger McGuinn or the sound of Steppenwolf.

The counterculture developed, found, and has managed its legacy in the media. Today, a generation later, it is judged by and through mediated forms ... whatever it is. Due to the potency of both music and film in the creation of ideology and perspective, it seemed natural to see how the two fit together to create texts that have (and sometimes have not) helped define major themes and points of identity when it comes to the counterculture. Each chapter thusly will see how a film or a small combination of films speaks to associated themes that have been established, maintained, and connected to the 1960 through 1970s counterculture. Key concerns like sex, authenticity, gender, race, and rebellion come up in these films and each of their messages that they create.

The book begins with a commonly referenced utopian and hopeful point for the counterculture in film: *Monterey Pop*. This usable bookend of a piece is used frequently as a common marker of potential beginnings, with *Gimme Shelter* acting as its other bookend. Like other concert films of the period, music itself and its ability to bring masses together becomes a main focus of the filmmakers looking to capture the ethos of the time. In numerous regards Monterey would establish essential foundations for music festivals to follow; *Monterey Pop* would in many ways establish conventions for concert films to come. Even if the event was not perfect and at times reflected some of the contentions that would be common in festivals to come, if not to the counterculture itself, its hope and naïveté have become its legacy, capturing on camera the sights and sounds of the counterculture of the time.

Gimme Shelter exists at the other side of the shelf, acting as a bookend for the life of not just popular music but of the counterculture itself. The sobering murder of a young man, captured by the camera's eye, became a poignant ending to an event that would help shape its presentation in the film and in the public's consciousness. Only two years after Monterey and merely a few months after Woodstock, a dreary day in December 1969 would become an oft-cited implosion point of a once-promising generational movement. Thanks to the presence of the camera's eye, an event that might have been lost in the narrative of the counterculture became a definitive, shared experience and reference point.

Even though *Woodstock* has also become a de facto referent when it comes to the times, it will be used in this book only as a comparative zenith from which to make sense of the narrative of the life of the counterculture, with

Monterey Pop as a useable cornerstone of hope and *Gimme Shelter* as its death knell. As will be demonstrated, both films and both events had commonalities with Woodstock that complicate their place as definitive bookends, as they have often been wont to do. Situating the two films' places in context to the celebrated, very well documented, and very successfully sold entity known as Woodstock will help to illuminate a narrative progression of the counterculture told in film that allowed for Woodstock to become what it is today.

The narrative is not always an easy one to follow, of course. It makes sense with the diversity and spectrum of counterculture participants, that the progression would not be smooth. The outright confusion, the realities of rebellion, and a demand for authenticity within the counterculture find an interesting battleground in which to negotiate these themes in *Head* featuring the Monkees. A band, regarded by some at the time as "plastic" and antithetical to the true power of young rebellion and authentic expression, wreaked havoc with their existing audiences by interrogating and deconstructing the very labels and concerns that critics had assigned to them. In the film, war, commercialism, marketing, drugs, and various other subjects are taken on through a series of vignettes that push the psychedelic visual, sound, and experience to audiences ranging from teen girls to Timothy Leary.

Next on the docket is an examination of the sexual revolution, where intimacy seemed to still heavily depend upon a vision of young, nubile, and sexually aware (albeit now with the modest veil lifted publicly) women. Free love, for many adherent and casual participants, didn't translate into a story involving a young man falling in love with, much less making love to, an almost octogenarian. *Harold and Maude* ultimately, even with the help of a soundtrack guiding the viewer through the film with emotion and direction, flopped but has existed as a testament to the time, with an important diplomatic link connecting audiences and the film: the soundtrack provided by Cat Stevens. For fans, it may be difficult to imagine the film existing without the soundtrack, as it plays such a key role in helping audiences decode and possibly even accept the narrative set out in front of them. The soundtrack has played an important part in keeping the film alive and audiences directed, even when dealing with a sort of unspeakable taboo. Yet, like many other films, the musical life of the film came together with some happenstance and somewhat late in the process. No matter, though; as part of the final product, it is an entrenched in consumer's minds as an expected part of the complete experience.

The next film dealt with possibly falls more in line with popular conceptions of the sexual revolution. The treatment and presentation of the sounds and the visions of psychedelia play a central role in envisioning the future and the future of free love in *Barbarella*. A campy look into a world devoid of war, it features a protagonist discovering the joys of her sexuality and in the process testing the parameters of gender in the counterculture. As the study suggests, the future featured, for many critics, an all-too-familiar vision of objectification when it comes to women. For others, the film actually speaks to an empowered woman saving the galaxy. How can such a spectrum of insights exist? Some of the responsibility rests with the music that guides us through these new lands. A mixture of peppy lounge music and psychedelic sounds (at times dissonance) speaks to both the contemporary world of women at the time and bespeaks of post-war visions of women as objects versus subjects. Playing a dominant role in the narrative, the film mixes these sonic cues to push the viewer while keeping them comfortably set in established gender norms. For all of the progressiveness associated with the counterculture, many traditional visions of the world continued to exist.

Easy Rider poses an important question about what a counterculture film means when it becomes so popular and iconic in mainstream American culture. The film is one of the first cited by some critics to use "heavy metal" music in its soundtrack. The musical genre, relatively new at the time, was a product of the countercultural era. The lyrics of the songs heard in the movie paint two main characters, Wyatt and Billy, as independent, free-minded, and untraditional. They try not to conform to the social norm by pursuing their own dreams. However, as Wyatt famously states, they blow it. Their eastward quest for the American dream is just another version of one of many American journeys. So the audience is left with the question as it considers the role of countercultural music in a film that became a part of the mainstream: Did the music also blow it by helping the movie turn into just one of many popular, commercially successful movies from the mid–twentieth century, or does it still continue to help the movie be considered "countercultural?" The chapter attempts to show how music is a vehicle with which the movie maintains its original countercultural identity.

The following chapter delves into film and music's ability to take on war. Robert Altman's *M*A*S*H* situates contemporary musical fare such as "Suicide Is Painless" along with Korean War–era popular music from both the United States and abroad. Music provides both juxtaposition and reaffirmation of the severity and cost of war. Like the film's humor, or the troubling depictions of war's costs, music is utilized to transition viewers from the highs and lows of a unit's experiences in a war zone. Becoming a brand of empty signifier, music, much like the action on the screen propels the narrative and its emotional polarities without offering redeeming morals or direction.

Compared to *M*A*S*H*, Roger Corman's *Gas-s-s-s* pushes the viewer through the narrative with clear lines of delineation separating the good and the bad, the hip and the square. Music only better entrenches a narrative meant to win over the "hip" countercultural demographic. There is no mistaking where the viewer is headed and what message to take away from the film. An overt homage to the saying "Don't trust anyone over thirty," *Gas-s-s-s* centers on and celebrates youthful rebellion in all of its commercial glory of the time.

In Gordon Parker's *Shaft*, Isaac Hayes played a significant role making the counterculture period memorable within the special context of the racial politics at the time. In the early 1970s, although it was past the Civil Rights era, the U.S. was highly racially biased. America's largest film producers were not exceptions. Hollywood continued to release films with no or very few African American characters. It was extremely rare to see a black role model. *Shaft* is one of the movies that could have made a change, even though its genre was soon considered as more detrimental than positive because of its perpetuations of African American stereotypes. Contributing the score of the film, Hayes well reflected this period of intricacy and uncertainty. On one level, Hayes portrayed Shaft as a sexual beast. But on the other level, he is shown as a caring and loyal person. He is also a hero who is shown breaking laws. As the third African American to win an Oscar, Hayes' contribution to countercultural concepts of race was immense.

Counterculture, of course, was not just about drugs, rock music, race, or the rise of the youth. It also offered the U.S. a new cultural perspective on sexuality. With *Deep Throat*, many Americans felt comfortable enough to admit to watching a pornographic film. It was a controversial movie. Years and decades following the release of the film, resistance to the film both inside and outside the pornographic industry appeared as media headlines. Aside from these controversies, the movie is unique with its use of preexisting music including Beethoven's Ninth Symphony, original songs for the film, and the sound effects of bubbles, rocket launches, and others. Frequently, lyrics of the soundtrack advance the storyline. They even instruct actors and actresses in the film what to do. Music in the film, for example the last movement of the Ninth Symphony, also challenges viewers to reconsider existing images about particular music.

Some familiar musical tropes also help to guide the dim and dirty world of *Midnight Cowboy* where western and cowboy cues help the audience negotiate a reverse course, looking for the American dream out east instead of out west. It is Harry Nilsson's cover of "Everybody's Talkin'" that highlights the futility of finding a place "where the sun keeps shining." When put together, the totality of the soundtrack provided a stark vision of a cynical point in American history where seemingly little ground had been covered in finding authenticity, utopia, and a place of acceptance for a generation in movement.

Music much more aggressively challenges the listener in the next film taken on: *A Clockwork Orange*. One name that is sure not to strike counterculture associations in the general public is Ludwig Van Beethoven. In the film classical pieces frame an "ultra-violent" dystopian future. Mixed with electronic compositions, classical music is incorporated into use that challenges the viewer to reconsider and reframe familiar pieces into new and sometimes disturbing circumstances. In the process, it challenges the listener to not only contend with the visuals and the narrative, but also to stomach it with works of familiarity in tow.

The last two chapters assist in the project of taking on music in countercultural film by checking in with some of those on the ground and in the nitty-gritty of the film-making experience. First, Country Joe McDonald sits down to discuss his experiences in both documentary and narrative film. From his performances on the stages of Monterey and Woodstock to roles as counterculture Svengalis in films like *Gas-s-s-s* and *Zacharia*, McDonald provides valuable perspective on the true nature of film in taking on music as a part of the film-making experience and in taking on the counterculture as a subject.

Finally, Robert Greenwald speaks about being on the other side of the camera and the utilitarian realities of making music a part of a film. He also assists in helping understand the ways in in which history is framed and sold to a film-going public. The counterculture, like other events in history, has been under the microscope of evaluation and reinterpretation in film. The brief interview with Greenwald reminds us the counterculture—its sound, its vision, its legacy—are an enduring and contested event that shows no sign of slowing in the public's want to claim and manage the meaning of a complex and nuanced entity.

In the end, this project does not assume the responsibility of isolating a single, clear meaning that links these bodies of works in an absolute way. Rather, the aim is to investigate the complex intertwining factors that contributed to this body of work and its enduring legacy. The counterculture, like film, was and is adept at avoiding being pinned into a singular corner of meaning. Yet, the potency of popular culture in creating ideology and historical perspective demands, much like the want to understand the counterculture, how parts to the whole combine to create seemingly uniform entities, easily glossed over on the surface.

1. Framing Utopia: *Monterey Pop* and the Heart of the Counterculture

> *There was a fantastic universal sense that whatever we were doing was* right, *that we were winning....*
> *Our energy would simply* prevail. *There was no point in fighting—on our side or theirs. We had all the momentum; we were riding the crest of a high and beautiful wave.* —Hunter S. Thompson, from *Fear and Loathing in Las Vegas*

Bookends can be quite useful; whether simply holding texts up or clearly defining a zone, an autonomous space for a collection of volumes, bookends order and neatly package the often weighty volumes, perceptions, and arguments they hold up. It seems, in numerous different lights, that we collectively appreciate intangible bookends, too. Historical bookends, for instance, neatly package history and provide starting and ending dates to the narratives of our experiences: Pearl Harbor and Hiroshima and Nagasaki; Yalta and the fall of the Berlin Wall; weapons of mass destruction and "Mission Accomplished." These bookends provide concrete parameters for historical circumstances, even if they sway far from the truth and the reality of the events themselves.

For some time, this process has been exponentially assisted by the presence of the camera's eye. Shared events on the screen like the assassination of John F. Kennedy; seeing the fall of Saigon; watching the Twin Towers fall, along with many other examples, reaffirm a collective experience and framing process. The media, an essential facet of the rise and fall of the counterculture, was used to discern the birth and death dates of the movement. Moments caught by the camera's eye can become collective experiences, and also can easily become bookends within themselves. To be able to *see* the birth, life, and death of something in the media like the counterculture empowers the viewer, giving the viewer a sense of presence and perspective. Of course, with a plethora of potential bookends to harvest from the media, there can also be sharp disagreement as to which one truly represents respective parts of a lifecycle for the concept or idea or movement, etc., taken on.

Monterey Pop (1968) is a text that represents, for some, a sort of organic wellspring of the counterculture that has been engaged as a usable, popular (but far from universal) representation of part of the counterculture's lifecycle. Coupled with *Woodstock* (1970) as a "critical mass" piece (Thurman), and *Gimme Shelter* (1970) as a chronicle of demise, the films are accessible texts that are often given great value as historical, documentary visions. Their ability to capture the counterculture with visuals and sounds abounding creates a neat, linear narrative and usable bookends to contain the life of this complex historical event that can be quite powerful. Thomas M. Kitts in an article dealing with this triad of films offers: "Much of what we know and think about these festivals comes from these films and recordings, which is not unusual as historians and film critics have long noted that Americans have been 'learning' more and more of their history from film" (715). Though not legitimate enough for some, films—especially documentaries—act "as legitimate histories, which is to say, as interpretations of major shaping events in the counterculture [sic] rise and decline in the 1960s" (715). In the process, audiences look for clear markers to cite and situate their interpretations of these historical events: the ability to label such events as good or bad, authentic or inauthentic, etc.

Monterey Pop especially has been used by numerous audiences both at the time of its release and in retrospect to help construct and represent the rise of the counterculture, a potential utopian vision, and often a more authentic expression of the times when compared to other texts. As Dennis Hopper reflected longingly on the festival, "It was a perfect experience. To many of us, it was the first and the last. I can't think of anything as special as that moment in my life," continuing, "We weren't making fun of the cops, either, who were amazed by it. It was a magical, pure moment in time" (Kubernik and Kubernik 232). Its connection to the Summer of Love helped establish a usable and visual mark in time for the counterculture. Chuck Thurman argued in a piece for the *Monterey County Weekly* that "Woodstock illustrated the peace-love-dope movement as it reached critical mass. But Monterey Pop showed us a generation bathed in idealism as it was born." Keeping such frames in mind, it can be argued that *Monterey Pop* acts as a beginning bookend. *Gimme Shelter* acts as the other bookend framing the counterculture, with *Woodstock* acting as a bridge from which to understand how these smaller-scale films compared to a musical, filmic, and historical behemoth. According to David Cotner of *L.A. Weekly*, *Monterey Pop* became a text that conveniently captures "those halcyon days of that loving summer," adding, "no one could have dreamed what was going to happen later" (Cotner).

Hence, the *next* chapter will look at *Gimme Shelter* with an eye on *Woodstock* and how these films have become reference points for the decline of the counterculture into dystopia. The triad of these festival films possesses a great power to situate and explore our history. It is essential that we look at it them as we would any other argument: a construction of ideas and thoughts meant to persuade and frame historical events that are sometimes assembled haphazardly, sometimes choreographed meticulously with hindsight in mind, and sometimes done with a combination of the two.

Formalizing the Summer of Love

Many popular accounts of Monterey attach an ethos of romanticism and authenticity that is echoed but not quite recreated in the same way when critics take on the latter two festivals in the triad. Monterey was not the first popular music festival of the time, but when compared to folk, jazz, and other festivals of the time, the sound and visions captured by the camera (in color) established some new standards in film and music. The Monterey International Pop Festival was as much "peace, love, and flowers" (an operating mantra at the event) as Woodstock, but it also faced challenges in the process. In the film, a few moments of attention are paid to the business of getting the festival together. Scott McKenzie's rendition of "San Francisco (Be Sure to Wear Flowers in Your Hair)" guides the viewer through a montage of moments leading up to the concert. After, in the arguably most utilitarian moment shown of the planning process, John Phillips, situated in a busy office, asks to speak with Dionne Warwick, who would eventually be one of the advertised acts (and who would eventually cancel due to a booking conflict). Much more went on behind the scenes semantically that brought Monterey together. These efforts and events were very much important in setting the tone for Monterey and assisting in framing the event as a utopian happening.

The original concept that eventually became the festival began as a for-profit initiative by promoters Ben Shapiro and Alan Pariser (Kubernik and Kubernik 12–14). The halo of authenticity descended upon the event shortly thereafter when Shapiro and his controlling ownership were bought out by a small team of buyers that included producer Lou Adler and John Phillips (of The Mamas and the Papas). The idea was to bring together groups that would frame pop music as a legitimate art form for a mass audience. All profits would go to the newly established Monterey International Pop Festival

Foundation. Groups agreed to play for free in exchange for national exposure (thanks to the cameras and a deal with ABC television) and "first-class travel and accommodations" ("The Big Idea"). The new blood essentially turned it into a charitable event focused on demonstrating the validity of popular music being considered art, aiming it at an immediate audience at the event itself and eventually to a much larger mass public via a planned television special.

Profits from ticket sales and television rights to ABC (ABC would eventually reject the footage, allowing for a feature release) went into the foundation to fund "music-related personal development, creativity, and mental and physical health" ("Foundation"). The fact that it was done for charity (though *Rolling Stone* would call the event an ego trip for Phillips and Adler) (qtd. in Thurman) helped to greatly create an aesthetic akin to rising countercultural values of authenticity, freedom, communitas, and rebellion against societal norms. As will be discussed shortly, such feelings were far from universal, but nonetheless these values would become the dominant and lasting themes in the historical situating of the event in American popular culture.

As Pennebaker attests: "One of the secrets of Monterey was that Lou and John Phillips took the money off the table. I knew they were hatching a real interesting game. Which was, from the beginning, *get rid of the money*. That was the big thing. Get rid of the money. And I could see that that was gonna make it work. It was a very Zen thing." According to Art Garfunkel, a performer at Monterey, this sent a message to those in attendance and one may suppose for audiences to follow: "The idea that the kids were going to know that we were doing this for the music's sake, that it wasn't a commercial endeavor—that was the essence of the show" (Kubernik and Kubernik 24, 26). Especially when compared to Woodstock, demand for authenticity and purity would be met with more poignancy, at least in the ways in which the event and film have continued to be framed for mass audiences in the media.

The idea of a countercultural baby-boomer utopian experience was furthered in promotional materials for the concert. One pamphlet offered: "Be happy, be free; wear flowers, bring bells—have a festival." The same pamphlet featured utopian reassurances of safety and detailed planning. It addressed the following: housing: "No problem.... More than 3000 hotel and motel units are available"; clothes: "Dress as wild as you choose. But remember that it's sometimes cool in the evenings. Maybe you should bring a blanket and sunglasses"; seating: "A matchless hi-fi sound system means that everyone in the new 7000-seat main arena can hear equally well"; transportation: "situated five minutes from airline, bus and train depots"; and made a statement that Monterey should be considered "EVERYONE'S FESTIVAL—Bring the family" (Kubernik and Kubernik 43).

An Eye on History: The Festival and the Film

Monterey, by most accounts, was a testament to the Summer of Love. Little violence, few medical issues, etc., plagued the event. The festival provided an important showcase for both established artists like The Mamas and the Papas as well as for up and coming acts like Big Brother and the Holding Company and the Jimi Hendrix Experience. Moments of perceived peace and transcendence, such as the ecstatic crescendo and response to Ravi Shankar's performance, packaged the possibilities of the Summer of Love, in all of its romanticism on celluloid.

The "peace crowd," as Otis Redding would refer to the audience at his performance at Monterey, lived up to their name on the national stage that was created for them. As Kitts argues, "Pennebaker develops and preserves the image of the festival as a peaceful and free-spirited phenomenon" where "everything at Monterey appears to run very smoothly and with little intervention from festival staffers or police officers" (716). Lou Adler recalls, "The Monterey Police Department had their own security, and the numbers employed were overkill the first day because, in Chief Marinello's mind, the hippies and the Hell's Angels were the same. However, their numbers were lessened dramatically after the first day of 'music, love, and flowers'" (qtd. in Kubernik and Kubernik 11). For a community and police force prepared for the presence of some troublemakers and for a strain on local services and supplies, peace reigned supreme.

Part of the general peace was thanks to a reported moratorium on arrests for marijuana usage and possession from Chief Frank Marinello (Thurman). The head of the police department was cited as saying the following to his officers: "We're not going to bust anybody unless they are out of hand or out of line.... This is going to be a love-in" (qtd. in Kubernik and Kubernik 158–159). The same kind of utopian possibility of a self-sustaining and respectful community also became part of the Woodstock lore. Pushing aside bad trips, the measure of possible success or failure of the events became closely tied and gauged to any reported levels of violence or trouble. This same focus would come into play at Altamont.

Pennebaker's film reaffirms these perspectives on the safety and fluidity of the event. Any dissonance created by the opening credits and its use of the initially accosting "Combination of the Two" is quickly resolved with Scott McKenzie's "San Francisco (Be Sure to Wear Flowers in Your Hair)" shortly thereafter. The montage that the song is played over presents an idyllic community of smiles, decorations, dancing, and even an amicable exchange between attendees and the police, the hip and the establishment sharing a laugh.

A group of security officers are shown entering the event. The concern shared by the authorities about the Hell's Angels, Black Panthers, and the sheer number of people coming are reflected in these establishing shots. It is left to the music throughout, as is the case with "Creeque Alley" to pull the viewer back into the peaceful realities and good behavior of the "love crowd." Lou Adler is even seen joking with an officer, playfully pretending to take his hat and badge. Shots featuring the Hell's Angels frame them as docile and well-behaved.

In essence, the narrative leaves behind any sense of confrontation in favor of a focus on the music and the good-natured crowd. It was, as Chuck Thurman wrote, "a never-repeated example of two generations working in harmony, even if they didn't understand one another." If any violence is to be had, it came in the safe confines of the stage where The Who and Jimi Hendrix provided a sharp juxtaposition with their destruction of instruments to acts like The Mamas and the Papas and Simon & Garfunkel. The stage and the performers occupying it throughout the three days are the dominant focus of the film with both utopian messages of love and expressions of unbridled rebellion. The sight of Hendrix sacrificing his guitar to the gods and Pete Townshend's efforts to bring an end to his guitar (and anything else within reach) was demonstrably enough to shock the audience, but the borders were neat, and save for those in the first few rows avoiding the rock and roll shrapnel, generally safe.

The incorporation of so many established acts as well as acts that would become canonical voices of the counterculture and the times offered a plethora of material to try to fit into the film. The acts featured, in many cases, became definitive voices of the time and the zeitgeist. The movement in its infancy, with the debutante, Janis Joplin, and the debut of Britain's sensational American export, Jimi Hendrix, spoke to a new era in popular music history, cementing the sound of the still emerging countercultural world. In Adler's mind, the event and ultimately the film's legacy are wrapped in this packaging of the sound of the times:

> Monterey was about the music—Woodstock was about the weather. Not many people remember the music that came out of Woodstock. They talk about the rain and the amount of people. Just the fact that it was East Coast and the sheer numbers is why it's talked about. But when anyone wants to talk about the music that was created during that period or the iconic groups that came out of it, they were at Monterey. Some also performed at Woodstock but not with the impact they had at Monterey [qtd. in Lacher].

There is naturally room for disagreement in Adler's diagnosis when discussing the legacy of the event and the life cycle of the counterculture itself. At the very least, some agreement might be found in saying that the event framed the counterculture, the baby boom generation, and the associated sounds of the times in a convenient, usable frame (for good or for ill). As *Big Picture Magazine* explained to its readers, the festival "has since come to embody the counterculture associated with the infamous 'Summer of Love,' and inspired a number of similar events, including the Woodstock Festival of 1969" ("One Sheet" 22). The film, as documenter, through the camera's eye, did bring music and image together into a text readily usable for those looking for Thompson's previously mentioned "momentum."

Associated ascriptions of romanticism, utopianism, are also joined by authenticity. Authenticity in the music, in the film, in the event, etc., are all aspects that assist in helping the event and the film maintain a place of prominence in the continued framing of the counterculture as a historical event and occurrence. The business, filming, and sound of the festival would become a mass-distributed text establishing various essential formulaic lines of vision when it came to filming the counterculture, hearing the counterculture, and determining the role of the music festival and film in the life of the counterculture.

As a well-documented text of the Summer of Love, the film orients the viewer into thinking they are seeing an untouched, unsullied, virginal countercultural utopia. Penelope Gilliatt, in the *New Yorker*, reflected upon the release of the film in this way: "When the film was shot, a lot of bad ground for America hadn't yet been travelled." Later, she adds: "In its way, it records the fact that the root of the great rising was in the mass possession of a gentler-natured idea of how to live," continuing, "It summons up not Chicago but the lunch counters."

The inclusion of Otis Redding in the festival and film drives this latter claim well, in that as Andrew Loog Oldham states, Redding was able to "amaze" the crowd: "We all saw the possibilities. You have to remember we were still not long past there being 'negro cinemas' in all of your major Southern towns, and the attitude, the racism, had kept on going" (Kubernik and Kubernik 30). Music was looked to as a force of change and challenge to the times ... a utopian idea of possibility and hope to create change on the stage and in the generation taking it all in. For those that would complain that not enough of the zeitgeist was captured due to the focus on the music in the film vs. the event in its entirety, the music became to some audiences the movement in itself.

The music/event itself has been regarded by some as a snapshot of purity at a time before commercialization was seen to have bastardized the music and life of the counterculture. Pennebaker in the 1980s pined, "The world is not quite so innocent now. Everyone would want a half million to appear. The big record companies would get involved. In the 1960s, rock was on much smaller labels" (Byrge). Moments of clarity and definitive experience were demanded by audiences that believed in the capability for true expression before cooptation by a suspected industry that, in their eyes, ruined the experiment. The regard for the zeitgeist of the Summer of Love wasn't universal, however. For example, Pete Townshend of The Who didn't find an overwhelming sense of possibility in the Summer of Love springing forth on the West Coast: "It was sad to go see the Haight-Ashbury, which was already very, very commercial." Later he gives a sense of context claiming Bill Graham was a "rock" in the middle of the scene and that "without him, all these airheads would fall to *bits*" (qtd. in Graham and Greenfield 190). Sentiments such as those expressed by Townshend tend to be ignored thanks to the march of popular culture's ability to frame the times in neater, mass-disseminated packages.

Robert Christgau explains in an article for the *Village Voice*, "Unveiled in 1968, Pennebaker's vision of the 1967 event was instrumental in convincing potential organizers and participants that music was the healthiest way to crystallize the energy of a counterculture that by then seemed both blessedly inevitable and dangerously embattled" (Christgau). A foundational collective text, *Monterey Pop* continues to act as a key demonstrative and readily usable text of the counterculture's adolescence and bright-eyed view of tomorrow. Still, some of the utopian sheen can be scraped away when looking at the seemingly smooth waters of musical collectivism and harmony displayed and often referred to in retrospectives of the event and the film.

The event itself reflected some suspicion and animosity from a few participants directed at what they saw as the corrupting influences of big business and commercialism. As mentioned, the event was for charity and was curated, according to Lou Adler, to feature the "growing sophistication and creativity" of the pop community, entrenching it as an art form meant to stay. Considering individuals like Adler and John Phillips "slick—too slick," several within the San Francisco scene drew a line in the California sand, agreeing to participate only after Ralph Gleason, a revered journalist with the *San Francisco Chronicle*, "gave his blessing to the festival, as did [concert impresario] Bill Graham" (Kubernik and Kubernik 11). Andrew Loog Oldham, an important figure himself in organizing the event, called the San Francisco scene a "little cauldron of insurrection" which he later states created "an underlying tension in this whole thing that was part of this culture war" (qtd. in Kubernik and Kubernik 31).

These suspicions of L.A. scene players among some of the San Francisco acts reverberated and showed itself quite forcefully in both the planning and implementation process. The Grateful Dead famously, for instance, are cited by Andrew Loog Oldham as having stolen equipment after their set. Jann Wenner, founder and editor-in-chief of *Rolling Stone*, admits, "It was prejudice, pure and simple. We assumed what we were doing was authentic, not part of the commercial machine" (Kubernik and Kubernik 33). Along with the Grateful Dead and their management, Julius Karpen, manager of the Big Brother and the Holding Company, had his own run-in with the perceived commercialism of the event. Karpen refused to let Big Brother and the Holding Company be filmed. He feared that they would lose artistic control and were bowing to the commerciality of Pennebaker's TV special and later film. The band would perform regardless of Karpen's concerns about being filmed and soon were on their way to national fame and significant record sales (Kubernik and Kubernik 94–95).

Lou Adler agreed the rift was palpable in a *Los Angeles Times* retrospective article in 1997: "San Francisco's bands had learned their trade at psychedelic street festivals, and concerts at the Fillmore Auditorium and Avalon Ballroom. They were suspicious of anything from L.A., and it didn't help that John and I had recently produced Scott McKenzie's hit, 'San Francisco (Be Sure to Wear Flowers in Your Hair)'" (Adler). The festival, a suspect gathering for many of the San Francisco acts, ironically, of course, gave many of the Bay Area bands their launch into stardom on a national stage first, and into theaters across the country later. Even in a perceived utopia, humanity found a way to rear its ugly head at times. The camera's eye has had much to do with how the event has been experienced and remembered as a collective cultural and historical event. Such bits and pieces, much like the Dead's frustrations at Monterey, have generally been left behind thanks to the definitive sights and sounds captured by Pennebaker and company, silenced in the framing of an event, a sound, a vision, and a time.

Much like the musical base of the event, the filming and framing of the concert was also met with some dismissal. From the initial cry of "sellout" by the Grateful Dead's co-manager Danny Rifkin when it came to dealing with broadcast rights for ABC to the film's release (Kubernik and Kubernik 34), a common undercurrent of debate concerning legitimacy and authenticity pervades public discussions of the film and the legacy of the event itself. As in retrospectives, initial reviews also inherently tie the event to the life, health, and prognosis of the counterculture and the 1960s as a cultural, political, social, and historical text.

To some, these things did not mesh that well. For instance, in *Life*, the true heavenly vision of Monterey was compromised by Pennebaker's want for the film to "play like putting on a record. The record never talked to you. It just played for you" (Kubernik and Kubernik 214). Richard Schickel laments that "Pennebaker and his huge crew utterly failed to probe into the spirit animating both the festival itself and pop music in general." What is offered does not encompass "the atmosphere in Monterey during what I am told was a beautiful weekend, socially and psychologically as well as musically" (Schickel).

Pennebaker and Christgau's focus on the potency of the music as an expression of the time was not enough for Schickel nor *Time*, where the following was written: "But Pennebaker ultimately lets down the present as well as posterity by refusing to probe any deeper than the onstage details" ("Drawbacks"). Charles Champlin of the *LA Times* echoed these sentiments in measuring the film's historical and cultural validity in capturing the "spirit": "Yet there is much less of an attempt to catch the whole underlying spirit of the event than there was in 'Festival,' last year's examination (at last deeply moving) of some Newport Folk Festivals." Other reviews seemed a bit more conflicted in deeming the film a proper time capsule of the time and the festival. Dale Munroe in the *LA Herald-Examiner* opened his piece by stating that the film had captured "much of the music—if not the sprit—of the festival" and then later pines that the film "delivers a timely sampling of modern rock" but "only a meager conception of what it was like to be a participant at the Monterey International Pop Festival."

Between filming in 1967 (and the subsequent rejection of the shot footage as a television special for ABC) and the film's release, as has been mentioned, much changed. Even if there was a sense of too limited of a view of the event by some, the film was generally celebrated and much of it was due to its ability to act as a time capsule of what the counterculture was in its halcyon days, seemingly the opposite of what some critics first thought that saw the film falling short. Dan Pasley of *Boston After Dark* wrote in 1969, "The film although slightly dated is carried by its authenticity" ("'Pop' Goes"). By the time of the film's release, it had become a valuable time capsule, containing a powerful (even if to some, too musical) look at a quickly changing and increasingly hopeless and cynical counterculture. For instance, promotional materials for the film frequently make use of a quote from the *San Francisco Examiner* that stated: "The 1967 Monterey International Pop Festival was a legend. Now the festival is a legend everyone can share." *Life* manages to make it on promo materials as well with the following: "D.A. Pennebaker's 'Monterey Pop' is one of the truly invaluable artifacts of our era. It is full of remarkable sights and sounds, some ridiculous, some sublime" (*Monterey Pop* Promotional Materials).

Fast-forwarding a few decades, most criticisms of the film have faded in favor of retrospective pieces that frequently push *Monterey Pop* as a somewhat lost artifact that speaks precisely about the utopian-focused counterculture. Compared to the overshadowing figure of Woodstock, the film speaks to some kind of innocence. The fact that Monterey has lived in the shadow of *Woodstock* in film and in American history tends to drive these familiar themes home, now retrospectively. Lou Adler himself reflects in the *Los Angeles Times*,

> It was a generation's coming out party, more than two years before Woodstock.... Millions of us came to feel a part of something bigger, with a collective sense of destiny and oneness. It couldn't last, and it didn't. But the music remains. And memories of the Monterey Pop Festival and the Summer of Love forever capture the energy, optimism and aspirations of a generation.

Sources that have taken on reviewing and situating VHS, DVD, Blu-Ray and connected vinyl, cassette, CD, and MP3 releases of *Monterey Pop* echo familiar themes. In an issue of the *Hollywood Reporter* in 2002, it is claimed that "Monterey the rock festival still stands in the shadows of the bigger and gaudier Woodstock, but 'Monterey Pop' the film has no rival as a time capsule of late '60s rock" ("Monterey Pop" 17).

It is intriguing to think of such a usable space from which to find an identity for a generation, for films to come, and for similar events, all in one packaged and relatively quiet expanse of three days in 1967. Thankfully, for those invested, the cameras were rolling, and bringing an eye to an event that may have been otherwise shadowed or lost in popular culture and American history. As stated in a blurb in *GQ*, "At the time, *Monterey Pop* helped turn the 1967 Monterey Pop Festival into a mythic event" (Carson 74): mythic not only as an event within itself, but also as a utilitarian marker to isolate the birth of a generational counterculture about to explode in often less innocent means and representations.

Some of this usability in the literature reflects upon the place and potency of music within the counterculture. Where some reviews are capable of separating the music from the culture, others squarely place music as a central organizing force in bringing the Summer of Love and the counterculture itself about. Complaints targeting the supposed inability of Pennebaker to capture the feel of the event have been largely pushed aside. The mythic event that Pennebaker captured, especially compared to the formality and production of the Woodstock film (not to mention its momentous size), now situates itself as a wellspring of authenticity for a massive collective audience.

The fact that the film has taken on such a foundational place in counterculture film history is a bit of miracle that Pennebaker himself calls "an amazing display of luck." Pennebaker's crew consisted of himself and five other people "who were friends and who were totally into the music." Richard Leacock and Pennebaker, according to Pennebaker, were the only card-carrying union members on the shoot, with the others, like Albert Maysles, there on Pennebaker's invitation. Additionally, little formula was set up for filming as Pennebaker "had never seen a music festival at all, not even Newport" (Kubernik and Kubernik 214, 216). With Owsley Stanley's Monterey Purple strain of LSD flowing through the veins of some of the filmmakers (and audience members and musicians, too), the door was open for interpretation.

In *Woodstock: Three Days That Rocked the World* it is contended that "the Monterey International Pop Music Festival (to give it its official title) was the first cultural manifestation of the 'alternative society' that reached its zenith two years later in Max Yasgur's field at Bethel, New York" (Evan and Kingsbury 30). The ability to refer to Woodstock as a "zenith" has been any easy thing for many to do, thanks to its consuming presence (when compared to Monterey Pop) in international popular culture, born on the back of an immensely profitable film and soundtrack chronicling this "zenith."

By 1969, the rock concert festival became much more formalized and standardized, built in many ways on the example of Monterey. As stated in Evan and Kingsbury, *Monterey Pop* "established the precedent of seeing the cinematic possibilities of such events and influenced the subsequent Woodstock movie" (30). In fact, an eye on the filmic experience was an essential component in the planning process itself, being one of several final consumable Woodstock products that were in the promoters' minds in the planning process. Of course, Woodstock also differed from Monterey in that it was initially to be a for-profit festival. Money and location issues affected the latter festival in the planning stages that had not been seen at Monterey Pop. Also, unlike Monterey, crowd issues quickly surfaced as the "hundreds of thousands more than anticipated or planned for" showed up for the festival, creating food shortages and sanitary issues. Still, the challenges that came in dealing with local authorities; setting a stage and lighting; film rights; questions of authenticity; and a never-ending attempt to create definitive meaning of the event, are all shared commonalities that unite Monterey, Woodstock, and Altamont.

Of course, as witnessed, the event was not perfect, no matter how much audiences may want it to be in retrospect. Regardless, the filmed event has endured as convenient, colorful, and usable bookend for witnessing the blossoming of the counterculture of the time in the United States. Whether seen through threats to hold anti-concerts, as the Dead's co-manager Danny Rifkin did in the planning stages (Kubernik and Kubernik 34), or being "bombarded by many a last-minute crisis (e.g., the renegade chemist Augustus Owsley Stanley III distributed free 'Monterey Purple' LSD)" (Adler), the innocence of the event has clearly overtaken negative ascriptions. Acting as a wellspring of countercultural hope and promise, *Monterey Pop* has packaged a common vision of a complex movement functioning within a complex time.

In the next chapter, the other side of the bookend will be established with more of Woodstock discussed, but now in the context of understanding the use and legacy of *Gimme Shelter* and the fallout from Altamont Speedway.

Popular culture has done a pretty effective job in pushing *Woodstock* as a zenith of the counterculture and thusly sharing utopian ideals with *Monterey Pop*. *Gimme Shelter* operates as the clearest form of discord, just as Monterey has come to represent a utopian birth of a media-friendly counterculture. The films chronicling these events and their ability to frame music as a cultural and potentially political force (as well as the associated choices of what to include and what to leave out) created commercial films *and* de facto historical documents that continue to frame and make sense of the 1960s counterculture.

2. Creating the Downfall: *Gimme Shelter* and the "End" of the Counterculture

> *Altamont, with its violent Hell's Angels and murder, became the embodiment of the death of the 60s dream.*—Alexis Petridis
>
> *Mick Jagger and the Rolling Stones attracted a throng estimated at 400,000 to the Altamont Speedway and, in the space of a few hours, deep-sixed the spirit of their generation.*—A.E. Hotchner

The release of *Gimme Shelter* (1970) defined the end of the 1960s, the end of the baby boomers' sense of innocence, and the end of the counterculture, or so it goes in the annals of popular culture history. Reflecting the end of the 1960s makes sense, as the concert, which the film documented, occurred in December 1969. It literally was the end of the 1960s and it makes sense to affix such a grandiose claim. *Gimme Shelter*'s examination of the concert at Altamont, instead of being a definitive text of the degeneration of a generation, is a vibrantly alive petri dish from which to examine the intricacies and contradictions of the counterculture, as well as acting as a testing ground for the potentialities and interactions of music, film, and social change. Though it functions as a convenient frame for many, representing the end of the counterculture, it may prove fruitful to refine the thesis a bit more. The film should shoulder only the lighter burden of being a moment of shared popular culture that did not kill the movement, but did show that one arm, popular music and its stars, could not accomplish the goal of solely leading the charge to a new utopia.

The film does not represent an absolute historical document but is instead an interpretation of a chaotic coming together of diverse influences and interests. Frankly, no more innocence than the innocence we are all prone to mislay in any kind of mass gathering was lost. Still the film is a ready-made package for those attempting to neatly put a bow on the package called "the counterculture" in America. With its focus on the event, the business of rock, and the audience, the film could be argued to be an important early testament to the fact that music should not be at the helm, steering, if the counterculture was to continue to exist. That being said, it was one of many important passages in the journey and life of the counterculture. The ability for the camera's eye to capture the events at Altamont and to present it as a narrative reinforces the ways in which film and music were and have been used as markers of a movement.

For better or worse, these creations and moments become useable media-ready fence posts for our collective memory, even if they may unjustly carry the benefits or burdens of history. A case in point: Rolling Stones biographer A.E. Hotchner's states:

> The Sixties Generation came to an abrupt, tragic end on December 9, 1969, on a desolate, barren field in Livermore, California, with the Rolling Stones presiding over the demise. What had started out, a decade earlier, as a surge of idealistic, carefree young people dedicated to a liberal romanticism and an aggressive idealism, ended up ugly, brutal and bloody, a Hieronymus Bosch madness accompanied by the impotent entreaties of a frustrated Mick Jagger [17].

The rhetoric here represents the pervasive power brought through media-based frames. The film, much like other frames, acts as a guide, assisting audiences "'to locate, perceive, identify, and label' occurrences with their life space and the world at large" (Benford and Snow 614). This process of framing and creating a linear narrative of the counterculture in the case of *Gimme Shelter* occurs thanks to film's ability to abbreviate, as Benford and Snow would contest, "aspects of the 'world out there,' but in ways that are 'intended to mobilize potential adherents and constituents, to garner bystander support, and demobilize antagonists'" (614). This process of condensing seems also to apply to the perceived degeneration of the counterculture. A vast array of perspectives and use values were present at the speedway that day. Pushing this diversity into one mass being, whose head (the only discernible part of the body for so much of the film) was composed of a small number of people within the halo of the stage lights, provided the means to create a "definitive" vision, and a de facto historical document for public use for decades to come. *Gimme Shelter* then, is a possible pan-ultimate text of conveniently framing the downfall of a complex entity which possesses numerous levels of identity and signification. The film provides useful media-friendly borders for such a large and complex social and political occurrence such as the rise and fall of the counterculture. The claims by Hotchner reflect a neatly-packaged frame that omits the continuous challenging of the counterculture and its identity within the mass media throughout its life, supposed death, and its carefully, continuously shaped legacy, thanks to the presence of the camera's eye(s). Documentary films like *Monterey Pop*, *Woodstock*, and feature films like *Fear and Loathing in Las Vegas*, and *One Flew Over the Cuckoo's Nest* maintain positions as accessible markers that inform, for better or for worse, conceptions and views of history, ideology, and meaning for the social movement called the counterculture. In combination with significant events caught by the camera's eye elsewhere, such as the assassination of John F. Kennedy or the evacuation of Americans from Saigon in 1975, these images and sounds become collectively owned and burned into the consciousness. Their potency comes in our ability to share in these common images and sounds, finding comfort in definitive narratives, and the prospect of feeling as if we have all collectively experienced these moments together. Combining the visual with the potency of music of the time made for some strong and affecting arguments. At the time, the music, like film, to many, was a commonly used frame in terms of bringing forth individuals' perceptions of the counterculture. It was also an easily identifiable and mass mediated scapegoat when things went wrong. In the end the question should be asked: How responsible was music in culminating the vision of the counterculture? What was the counterculture and how do the filmmakers wish to portray this and how does it interact with music at the time? To begin this examination some background on music festivals themselves and Altamont should be discussed. The violence and confusion at Altamont were not isolated affairs or an island of bad vibes in an ocean of peace, love, and music.

Instead, throughout the 1950s and 1960s music festivals had established a penchant for death, rebellion, violence, and drug and alcohol use. Burt Goldblatt, for instance, in his chronicling of the Newport Jazz Festival, cites a rich history of alcohol consumption and youth violence over the years. In 1954 the *Providence Bulletin* cited beer tents at the festival, run by the Kiwanis organization, as selling beer to "one and all" (67). The 1957 festival was fueled by sales of up to 2,000 bottles of beer an hour, resulting in numerous "battle causalities" of "revelers who were bent on getting their jazz kicks in a physical way" (67). Beer sales were also a factor in the 1959 festival, resulting in "wild-drinking, brawling, and 24-hour reveling." The debauchery at Newport culminated in 1960 when an estimated crowd of 12,000 youth rioted in the streets, and the National Guard was deployed to contend with the situation (82–83). Festivals saw a plethora of violence and disarray elsewhere throughout the 1960s as well. At a music festival that took place in Denver, "fighting between bikers and would-be gate-crashers and enthusiastic troops of club-wielding, tear-gassing, Mace-spraying police officers had turned an otherwise excellent three-day gathering into a bitter battlefield" (Goldblatt 44). In California at another festival 300 people including fifteen police officers and youth as young as fourteen were injured in rioting and "another 75 had been placed under arrest, about half of them on charges of assault with a deadly weapon against a police officer." The Street Racers, a biker gang, had been hired as security for the affair (Marshall, Wolman, and Hopkins 56). *Rolling Stone*, seeing the realities of the festival scene, issued the call in 1969 for festivalgoers to prepare for a "Bummer this Summer. Festival? Be festive and be hopeful, but also beware" (Marshall, Wolman, and Hopkins 47).

Held that same summer that the warning in *Rolling Stone* was heeded, the Woodstock Festival was relatively peaceful compared to some of these previous examples discussed. However, the event was far from utopian; *The New York Times* reported after the event that there had been "at least two deaths," three drug users left in critical condition and "4,000 people treated for injuries, illness and adverse drug reactions over the festival's three-day period" (Colliler A1). A significant portion of medical treatment administered was for the "adverse drug reactions." Greil Marcus in his *Woodstock* reminds the reader that "several thousand" among the total population "left in disgust, oppressed by water shortages and ninety-degree heat and ninety-nine percent humidity and the crush of bodies" (14). Marcus also encourages the reader to recall that: "Dreadful scenes of death and fear were part of the price of three days of peace and music—they will be forgotten, but they were real and they too were part of the festival at White Lake" (16). Like Altamont, changes of venue, use of drugs such as mescaline and LSD (sometimes by those that had never tried the substances before), and a lack of facilities and supplies, created annoyances for many and tragedy for an unfortunate few when looking at the crowds gathered at both locations. Negative remarks about Woodstock, like one concertgoer's perspective that "I love all these people." "They're all beautiful, and I never thought I'd be hassled by so many beautiful people," were historically overwhelmingly lost as a universal, single ethos was sought, so that the public could collectively start making sense of the events, regardless of one's presence or absence (16).

Hence, if the parameters of tragedy and failure that continue to surround Altamont as the great killer of the 1960s are looked at practically, it would seem that the 1960s could have died as early as 1954 and reoccurred countless times throughout the 1960s. Less to blame on organic expressions of idealism, the violence of Altamont and many of these other gatherings was due to poor planning, at times greed, and the commingling of hundreds of thousands of temperaments, personalities, chemicals, and experiences. Within the film, these themes are established heartily in allowing the camera's eye to lazily rest on scenes where planning and development are in process.

Gimme Shelter, perhaps because of its outcome, is able to feature these scenes in elongated detail. The focus on planning allows for a fascinating glimpse into the preparatory stages of a major festival, especially through the film's focus on Melvin Belli, an attorney who represented Jack Ruby and during the filming of the scenes within the film was actively involved in the Manson murder trial (Norman 382). One can see a flurry of activity as deals are made to harness a viable location. The viewer is put into the cacophony of a busy office and its urgent tones.

The original location of Filmways' Sears Point (Golden Gate Park was not available due to the refusal of the necessary permits) was nixed after Filmways demanded the film rights and "three million dollars for cleaning, three million dollars for insurance" (Russell 164). It was at this point that Belli was brought into the fray, retained by Mick Jagger (Norman 382). Charity was to be the "official" beneficiary, but economic interest did not end there. The promise of a "Woodstock of the West" could bring in a great deal of money in capturing the event on camera and on tape. Sensing a good promotional event himself for his newly acquired race track, Dick Carter offered Altamont Speedway.

The move from the Sears Point location to Altamont showcased the haphazard methodology occurring between the location owners, lawyers, and band representatives. In an article marking the 37th anniversary of Altamont, Peter Howell comments that "Jagger and company may have been foolish and arrogant to think they could pull off a party for 350,000 on a cold winter night without due regard for such human necessities as food, sanitation, medicine and police security. But they had the Woodstock miracle of just a few months earlier to guide them." At the same time though Howell balances such sentiment with, "You can't put 350,000 people together in adverse circumstances and expect them all to get along, no matter how much peace, love and understanding you profess to have. Woodstock had summer warmth and months of planning behind it; Altamont had neither" (E01). Of course, Woodstock, as discussed, faced its own planning issues and weather-related havoc, but Altamont seems to retain these themes prolifically in public memory also.

Unlike *Woodstock, Gimme Shelter* captures on film the legal and economic bargaining session where the plans were hastily put together. Altamont is shown as not being based upon the hope for a communal gathering. This distinction needs to be made as the "lemmings" that are referred to in Belli's office are not having a community built for them through music, but are having a large scale marketing and media event constructed around their "spontaneous gathering." The legal frameworks and monetary negotiations that are part of any large scale gathering, whether free or not, found a place of significance in the film due to the unfortunate outcome of the event. Perhaps if the outcome had not involved a murder on film, this process may have been dealt with more in the tradition of *Monterey Pop* or *Woodstock*, as a more benign undertaking compared to the event itself.

The unfolding of the rest of the film leads to the unleashing of the "Woodstock of the West." As would be soon surmised by the filmmakers, the groups, and the crowd, the event was marred with poor parking and traffic quandaries, poor medical and sanitation outlets, and of course, violence. Chip Monck, who had also presided over Woodstock as an emcee, as well as being responsible for the lighting there, described the grim nature of the new location as such, before the concert even occurred: "But when I get to Altamont I see the place hasn't got any toilets. It's got no fencing. It's wide fuckin' open. We're not in a building. We have no security whatsoever. What are we going to do?" Tony Funches, in charge of the Stones' personal security, on a trip out to the site, echoed Monck's concerns and more: "I'm thinking to myself, *These motherfuckers have got to be out of their minds*. My assessment is that it's a complete disaster in the making, so I drop back into fail-safe mode of accomplishing my primary task—making sure that nobody tags the band members" (Russell 170). The potential for disarray and excess abounded even before the first chord was played.

It seemed the only item not in short supply was the immense amount of drugs. Again, this was nothing new to the festival scene. At Woodstock for instance, estimated use of marijuana by the crowd was at 99 percent (Special Correspondent, 25), as well as the aforementioned presence of tainted acid and many other drugs. These substances were present at Altamont along with DMT, mescaline, and alcohol (which was the drug of choice for the Hells Angels at the Altamont debacle). Audio of an interview with Sonny Barger of the Hells Angels is played for Charlie Watts at the beginning of *Gimme Shelter* highlighting the presence of these substances at Altamont. Before we see a single frame of Altamont, Watts, overwhelmed, hears Barger complain of being "used for dupes" by Jagger and the Stones. Besides Jagger, the blame, according to Barger, needs to be placed on people using drugs:

> I am not no peace creep by any sense of the word. You can call them people flower children and this and that. Some of them people was loaded on some drugs that it is just too bad that we wasn't loaded on because they came running off the hill yelling ahhhhhhhh ... and jump on somebody and it wasn't always Angels but when they jumped on an Angel, they got hurt [Maysles].

Barger shares that the draw for the Angels came in the organizers' promise that they could drink beer by the stage. The centrality of drugs and alcohol were a central focus for the filmmakers that, like the violence, was present from the beginning of the narrative. The effects of these substances can be seen especially in pre-performance shots of the crowd as well as in the arena of the stage for the rest of the film.

The confusion brought on by the drugs and by the realities of planning such an event did not leave much room for the filmmakers to comprehensively present a linear picture of the counterculture (not that they were aiming to do so). Still, critics would be able to ascribe the collective death of the counterculture to the event thanks to the camera's eye being present and framing the event. Instead of being a unique representation of the counterculture and utopian ideals, the film and the event itself points out the inherent complexities of defining the counterculture. It was more than drugs; it was more than the music. Perhaps the real death of the counterculture that Altamont and its documentation in *Gimme Shelter* signified was the death of *publicly* viewing music as the key unifying component for the desired revolution. The film exemplifies the real contention of Simon Frith that music is inherently "a commercially made mass music and this must be the starting point for its celebration as well as for its dismissal" (54). One can see in the documentation of the event's planning, as well as within the concert itself, how dependent on the entertainment industry these events were. Very real considerations of adequate parking, film royalties, and liability insurance commingled with the hope of press coverage by the bands, venue owners, and film interests.

In fact, these issues are the predominate focus of the first half of the film. Interspersed with concert footage of the band's earlier tour, an edgy mood is created poignantly mixing filmed reactions of the group to reports following the concert and to the footage taken. The confusion and violence of Altamont is with us from the beginning, joining the viewer throughout the narrative. Momentary escape is offered in those scenes of concert footage from earlier in the 1969 tour, as well as seeing the band doing some daily activities and in the recording studio. The music is constantly interrupted with the developing narrative of bringing Altamont into fruition. These preparations for the concert ominously push towards the anarchic second act of the film.

Compared to earlier cinema vérité efforts like Pennebaker's *Don't Look Back* and *Monterey Pop*, a great deal of attention in *Gimme Shelter* has moved away from the music and has settled on the crowd, a trait also seen in *Woodstock*, though not to such an extent. The music becomes, quite arguably, secondary to the cast of characters developed both behind the scenes and out in the crowd. Bill Wyman, bassist for the Stones, laments the musical output from the '69 tour appears to have fallen off the face of the earth in the wake of the events at Altamont: "The '69 tour was the best tour until then, which gets completely overshadowed by what happened at Altamont. We had Chuck Berry, BB King, Tina Turner, and Terry Reid, a young, upcoming British star. It was a fantastic tour" (Russell 107). Such was not to be the focus of the final product. To not focus the film on the events near the stage, and to not use the murder of Meredith Hunter as the crescendo, would be to ignore what

Pauline Kael would label as the Maysles hitting the "cinema-vérité jackpot" via capturing the discord around the stage, culminating in Merideth Hunter's murder (112). The music was still there, but was metaphorically turned down in the wake of the drama at hand.

What was captured on film as well as what the filmmakers decided to leave on the editing room floor naturally established the dominant narrative of dark foreboding that has so famously stuck with the event, the band, and the film. Such narratives, especially when associated with cinema vérité can lend a comforting hand to those that had not constructed their own narratives from being there that day in December. There are many accounts taken after the show that definitely agree with this narrative, but there are also many that dispel the notion of a natural aura of destruction hanging over the event bookending an entire generation's idealism.

As discussed, those involved in the festival's planning stages like Monck did see a myriad of issues, but some also viewed the great possibility of Altamont as well, a part of the experience that may challenge the narrative or presentation of the events and narrative to a larger audience. Ronnie Schneider, who played an instrumental role in bringing the concert together, discussed that he did not sense an ominous foreboding up to the night before the show:

> The night before the concert was just mystical. There would be three or four of us walking around the land at Altamont and people would come up and follow ... a quiet procession just following us around. It was so nice and laid-back and beautiful, sitting around the campfire, drinking wine, everybody talking. That's why Keith [Richards] decided to stay because it was so fantastic. The night before was beautiful: a great prelude to what we all *thought* was going to happen [Russell 171].

Mick Taylor on the helicopter en route to the venue the next day reinforced the notion of possibility asking, "Have you noticed there's kind of an atmosphere over the whole city like a carnival?" (Booth 352).

Taylor and the other Stones in the film are shown flying towards Altamont Speedway; Taylor's perception was not featured or caught as part of the diegesis. The flight in, opposed to Woodstock's utopian use of "Goin' Up to the Country" shows the band approaching with only mechanical hums and whirs providing the soundtrack. Miles of cars and humanity are flown over through an eerily silent perspective. No promise is offered of a community waiting below. In fact, when the helicopter lands, the Maysles provide an excruciatingly long look into the hell that waited below for the group. Jagger is punched in the face, acid is sold, numerous cases of acid freak-outs are filmed, individuals walk by lost, or bloodied or nude and confused. Such accounts very much agree with some attendees' views of the dystopia of Altamont, especially those near or on the stage. Naturally with the "unpaid cast of thousands" not all experiences were felt the same acute way that confronted the band and those surrounding them (Kael 112). In *The Village Voice* for example, Grover Lewis describes a slightly different diagnosis for the day:

> In the crush of the amphitheater, my friends and I found a place to sit perhaps a quarter of a mile away from the bandstand. I scanned the crowd with zoom-lens binoculars. The sheer magnitude of the gathering was awesome and, as the day progressed, not a little disquieting. In the main, the audience struck me as benign, passive, and unutterably stoned.

Citing a lack of toilets, food, and a water supply, Lewis does find some agreement with the narrative provided in the film when he continues: "But more than once, I had the troubling feeling that if the mammoth crowd was itself capable of feeling anything on a mass gut level, the mass gut immediately devoured its own feeling, swallowed up by its very enormity. It wasn't a good feeling to feel." In hindsight Lewis can definitely place an ill feeling surrounding him, but also admits to a sense of the "benign," a term not used much in reference to Altamont and the crowd that day. With Lewis we see a different experience for an individual a quarter of a mile away from the four-foot-high stage. Other comments in literature concerning the concert such as the Rolling Stones' equipment manager, Bill Belmont's perspective that "the people who weren't near the stage had a good time" (Gleason), challenge the frame definitively provided and the investment in the events of that day in December 1969 that audiences have created thanks to watching the film. This is not to say that the mood may have been ominous or joyless for some, but the point remains that diagnosing the events of that day for 300,000 plus people is a tough project to try to take on through the camera's eye.

The images of the crowd are soon interrupted and somewhat left behind with a new cast of characters: the Hells Angels. Their presence has been cited by some in related literature as replacing the void created by the Stones' policy of no uniformed police in front of the stage at their shows (i.e., see Russell 62). Disagreement ensued on who exactly was responsible (The Grateful Dead, Mick Jagger, etc.). The role that the Angels were supposed to play has also been the subject of debate and discussion. Amid the roar of engines, the Angels enter the narrative with a cut to two pensive individuals and their looks of concern as motorcycles charge. The bikers silence the fractured and confused community, cutting the action off. Later the Angels cut a line through the crowd as night descends, engines roaring again. As Charlie Watts remarked about his experience getting to the stage, "I mean the way they cleared the path was just incredible" (*Gimme*).

The apparently lone theme that unifies the Angels, the drugs, the sex and the violence presented is a general reverence for the gods of rebellion and darlings of the counterculture: the Rolling Stones. The Stones throughout their career in the 1960s firmly established themselves as *the* "bad boys" of rock. What this label meant was not completely communicated by the Stones and seems to have been built up with a multi-faceted usability. Sheila Whiteley argues that the band, among other acts, possessed an image based upon motifs that emphasized "death and/or satanic ritual" (85). At the same time the sexuality of the Stones and their music was also another level of an ethos built upon rebellion. Politically, an aura was fostered thanks to events, for instance, like Jagger's participation in the Grosvenor Square riot, an event that eventually lead to the penning of "Street Fighting Man." As Whiteley states,

> The association of political progressivism and cultural subversion with overt sexuality may well be the reason why the Rolling Stones were acclaimed by the more militant branches of the counter-culture. With the recognition of rock as a means of liberation for the young from adult repressions, the Stones' sexuality was seen as a challenge to the establishment. Their confrontational style equated with sexual freedom, relating strongly to the senses [Whiteley 87].

Being such pied pipers of motifs relating to a generic sense of rebellion and the counterculture, the Stones represented a coming together of the disparate and sometimes contradictory audiences that found promise in music's assertion of subversion, whatever that was going to turn out to be. Not to mention there were inevitably those that were there with little regard or care about the music that day. The idea of a discernable counterculture being in attendance for the "death of the 1960s" becomes muddied with the term "rebellion" at Altamont. How could the Stones be responsible for roughing out the hastily formed pieces of the puzzle from the bottom of a hill, perched on a stage a few feet off the ground?

Perhaps the counterculture could have been cited as being in attendance at Woodstock under the generic guise of the mediated idyllic community. However, when such a large and diverse grouping of people experience the problems that have historically accompanied mass gatherings with only music to lead them, labels of "community" are quickly left by the wayside. In this case, the music, simply put, was not enough to quell the masses into an organic collective. One could see clearly through the Maysles' cameras that a generic gathering under the Stone's marketed sense of subversion and maybe even "counterculture" was not enough to create an alternative community; the idea was pushed asunder in favor of personal paths of subversion and personal experiences for those gathered at the racetrack. What their individual paths were to mean was up to the participants and eventually the audiences watching the events on the screen.

For those invested in the Stones, in the ethos of rebellion, etc., as part of the counterculture, it may still have been difficult for such concertgoers to find others with the exact same conceptualization of counterculture that they were carrying around in their own heads that day. Could it be done through drugs, political change, sex, or biker gangs? The Stones would never say themselves. The crowd was willing to demonstrate their personal interpretations of these investments and ideologies to the camera though. In addition, large throngs of people that did not feel such tugs of rebellion or that did not necessarily find themselves within a "counterculture," would inevitably make for less interesting parts of a narrative in popular culture, for an event eagerly providing an accessible and well-edited take on an enormous gathering.

By focusing so much on the events of the day, the film makes a good case for music's inability to unite a common countercultural community; music is remarkably impotent within the film. The film's first documented performance by the Flying Burrito Brothers portrays the crowd as close to utopian as they were going to get. "Six Days on the Road" plays over shots of audience members blowing bubbles and dancing. As portrayed, the Burritos finish the song and violence breaks out in the crowd with Angels in the center of the disruptions. This sets the stage for the Jefferson Airplane's appearance. Fights involving the Angels policing the stage mar their rendition of "The Other Side of This Life." Marty Balin, the group's lead singer, is punched in the face as Grace Slick repeatedly coos, "Please be quiet." Slick tries then to act as moderator:

> You gotta keep your bodies off each other unless you intend love. People get weird and you need people like the Angels to keep people in line but the Angels ... also, you know you don't bust people in the head for nothing. Both sides are fucking up temporarily ... let's not keep fucking up! [Maysles].

Slick's soliloquy apparently falls on deaf ears as the violence continues. The ineffectiveness of the Airplane, a band that presided over the Monterey Pop Festival and Woodstock, represents the stark reality that music may have lost some of its voice as a natural leader in such mass demonstrations of supposed generational cohesion. The more the camera turned to the audience, the less the music spoke for the framed masses. The loss of musical potency is highlighted even further before the Stones' set by the arrival of the Grateful Dead. A confused and shocked Jerry Garcia and Phil Lesh are briefed on the troubles with the Angels. The only comment Garcia can offer in the film is an "Oh man....really?" The Grateful Dead famously then refused to play following Balin's attack, realizing the possible dangers.

When the film's main protagonists, the Rolling Stones, take the stage with "Sympathy for the Devil," Jagger pleads, "Will you cool out?" and "We don't want to fight ... come on." Spotlights blind the Stones and heads are busted open with weighted pool cues just past the stage. Due to the lack of lighting beyond a certain threshold in the crowd and because of the blinding nature of some lights trained on those on the stage, what was transpiring near the stage was not fully apparent to all of those on it, performing or not. The stage increasingly becomes a cramped, chaotic atmosphere with Hells Angels enveloping the band, speakers toppling off the stage and a dog wandering through the mire. One of the more frightening scenes shows a man apparently experiencing a bad acid trip, fuming, ripping off his jacket, and glaring at Jagger, who is only an arm's reach away. The very real feeling of threat to the band and to those near the stage, within the halo of the stage lights, is palpable. The Maysles put us on stage or looking down on the stage, bringing in the viewing audiences onto the small platform separated only by a few feet to the ground. Keith Richards is made into the authority figure, threatening to stop playing if people did not settle down. Jagger asks the crowd to sit down. Among the pleas and demands from the band, the Angels strip the Stones of their maverick romance with their very real defiance. Like the band members themselves on stage, the music is lost within a confused mass of humanity. Here, Jagger is rendered incredibly small in scale to the realities of drug use, the massive size of the crowd, and the conditions of the day for attendees. Music does not provide a way out of the mire, and the audience is left perplexed as their music gods lose their immediacy and power beyond the spotlight. Vitality is lost when the music is confronted by bad trips and the unwanted actions of a group that was seen as semiotically romantic incarnations of rebellion, the Hells Angels (a group far removed politically at least from traditional notions of the 1960s counterculture).

Opposed to collecting the broad and sometimes disparate goals and uses those individual audience members have when attending a concert event, media has sought to give such massive events a singular voice comprehensible to diverse audiences. Throughout the film, one can see the need for media outlets to frame the event into an understandable context. The viewer can see this occur when the press at numerous points tries to lead organizers and participants in labeling the event as a "Woodstock West." Labels and an official documented narrative are craved as the event unfolds, and naturally are just as demanded in making sense of the wake that the concert has left behind.

Gimme Shelter provides a visual documentation for those seeking to neatly package a broad and disparate movement and an entire generation. This is saddled on the backs of the filmmakers as conveyors of truth through vérité. Such a media frame can successfully create borders in social and cultural movements thanks to the presence of easily understood, orchestrated mixtures of visuals, values, and the music. The Stones, as false idols, and Altamont are the stars of the film; the music simply is not. Instead, semiotic representations of rebellion and the "counterculture" are intertwined into a tangled mess that can easily place the blame of killing the counterculture and the innocence of a generation on The Rolling Stones, on their management, The Hells Angels, or the thousands of individuals taking drugs, or perhaps even the Maysles brothers for capturing the event and establishing a narrative that we all can share in together.

The media and indeed the counterculture (admittedly, the very term being an attempt to group) had an increasingly difficult time framing itself as "the whole world was watching. "*Gimme Shelter* is merely another frame in this process. Like music, film would prove to be a powerful molder of form, intent, vision, and meaning. The events of that day, including the visuals and music captured in the film helped those demanding an absolute meaning of the event and of the times. As Mick Jagger contends, "Of course some people wanted to say Altamont was the end of an era.... People like that are like fashion writers. Perhaps it was the end of *their* era, the end of their ... naiveté" (qtd. in Davis 325). The Maysles actively helped to create this dramatic renderable frame for audiences. Howell describes that some critics also saw an intended frame:

> Chief among the appalled was Pauline Kael of *The New Yorker*, who argued that the violence had been "manufactured for the cinema" and thus the film was not a true documentary. She compared the staging of Altamont for *Gimme Shelter* to the way the Nazis put on the Nuremberg Rally in 1934 "so that Leni Riefenstahl could get the great footage that resulted in *Triumph of the Will*" (E01). The Maysles' dramatic positing of the violence at the beginning of the film gives the audience a dominating theme. Music simply becomes a backdrop to drama that gradually unfolds. As Howell states, "The violence was equally unscripted," but the violence did provide a script from which the filmmakers could work, and from which audiences could find a focus.

Like many others of the time, activist Todd Gitlin, in his experience, found out the power of such frames in shaping public perception. Gitlin states, "I worked in a movement and watched it construed as something quite other than what I thought I was" (17). Instead, "mass mediated images were fixing (in the photographic sense) the terms for internal debate" (31). A generation's challenge to the status quo of the time lived and died by these media frames. These said frames have played and continue to play an intrinsic role in the reception of Altamont and *Gimme Shelter*. The frames allowed the creation of both the pinnacle of countercultural ideals at Woodstock (a film which generally denies the realities of the festival experience that *Gimme Shelter* is required to include) and the nasty underbelly of a movement that felt some legitimacy in its efforts to change the world.

In the end we see the true disconnectedness in this film of rock icons from the hundreds of thousands that came to see them. As a July 1969 *Time* column quoted, "A rock festival is like a football game now. It doesn't have anything to do with the music any more. It's just a scene" ("More Wrong"). Music was shown to not be the autonomous leader of a revolution; though essential, it could not lead the way on its own. When these two worlds—the musician on stage and the audience there to hear them—meet literally beyond the fourth wall of the stage, confusion and disappointment resulted.

Opposed to being the holistic end to a utopian vision, music, like film, must be considered part to a whole in a counterculture that sought both political and cultural change. The constant defining of the movement, as media frames both empowered and castrated the counterculture in its life in the 1960s and into the 1970s, was not to stop in the following decades either. To assign one media frame as the death call for the entirety is to ignore the inherent complexities in how individuals and the media make sense of meaning around them in everyday life. *Gimme Shelter* allows, through a mix of visuals and a distant soundtrack, a revenue-producing frame as a way to seamlessly meld together any differences or contradictions into a general narrative of loss and dis-allusion. In *Gimme Shelter*, it appears as if music itself is one of the casualties of the day, incapable on its own of forming the utopian world so hoped for by audiences worldwide. Rather than following and capturing the complex currents flowing through and around Altamont, the film, thanks to its ability to frame, is much more usable to audiences as a definitive narrative and last nail in the coffin of the counterculture.

3. Searching for the *Real* Times, Baby: *Head* and the Unmaking of the Monkees

There might be some out there that would question why one would discuss the Monkees in context of the counterculture or in respect to a canon of films that are situated prominently in reflecting and perpetuating the concept of the counterculture. What does a group that was formed and sculpted by corporate interest and money have to do with a movement in film that sought to celebrate rebellion, authenticity, and films that would challenge the conventions of Hollywood? Often viewed as a less-than-legitimate or authentic musical and television product of its time, the Monkees didn't quite fit into the demand for the authentic that was so prevalent for those that identified with the counterculture as a movement. Yet, it was exactly this denouncement and interrogation of authenticity into their musical production, especially, that placed their feature film, *Head*, into the ranks of films maintaining some lasting, if at least cult, influence, capable of shaping visions and sounds of how one conceives of the counterculture through film.

This chapter builds upon important and detailed work by authors like Eric Lefcowitz (*The Monkees Tale* and *Monkee Business: The Revolutionary Made-for-TV Band*) and Paul B. Ramaeker ("'You Think They Call Us Plastic Now...,' The Monkees and *Head*") to posit that *Head* has both assured its place as a film *of* the counterculture, and has functioned as a usable historical document for numerous audiences making sense of the life and legacy of the counterculture. This is the case thanks to the discussion of art versus commerce that so many have been caught in when focused on the band and the movement itself. Thanks to their continued legacy, spurred on by a notable comeback in the 1980s, the band has remained an active text and an excellent case study in examining authenticity and rebellion via a multi-mediated product.

By examining briefly the life of *The Monkees* television program, which aired on the National Broadcasting Network (NBC) from 1966 to 1968, and more importantly their jump to film with release of the movie *Head* in 1968, we will see how countercultural values were communicated with the Monkees. Also discussed will be how the group resisted their handlers in the name of claiming authenticity, a key component of espoused countercultural values. Ultimately at the time, the soundtrack, the film, and the Monkees themselves would be left behind amid a narrative of commercial failure and alienation of their teenage base (Lefcowitz, *Monkee Business* 168).

For those dismissing the group or the film, the manufactured Monkees smacked of corporate greed and exploitation. For those fans taking part, many would be disappointed that the film was a far cry from being an elongated episode of the television show that they may have hoped for. As Michael Nesmith stated, "The film was tackling the blurred line between fact and fiction. This fictional band, The Monkees—which never existed and was the construct of a TV show—was coming to life and the machine couldn't handle it and kept trying to put it back in the box" (Watson 30). The group's critics became more entrenched or simply confused. The sights and the sounds to come would be a challenge for many of those that had comfortably invested in the band as a ... band.

In 1964, the nation was in the grip of the British Invasion. British rock, spearheaded by the success of the Beatles, dominated American music charts. Many American recording companies were concerned and were left asking themselves, "How can we regain control?" Richie Unterberger reflects, "In fact, all areas of American music were reeling from the Beatles' takeover, even more so when equally unsuspected hordes of British acts followed them into the U.S. charts throughout 1964. The British Invasion, as it was dubbed (in the UK it had been called the Beat Boom), blindsided the whole business" (66). It was in this want for reclaiming the American charts and sales that the Monkees came into existence.

The mass-market success of the Beatles and especially of *A Hard Day's Night* exposed the incredible selling power of the music and image of a popular music group. Two young producers, Bob Rafelson and Bert Schneider, pitched the idea for a television program that would both be able to exploit the music and image of a band to an American audience as the Beatles had done: now dominating on vinyl, in merchandising and on the screen. They took what they had seen with the Beatles and began auditions for their assembled group. Along with the search for a group, songwriters were hired on for the show as well, given instructions to "make it sound fresh, like early Beatles" ("Pop").

The audition process culminated in the hiring of four predominately unknown individuals: Micky Dolenz, Davy Jones, Michael Nesmith, and Peter Tork. Jones and Dolenz both came from predominately an acting and stage background, while Tork and Nesmith both shared more of a popular music background before the auditions. Nonetheless, the respective backgrounds of each would have little influence on the music in the early life of the Monkees. With the addition of record producer Don Kirshner soon after the debut of the Monkees on NBC television, the reins of the group were systematically defined so that the only musical contribution the four members were allowed to make to the recording process was their vocals. The group would have their music written for them by such song writers as Gerry Goffin, Carol King, Neil Diamond, Barry Mann, Tommy Boyce and Bobby Hart (Ramaeker 82–83). In addition, the music was performed for them by session players including artists like Chet Atkins. Due to this, the Monkees faced press, often from newcomers like *Rolling Stone*, that they represented a capitalist, corporate perversion of rock 'n' roll. A review of the Monkees' show by Cleveland Amory at the time established a narrative of corporate greed at the very heart of the show:

> It had to happen sooner or later. Some big boy upstairs saw a Beatles film and he called a network meeting. "Get the Beatles," he snarled. Whereupon everybody agreed it was a terrific idea.... All except one little guy. "I don't think we're going to be able to get the Beatles, Boss," he said. "They're richer than we are."

This resulted in Amory's mind with "The Beatles Next Door!" (qtd. in Greenwald 99).

Even though only broadly approaching the subject in terms of this chapter, it is important to note that developments in popular music in the nineteen sixties allowed for the expansion in the music community of conceptualizations of authenticity. With the advent of the "Folk Revival" including artists Bob Dylan and Phil Ochs, and the rise of the "San Francisco Sound" which included artists like the Jefferson Airplane, The Charlatans, and the Grateful Dead, an emphasis was put on the artist not only as performer but also as a creator. As Ramaeker discusses the connection was a direct one: "The folk ideology of musical production of, for, and by a community had begun shaping the development of rock 'scenes' in cities such as San Francisco" (Ramaeker 81). This emphasis, pushed publicly by growing music publications like *Creem*, *Rolling Stone, Crawdaddy*, etc., identified the Monkees as imposters in a musical community trying to reflect its values and ideologies in an idealized "pure" form (Ramaeker 75; "Non" 18).

Artists like Big Brother and the Holding Company and Country Joe and the Fish reflected the rise of the counterculture in the 1960s, and acted as minstrels of the times, bringing an aesthetic or valuing of supposedly organic and true creation, originally rooted in the authenticity-crazed hunt of the folk revival. It was rebellious music that challenged convention and technology of the time. The music reflected the values, concerns, and questions that a growing number of baby boomers (especially on college campuses nationwide) had amid a climate of political and social turmoil in the United States. Also reflected, in numerous instances, was the growing drug culture including the use of marijuana and psychedelic drugs like LSD and mescaline in the hope to explore and expand consciousness. As highlighted throughout this book, the debate as to what constituted and what was excluded from individuals' perceptions of the counterculture was prevalent then and is prevalent still. For a movement dependent on authenticity and rebellion, the debate was inevitable, and would be fought out in many places, including on the screen and on turntables across the country and across the world. For the four young men in the Monkees, there would be no shortage of attention and criticism as to whether they could be trusted or welcomed at the varied and sometime disparate table of the counterculture.

The Monkees television series lasted only until 1968. In their two years on television, those behind the creation of the Monkees used the half-hour comedy about an out-of-work band as a launching pad that secured economic success not only in the medium of television, but also in concert, record and merchandise sales. As stated before, there was a significant backlash from some critics. Yet as we will see momentarily there was also a significant amount of support from what could be considered countercultural sources. Regardless of critics' opinions, the Monkees machine was becoming an enormous success.

Although the show's debut ranked only sixty-fifth on the Nielsen scale, and it would never be able to break into the top twenty-five, the Monkees as an entity were meeting unprecedented commercial success (Ramaeker 77). This was due to the show being specifically targeted to a key audience, teens and preteens. Although never asserting itself as a show with wide appeal to multiple age groups, the show was able to exploit a specific devoted audience that invested high levels of disposable incomes into record sales and merchandise. Here we see the creation of niche markets, the targeting of certain audience segments, which would soon become the norm in many media sources in the coming decades (for example on television when the cable industry became more widespread). The true success of the Monkees could be and was measured by corporate interest in record sales (the first LP stayed on the charts for 78 weeks) (Lefcowitz, *Monkee Business* 53).

What was the appeal though? Most of the discourse concerning the Monkees on television contains a reoccurring theme of "freedom." Utilizing the traits which made movies like *A Hard Day's Night* and *Help* successful, including visual and camera styles and the use of dialogue which often comically questioned older generations' values and authority, *The Monkees* was a testament to youth culture and its values. Matthew Stahl in his examination of the life of so-called commercially intended "boy bands" called "Authentic Boy Bands on TV?" comments,

> The producers of *The Monkees* wanted viewers to see an "authentic" youth cultural expression—the rock band—based on their belief regarding what was required for market success, that is, the story of young musicians "doing their thing" without the intrusion of "the man" in the form of the culture industries (only a small number of the over fifty Monkees TV shows made any reference at all to the music business or the commodification of music necessary for the survival of a professional musician in a capitalist regime) [319].

With this kind of corporate orchestration it may seem that we have met a dead end in terms of the group truly representing and conveying countercultural values. Partially through the first season, the Monkees enacted the most corporately feared undertaking they could have: they began to think and speak for themselves. The *New York Times* in an article entitled "The Monkees Let Down Their Hair" quoted Peter Tork as saying, "I stand for love and peace. To my way of thinking, they're the same thing. But the man who said 'My country, right or wrong' made a slight error in judgment. My country wrong needs my help. Well, I guess I've got myself in hot water" (Lefcowitz, *The Monkees Tale* 24).

Yet, it would be Michael Nesmith in an interview for the *Saturday Evening Post* in early 1967 that would most infuriate the corporate moneymaking machine behind the creation of The Monkees. Nesmith was becoming frustrated with criticisms that pointed out the Monkees being a prefabricated band, as well as becoming increasingly upset (along with Tork and Dolenz) with Don Kirshner. Kirshner refused to allow any creative control of the band fearing to upset the money-making giant he was so central to at the time. Nesmith lashed out in the interview: "The music has nothing to do with us. It was totally dishonest. Do you know how debilitating it is to sit up and have to duplicate somebody else's records? That's really what we were doing." Nesmith continues,

> Maybe we were manufactured and put on the air strictly with a lot of hoopla. Tell the world that we're synthetic because damn it, we are. Tell them the Monkees were wholly man-made overnight, that millions of dollars have been poured into this thing. Tell the world we don't record our own music. But that's us they see on television. The show is really part of us. They're not seeing something invalid [Lefcowitz, *The Monkees Tale* 25].

An escalation of these tensions among Kirshner and members of the Monkees only progressed further in the coming weeks and months. Producer Bob Schneider explains the circumstances behind the growing tensions by stating, "It was like walking a tightrope all the time, because on the one hand, we wanted to encourage the creativity of the Monkees but, at the same time, we wanted to keep it manageable so it didn't end up with a phone call that said 'you're cancelled.'" He continues, "We were walking the line between industrial America, on one hand, and rebellion, on the other. What we stood for was the rebellion, but at the same time, we were dealing with the real world. I was very personally desirous of manipulating the situation so that we wouldn't get our heads chopped off" (Lefcowitz, *The Monkees Tale* 23).

Schneider's fears would soon come to pass. In an attempt to reassert power over the group Kirshner opted to release a single "A Little Bit Me, A Little Bit You"/"She Hangs Out," violating an agreement between Colgems and the Monkees. At this point Kirshner was dropped and the Monkees were allowed more artistic control (O'Neal). The group enacted their new power in the recording of *Headquarters*. Along with penning some of the songs and being able to select the others themselves, the Monkees also played instruments on the recording. Many saw this as a turning point in which the band began to function more like an actual group.

The Monkees were also awarded more control of the television program as well. With more ability to ad-lib and the personal selection by the Monkees of guest stars including Tim Buckley and Frank Zappa, the group was able (at the very least) in a limited fashion to publicly assert themselves over the corporate regime that created them. By determining more their musical path as well as the path of the show, the Monkees made a very public claim for authenticity. The Monkees were seen by figures like Timothy Leary (who will be quoted shortly), as now exploiting corporate interest for their own purposes.

The group's departure from a tight corporate grip and their reflection of counterculture themes in their career, including drug use, political concerns, and assertiveness of the self simultaneously garnered them more respect among a select number of the counterculture intelligentsias and alienated their intended base audience composed of "teeny-bopper" pre-teens and teenagers. Yet, they were far from being universally accepted as part of the counterculture by adherents at the time.

Yet, in terms of a growing countercultural respect there are numerous examples. Included among these are articles by Paul Williams in a July-August issue of *Crawdaddy*, which placed much of the blame concerning the themes of falseness with the group on Kirshner's shoulders almost exclusively. The participation of Dolenz and especially Tork in the Monterey Pop Festival of 1967 highlighted their connections to "hip" acts; there they situated themselves with and encouraged up and comers like Jimi Hendrix and Big Brother and the Holding Company. Perhaps the most poignantly stated commentary of acceptance came from Timothy Leary, who after describing the band's corporate rise to fame in *The Politics of Ecstasy* posits: "And what happened? The same thing that happened to the Beatles. The four young Monkees weren't fooled for a moment. They went along with the system but didn't buy it." He continues:

> The Monkees television show for example. Oh, you thought that was silly teen-age entertainment? Don't be fooled. While it lasted, it was a classic Sufi put-on. An early–Christian electronic satire. A mystic-magic show. A jolly Buddha laugh at hypocrisy. At early evening kiddie-time on Monday the Monkees would rush through a parody drama, burlesquing the very shows that glue Mom and Dad to the set during prime time. Spoofing the movies and violence and the down-heavy-conflict-emotion themes that fascinate the middle-aged [Lefcowitz, *The Monkees Tale* 35].

Regardless of such praise, the television program failed in a milieu of corporate challenge (CBS moved *Gunsmoke* into the same time slot as *The Monkees* over on NBC), and decreasing album sales. The Monkees were a far cry from being out of the public eye, thanks to the popularity of repeats of the show and interest in their music (though selling fewer albums). At this point of their career, the Monkees geared up for what some would come to see as a counter-culture cornerstone, and, at the time, career suicide: their first feature film, *Head*.

With the assistance of Schneider, Rafelson and a young actor and screenwriter named Jack Nicholson, the Monkees formulated a plan for their film (Stafford). With a healthy supply of marijuana and alcohol, the group went to Ojai, California, to stay at a golf resort. Gathered around a tape recorder the group had "stream of consciousness sessions about television, movies, music, art, love, lust, good, bad, evil, life, and death" (Dolenz 146). A disagreement on how much the four Monkees contributed to the script resulted when they were not granted writing credits in the film. As Nesmith shared in an interview, "It's not like we were the creative force behind this whole thing, but it came down to a situation of credit where credit was due" (Finn and T. Bone 32). The writing and production credits were listed as Bob Rafelson and Jack Nicholson's. Nesmith qualifies it further in *The Monkees Scrapbook* that "essentially if you want to say whose vision it was, it was Jack Nicholson's" (Finn and T. Bone 32). The film, although likely funded by Columbia Pictures in the hopes of producing an exploitation film to sell records, like the ones Elvis had become widely known for by this time, was to be a far diversion from such standards. Even with songs from familiar songwriters to the group such as Gerry Goffin and Carole King, as well as Harry Nilsson, among pieces composed by Peter Tork and Michael Nesmith, the soundtrack would also be a challenge to some fans. As Lindsay Planer puts it on Allmusic, "The music featured on both the screen as well as this album is a long strange trip from the Farfisa-driven bubblegum anthem "I'm a Believer."

Playing on acceptable norms of film genres and possessing an urgent sense of self-awareness and self-deprecation, the involved parties created a post-modern assault on the senses. The Monkees created a hyperreal atmosphere dispelling the myths about the band. Those behind the film took extreme measures to break down the goofiness of the group that had been defined in the last two years on television, music, and merchandizing. Throughout the film the creators test the audiences' sense of comfort in the Monkees' image and aura that had been created by corporate interest to sell associated products. By taking on political and cultural concepts central to the creation of and negotiation of a movement, such as drugs and the war in Vietnam in the film, the Monkees started another round of possible consideration for those gatekeepers aiming to draw the lines of inclusion and exclusion in a powerful but amorphous countercultural movement. Ultimately, critics' capabilities to focus on the theme of authenticity has since helped put the film into the canon of filmic works associated with the time and the zeitgeist despite the film's initial failure at the box office.

The opening scene, a far cry from the content of the familiar and safe television show, surely must have been quite disconcerting to their traditional fan base. To see a Monkee jumping off of a bridge, with a look of panic and terror in his eyes (even if he is saved by psychedelic mermaids) was a potential sobering image when compared to what had been generally seen on the TV show. To see the group jumping off of a bridge, according to Dolenz, is part of the larger project that describes the "story of the Monkees: our birth, life, and death, as metaphors for all of Hollywood and its tinsel-and-fabric manipulations or people, images, and ideas" (146).

The use of "Porpoise Song" and the "saturated negative colorizing hippie trippie photographic technique" of solarization (Dolenz 148) in the first moments of the film set a surreal and some may say discomforting tone. Later, the Monkees, speaking over a wall of small screens depicting the events to come, break into a unison rhyme, the "Ditty Diego Chant" that mentions their "manufactured image," their plastic-ness, the cash rolling in, and their lack of any guiding philosophy or meaning. The other half of the rhyme describes how the Monkees, with this knowledge of their falseness, plan to structure the film to reflect upon these values; they let the audience know they are in for a potentially rough ride, without a story, and one that will easily buck traditional narrative conventions. By first claiming that they have "no philosophies" the Monkees then begin to crack the image that has been so carefully orchestrated by the Establishment to sell them as a product. The group begins to challenge the conventions of the group that were created to generally live comfortably outside of the social and political turmoil of the late 1960s.

Throughout the rest of the film, the Monkees find themselves in an ever-changing milieu of series of situations, themes, and sets. For example, the band act as soldiers on the war front, they play in front of a crazed audience, are stuck in a black box, in a desert, and so forth. Musical instances, like the performance of "Circle Sky," "Can You Dig It," and "As We Go Along," are wrapped into the stream-of-consciousness development of the film. Framed among what could be best described as several small vignettes, the film jumps radically, being strung together only with the re-emphasized statement of the Monkees acknowledging and toying with the concept of their fabricated past. As promised, the narrative constantly morphs, and reconfigures itself numerous times. While one may begin to ponder if the drug use of the individuals involved in its creation overtook any coherence of the film (which will be explored shortly), a closer examination shows that several themes are developing within the anarchistic flow of the film. Three thematic areas associated with the film speak to countercultural life especially: authenticity, drug use, and opposition to the Vietnam War. Whether perceived as a hedonistic, nonsensical mess by critics and audiences, or regarded as a critically aware, wary, and cynical time capsule from 1968, *Head* solicits continued interpretation, meaning, and debate thanks to the presence of these themes.

Although stating there is no real meaning behind their "plastic" facade as a band under corporate control, the film uses authenticity as its crutch to link these disparate events. According to Nesmith, he was on board with the plan as the inward-focused interrogation of the Monkees was going to "set us apart, make us a valid member of the community" (Finn and T. Bone 32). Bert Schneider and Bob Rafeleson, who were looking to explore other business avenues, were on board as it could provide a bookend for their time with the Monkees. As Schneider stated, "This was the cap and then we're finished and if we can destroy the group in the process of making the movie, all the better" (Lefcowitz, *Monkee Business* 172–173). To mock their validity fulfilled both the aims of those "hung up on this manufactured Monkee business" (Dolenz 154) as a way to kill the experiment, and for those hoping for something more (with many between as well).

A meta-commentary on the nature of authenticity, *Head*'s meaning and legacy has certainly encouraged a continuing debate concerning the authenticity of the band and their place within the countercultural zeitgeist of the time. Perhaps even more so, by taking on themes prevalent in countercultural life of the time, such as drugs and the Vietnam War, the film has come to be a historical text, capable of measuring the authenticity of the movement itself. Cynical at times, politically alive, culturally contextualized, *Head*, at first about a group, has now become about a time and a place in American memory and the fevered debate about its legacy.

Deciding that their existence as a group was not a closed one, the Monkees wished to exercise the power of choice in a world where power was thrust down upon them. By rejecting themselves as an entity that existed within a closed sphere of control, they instead sought individualism by dispelling the characters that were created to represent them. "In form and subject, *Head* plays with, and blurs, the distinctions between the reality and illusion of the fiction of the Monkees" (Ramaeker 91). In doing so they were able to create a product which they felt was a true representation of themselves for once in their careers as "Monkees," while at the same time toying with the characters created for them and in the process dismantling those said "plastic" figures (Finn and T. Bone 32). In essence, the Monkees had used *Head* as a vehicle to play with, and in the end, declare their authenticity.

Another way in which these parameters could be tested was to overtly deal with a countercultural staple, drug use. From Davy Jones remembering that they smoked "a ton" of dope to claims that Rafelson and Nicholson utilized LSD when drafting the script, the product is conclusively attached to drug culture of the time (Stafford). Since, various accounts and retellings of the film's creation, drugs have been become part of the central mythology surrounding the film.

For instance, Paul B. Ramaeker argues in "You Think They Call Us Plastic Now...," that the Monkees had an eye trained on dealing with psychedelics. Citing Timothy Leary's "adaptation of the Tibetan Book of the Dead for his 1964 *The Psychedelic Experience*," Ramaeker connects the book and the structure of *Head* as the film wrestles with the self and reality. The movie is meant to reflect or "mimic" the stages of experience under LSD that Leary laid out for the reader. Ramaeker outlines the map:

> The first stage involves transcendence of the self, with the onset of the drug; the second, facing up to and dealing with the self; the third, return to the self, but a self that can, he wrote, be radically transformed. During the "trip," if one approaches it correctly, one's entire relationship to the self and the culture that surrounds and helps to comprise it may be altered; the consciousness can be freed from "the games that comprise 'personality.'" On the way back from this journey, the consciousness will reconstitute the personality, in the process allowing one to freely choose a new identity, one that has been liberated from the deadening oppression of Establishment culture [86–87].

This is an association that has assisted the film in being seen as a historical document of the counterculture, and as an example of countercultural film. Nesmith contended in one interview that the centrality of drugs was overstated: "The only mistake is to ascribe it to a drug culture." Rather the film in his eyes was creating a postmodern pastiche of the band (qtd. in Watson 30). Any such qualifications, however possibly valid, have been lost in the vast predominance of sources consulted for this study and in numerous fan reviews and discussions online. Some level of authenticity appears to have accumulated with critics and fans and is contingent on a great deal of emphasis on drugs in the creation of the film.

Later accounts and descriptions of the film have often prominently featured drugs as a key concept in even beginning to approach the film. Michael Dwyer in *The Age* sets a good example of this language in his review of the DVD in 2004: "Warning: any resemblance between this film and the zany TV show starring the same lovable prefab pop group has been twisted by recreational chemicals." He refers to the creation of the film as being done "in a rush of dope smoke and LSD in '68." The psychedelic lightshows, saturated colors, and "a different trip entirely from Last Train to Clarksville" (Dwyer) musical creations, along with the many stories concerning the film's creation, have stuck with the film. These surrounding drug myths, stories, and details are at least responsible for some of the use of the film as a counterculture period piece.

The group further challenged conventions of their plastic origins, through their prominent anti-war stance within the film. Here was a group designed for a pre-teen and teenage crowd, editing in actual news footage of the Vietnam War. Scenes of bombings, shootings, and suffering were spliced into the film to testify to the atrocities of war. The use of the famous clip of a Vietnamese general executing a Vietcong prisoner was especially problematic for some audiences. Dolenz recounts, "It has been argued that that image profoundly altered American public opinion about what was actually at stake in the war, and Bob used it to death (no pun intended). At one point in the movie it is shown thirty-two times simultaneously in split screen" (151). The use of anti-war themes, as Lefcowitz claims, "were generally misinterpreted by critics, who perceived them as smug and flippant commentary on the burning issue of the times" (*The Monkees Tale* 57). The usability and interpretation of these encoded messages by audiences varied, based upon age, perception of the band and show, and other concerns.

This exercise in self-reflection and cynicism, even while espousing countercultural themes, ultimately doomed the film. *Head*, to put it mildly was a commercial flop. Their predominately pre-teen and teenage audience did not take kindly to the existential and postmodern feel of the film. The cynicism of the film as well as the lack of *A Hard Day's Night*-like themes, which had made the television series a success, alienated their core audience which expected a film adaptation of the series. Critics also lambasted the film as a drug-induced waste of time, which as indicated by this review in the *New York Times*, "might be a film to see if you have been smoking grass or if you like to scream at the Monkees, or if you are interested in what interests drifting heads and hysterical high-school girls" (qtd. in Baker 58). *Rolling Stone* declared the film and the departure of Tork shortly after as "The Non-News Story of the Year" ("Non").

Though the film continued a tradition of the Monkees being dismissed by critics, in the coming decades *Head* would build a cult following. Ramaeker argues that the film was "arguably even too sophisticated, for its moment" (99). This would especially be the case as Nicholson, Rafelson, and Schneider, whose names would be forever connected to the film, went on to successful careers in Hollywood. Aside from being cited as a film created within countercultural surroundings, the film has also become a historical document of sorts, measuring a pinnacle of debate in the realm of art versus commerce, rebellion, and the fevered passion for the "authentic." The fact that the film dealt with a central and sacred expression of countercultural thought, popular music, made it a multi-mediated experiment in meaning and identity. Much like other Hollywood films, *Head* can be seen as a detriment or a gift to historical perspective, putting its finger on the pulse of the time or being allotted too much responsibility for a mere film. When defining a broad movement, one cannot help but want to listen and watch, in the hope of figuring some things out.

The history of the Monkees allows for a varied reading. While it is common for the Monkees to be viewed as a purely saccharine treat, heavy on humor, light on thought, they also publicly examined countercultural themes, and basic conceptions of free will, and existentialist lamentations in understanding the self. We can see that the group, although born from a specific formula orchestrated by corporate concern, consistently fought for greater levels of control and respect from their own peers. The tensions created in this search for a voice and for something *real* made the Monkees a perfect text from which to explore the earnest means by which the counterculture's borders and meanings were and continue to be managed. The want to challenge convention and to do something real, in a world perceived as plastic and hypocritical, demanded an interrogation of all facets of life, whether it was political, cultural, social or personal beliefs and expressions. In the case of the Monkees, the struggle was personified by a group locked in a metanarrative of authenticity. *Head* represented a damning end for the Monkees for some, and for others it was a moment of potency, as here was a group pointing out the futility of pointing out absolutes in a movement so disdainful of the absolutes that had been placed on them by their parents, country, etc.

Yet, throughout their careers the Monkees were able to remain introspective in terms of realizing their identities within popular culture. Never fighting off but instead embracing their manufactured-ness allowed for statements, especially in *Head*, concerning the fallacies and promises of popular culture.

Today, *Head*, *The Monkees* television show, and recordings of the Monkees are the subject of interest for several generations of fans. Rhino records re-release of their catalog including *Head* on DVD demonstrates the continued effect and popularity the Monkees have had on popular culture. While it is true that much of the sales can be attributed to the pop anthems created for them, there is also a growing tide of interest into the political and social implications of the Monkees and their place within the late 1960s counterculture as a group confronting themselves and the tumultuous time period in which they found fame.

4. Love in Counterculture Film: Music's Diplomatic Role in *Harold and Maude*

Music can fulfill a host of responsibilities during a film. It can contribute to a narrative, mold and shape viewer responses, or throw popular standards of the time in as an afterthought to make a buck, along with numerous other possibilities. The increasing use of popular or rock music in the 1960s and early 1970s was a flashpoint of debate concerning the supposed "New Hollywood." The music was partially displacing what James Wierzbicki calls "Hollywood music" that cinemagoers had become accustomed to hearing in the theater. Is it possible that this turn reflected a working knowledge of niche markets, where filmmakers and studios were looking to bastardize the role of film music out of ignorance and greed? (189, 192). Quite possibly in some cases, yes, this was absolutely true. However, the rise of the New Hollywood also pioneered uses of popular music that elevated narrative, meaning, and emotional investment into the Hollywood film. In the case of Hal Ashby's *Harold and Maude* (1971), music took on a central role in facilitating the reception of a remarkably unconventional love story for a vast array of audience use values.

In contemporary cinema, a project where the protagonist, a young man, falls in love with an elderly woman would still have a tough time being green lit in the modern film industry. Its utter failure at the box office when first released in 1971 perhaps also points out to the fact that even an era of concentrated social challenge and change was not ready for it either, or simply the audience did not bite. Among films dealing with sex, drugs, and rebellion, the taboo of age dealt with in *Harold and Maude*, simply pushed too far. So why discuss such an utter initial failure? As many know, the film tenaciously held on, becoming a cult classic that spoke to an array of viewers. One important responsible party involved in successfully translating this film to numerous audiences and generations of fans came in the authorship of Cat Stevens' leitmotif of freedom and musical narration of a film running over with morbidity and sexual taboo.

In 1971, the outlook for *Harold and Maude* was about as dim as Harold's world outlook. *Harold and Maude* was panned by critics like Roger Ebert and *Variety*; the latter stated that the film "has all the fun and gaiety of a burning orphanage" (qtd. in Patterson). In *Easy Riders and Raging Bulls* Peter Biskind quotes producer Charles Mulvehill as saying: "You couldn't drag people in…. The idea of a twenty-year-old boy with an eighty-year-old woman just made people want to vomit. If you asked people what it was about, ultimately it became a boy who was fucking his grandmother" (174). With such sentiments abounding, the film met an early end, closing quickly in theaters.

Indeed, the film was initially funded, thanks in large part to the lack of detail provided to Paramount. Nick Dawson, in *Being Hal Ashby: Life of a Hollywood Rebel*, said the film was given "a meager $0.8 million budget," "without the front office knowing what it was about" (120). Originally penned as what "had begun as the master's thesis of UCLA student Colin Higgins, who was working as producer Edward Lewis's pool boy," the movie would be a possible gamble for all involved due to the "bizarre nature of the material" (Dawson 122). If the "New Hollywood" was about upsetting convention and testing the parameters of film, *Harold and Maude* tested a status quo that apparently many audiences of the time were more than happy to leave alone: aging.

One of the unsure parties involved at the time was Cat Stevens, himself. Stevens was somewhat surprised with the request from Ashby to consider the use and incorporation of Stevens' music in the film. In his interview for the Criterion Edition of *Harold and Maude*, Stevens (Yusuf Islam as he has been known since 1979) recounts being approached about contributing music to the film, thanks to Ashby's growing fondness for his work: "He seemed to be living with these two albums: *Mona Bone Jakon* and *Tea for the Tillerman*. I think when he made the film looking at the rushes, he never stopped playing my records at the time. He kept on putting on my records while he was watching the film. So it became an indelible part of the vision that he saw."

Though encouraged by the idea of having his music utilized in a feature film, Stevens/Islam at the time felt a sense of anxiety about moving forward with the project. He agrees that he did see some connection in Harold and some of his own work in that they both take on "playing with the idea of death: the whole idea that you are going to leave this planet. And so there are threads of similarity, and just the approach, which Harold had towards life, which was to get as close possible to the edge to find out something he didn't know" (Islam). He recounts that he was encouraged by the interest, but after reading the script he still felt some trepidation:

The juxtaposing of songs in film is a kind of dangerous business, because as a writer you've got your own vision and along comes a director who kind of sees it in this other way. I wasn't certain if we were going to do this or we were going to say yes, so he really wanted to convince me.... Hal really wanted to convince me that this was the right thing. So, he invited me to San Francisco [Islam].

Eventually, he was successfully harangued into the project. Works from Stevens' first two already recorded albums would be used in addition to him recording two new tracks for the film. One of those, "If You Want to Sing Out, Sing Out," would become an important, life-affirming musical focus for both the audience and for the characters within the film themselves. The other song, "Don't Be Shy," would set the tone for the film as the musical accompaniment to the title sequence in which Harold stages his first fake suicide.

The recording of these tracks became a troublesome issue as Ashby decided that the rough demos that were recorded at Wally Heider's in San Francisco were a good fit with the film or at least fit in with the wrap-up schedule. Much like the film, the songs and the soundtrack began to take on life of their own with audience:

> ... he said that's great! I said don't worry, I'll record them properly and my whole intention was to go away and do this. But then of course the whole wrap up of the film that happened and suddenly it was out! And I was kind of a little bit upset about that because I wanted to do the songs properly. The songs they finally used were kind of the original demos, they might have been dollied up a little bit, but they were the same rough pieces of work which I meant to finish. But then it came out and everybody wanted to have the soundtrack and I said, "No way! I never finished those songs!" [Islam].

In the end, at the time of its release, even with a highly regarded soundtrack in tow, the film failed at the box office and the short life of *Harold and Maude* appeared to be over.

Somehow rising from the ashes of the "burning orphanage" referred to so poetically earlier, the film and its soundtrack would hang on to resonate with audiences in the following years and decades. *Harold and Maude* spent time after its initial release in art house showings for years, stage musical adaptations, and numerous editions produced for home viewing. The film continued to live on in VHS and DVD formats, undergoing a Criterion edition in 2012. As we will shortly see, the demand for the film has been met with a demand for a formal soundtrack release, a continued pull that has become a main artery in the life and legacy of the film.

What has been the continued draw then, if this is a film that was met with such an overwhelming sense of dismissal? The answers, based upon the film's potential audiences, are plentiful. The film can be regarded as a work of dark humor, a highlight or lowlight of Hal Ashby's body of work, a touching romance, a film acutely dealing with taboo, a film overtaken with death, a life-affirming tale, or a film, much like other works within this canon of films of and in the counterculture, that represents a search for a true and lasting freedom. Both positive and negative reactions and many perspectives between have kept the film alive and well in the realm of popular culture.

Of these many perspectives, there is one theme that resounds with many of the audiences studied that features most prominently: the search for freedom. Among these other insights garnered by audiences and critics, the film's theme as exemplified by Stevens' "If You Want to Sing Out, Sing Out" has continued to be a hook to the film that resonates with a diverse set of audiences that seems to center around, according to Diane Jacobs in *Hollywood Renaissance*, the ability to "'Do your own thing'" (222). Sometimes seen as cliché, and sometimes as an inspiration, the film depends on this unifying voice both in the world of the film and in the world of the audience to guide them through peculiar but also conventional lines of a comedic romance.

For some viewers an enduring idea in the song that "there's a million things to be" is a statement of questioning the status quo. Decades after its release this loose but resonant ideal has manifested itself in a variety of audiences through the current day. For example, in Belfast, Ireland, the movie was played as part of "Age Awareness Week." The reasoning given was that the film "challenged the stereotypical ways in which older people are portrayed in cinema" (Quigley 12). *The Advocate*, in an interview with Broadway's Harold, Eric Millegan (an openly out male), stated, "It's about 'Be the person you're in love with.' It doesn't matter if she's 60 years older than you or, if you're a gay man, if it's a man" (Glitz 55). The *Daily Telegraph* goes so far as to cite the film and music as a cornerstone work of countercultural life: "'If you want to sing out, sing out/If you want to be free, be free;—Cat Stevens' hippy anthem forms the leitmotif of a movie directed by Hal Ashby which stands along *If...*, *Zabriskie Point* and *Alice's Restaurant* as one of the most enduring cinematic embodiments of the libertarian counterculture of the 1960s" (Christiansen 30).

Obviously, there were many "burning orphanage" interpretations of the film as well, and this same notion of "doing your own thing" has not translated so well to all audiences. Diane Jacobs in *Hollywood Renaissance* called it Ashby's "least interesting" film (222). One of the reasons that the film disappoints in Jacobs' mind is due to the fact that Maude "has a beneficial effect on Harold and it's nice to watch Bud Cort's face open up as he reacts to her. But the Sixties clichés become oppressive" (225). In addition she criticizes that Ashby is not fair in terms of examining the characters, clearly favoring the "cool" versus the "straight," whereas in other films like *The Last Detail*, he is "almost always fair to both sides" (224). One would be hard pressed to argue that

Stevens' simplistic message in "If You Want to Sing Out, Sing Out" would not have played a role in helping to assert this expression of Sixties clichés and the dividing line between the repressed status quo and the utopian ideals of the counterculture.

Jacobs, in isolating the film from the rest of Ashby's efforts, brings to mind questions of legitimacy and authenticity within his body of work. Such questions of merit and quality demonstrate the continued struggle over the inclusion and exclusion of works within a canon of texts as worthy, unworthy, or resting somewhere between in numerous contexts. From those that saw, such as Ellen Harrington of the Academy of Motion Picture Arts and Sciences, a film that showcased a "life-affirming connection that finds beauty in tragedy and dark humor" to those that have panned the film over the years, the lasting legacy of the film is still up for grabs (qtd. in King). As a text of great American film, as a text of the counterculture, etc., *Harold and Maude* is welcomed by some, but not all.

Cat Stevens/Yusuf Islam has not been immune to such questions of legitimacy and proper place that Ashby and the film have faced. Dave Thompson in *Hearts of Darkness: James Taylor, Jackson Browne, Cat Stevens and the Unlikely Rise of the Singer-Songwriter* describes that Stevens was trying to escape his commercially successful past in the late 1960s, a few short years before the release of the film. Thompson describes, "He sought, he said, a whole new audience, a crowd that might have overlooked him completely in the past not because they didn't like his music, but because they didn't like what he was perceived as representing, the teenybop poster boys with their pictures in *Fabulous 208* every week" (177). Stevens aimed to create a "personal" and "good music" that could resonate with peers and audiences that he could feel proud of and in control of in the face of label pressure (178).

Though playing to the much demanded want for authenticity from baby boomers, Stevens proved to be a bit of an odd fit when he made his way to the U.S. in 1970. Bud Scoppa noted that at the iconic Fillmore East, "Cat Stevens and [Alun Davies] looked hopelessly tiny. Just two seated figures holding guitars; no banks of amps, no massed drums, no sparkle suits." (qtd. in. Thompson 185). The intimacy of the event "was practically unheard of at the Fillmore, with its reputation for toughness. The kid must be awfully naïve," but Scoppa notes Stevens easily won over the audience that evening (185). The relative calm of intimate acoustic performances at a time in which rock was finding a new level of spectacle, formalization, commercial potential and appeal, awakened a folk-style revival type of response: simplicity in contentious times. Stevens, of course, thanks to this simplicity, would ultimately become a phenomenal success in the United States and elsewhere internationally.

The film, hence, encompasses a host of potential legacies for a variety of audiences, whether as a text reflecting the shifting aims of legacy reflected in Stevens' work, Ashby's legacy as a director, or as a part of canon of films defining a movement and a time. Each is ultimately connected to use and place. In terms of the "New Hollywood" and in terms of the body of work dealt with in this book, these questions of place become paramount in discussing both aesthetic merit and the validity of these texts as cultural markers of the times they chronicle or exist within. Lines of inclusion and exclusion in an identified movement like the "New Hollywood" or the "counterculture" are fiercely protected by those that took part, as well as those that celebrate the film or damn it, and for those that look or don't look to these texts for placement, context, and identity. Whatever trajectory, Stevens' music and "If You Want to Sing Out, Sing Out" provide a forthright cornerstone for multiple audiences to measure the validity and legacy of the film.

Harold and Maude demonstrates the centrality and place that popular music can have in constructing narrative and mediating what is going on screen for audiences in need of some guidance in terms of their reception of film. Ashby, along with numerous factors and influences combined to create a film that lives and breathes almost forty years after its release. It is the soundtrack of the film and this repeated leitmotif that has acted as a diplomatic and guiding force for audiences, shaping reception and becoming a definitive part of the narrative that has significantly helped lead to the film's success and perhaps to its dismissal by some viewers. A discussion of instances where sound and vision connected will help to make sense of the diplomatic role played by the music.

Harold and Maude makes use of music to transition the viewer between sequences, neatly, in a 91-minute film concentrating on the process of self-discovery and love that the protagonist encounters. This is a difficult task, as the viewer is supposed to not only accept an unconventional relationship, but to also find a connection with Harold amid self-inflicted gunshot wounds, and self-immolation. This mirrors Peter Larsen's perspectives on film music generally that are discussed in his book *Film Music*:

> The forward-looking musical progression sets boundaries, it measures out and rounds off the individual narrative event, but music's own, internal arcs of tension are also used more generally to "scan" the course of events. With the aid of its own structure, the music structures the events on the screen, separates them from each other or links them, points out connections and transitions, closes sections off and opens new ones [209].

In the case of *Harold and Maude*, this is pronounced. The music boldly takes us from psychiatrist's office to funeral; from funeral to home; it connects a somber military graveyard to a joy ride where cops are comically messed with and urban trees are liberated; and it transitions the drollness of Harold's home life to visits with Maude. It is also the music that links together the montage of Maude's death. All the while, Stevens' work cuts through the cloudy skies, funeral processions, and dark recesses of Harold's mind. "Don't Be Shy," "Where Do the Children Play?" and other songs by Stevens play into the emotionality and warmth of Maude, and the process of self-discovery that Harold goes through to find the authentic. The specific sound of Stevens' musical work does fulfill Craig Sinclair's claim that "a picture may paint a thousand words, but when it is 'accompanied' by sound, it is the sound that tells the experiencer how to paint them. When linked to the image, the sound provides and writes the narrative, directing, constructing, and emoting these words perceptually" (27). Indeed, as audiences have often proven, the music is used as a key feature in terms of perpetuating the film's reception and legacy.

Stevens/Islam describes that when invited to San Francisco by Ashby, it was one of these instances that affirmed his music would be a good fit with the film: "I think it was 'Miles from Nowhere' and the hearse and I went 'Oh ... that's good'" (Islam). The scene, opposed to offering overt commentary or assisting in clearly further defining the narrative, demonstrates music's ability to guide and establish a film's pathos. He was comfortable that the song was not used as an overt narrative trope to reaffirm what was going on in the film: "It doesn't describe what's going on and it shouldn't in some way ... but there's a spirit, there's a meaning, there's something so subtle about the core of that song which hits that strength and that scene and tells you everything about it" (Islam).

He mentions a certain pathos was certainly shared by the film and music and it allowed for a comfortable fit, without reverting to cliché: "There was some kind of real synergy also with the kind of strange sadistic humor, dark humor, which I kind of had a kid as well. So I kind of recognized all of this rebelliousness and wanting to turn things upside down and to not accept what the great world was telling me" (Islam). His canon of work was able to address the early frustration and despondency of Harold early in the film with "Miles from Nowhere" and later "Trouble" as Harold awaits news of Maude's inevitable death. These darker moments expressed in the commingling of the visuals and of the soundtrack are always temporary though thanks to its reoccurring leitmotif.

Unlike examples that may speak more to the macabre nature of the film, the incorporation of "If You Want to Sing Out" becomes the central, discernible link in the narrative that propels the viewer to the ultimate life-affirming thesis. As a song recorded for the film, as opposed to the use of Stevens' prior work on his first two albums in the film, the ability of the director and the musician to frame the events viewed through the camera's eye was much more potent, as it was directed for this use. Due to this process of production, the song could be used to address or guide several narrative turns within the storyline for the audience. Speaking both to the seriousness of the images presented, as well as to the current of embracing and living life, so exemplified in "If You Want to Sing Out, Sing Out," Stevens' musical shorthand provides this guidance in the film that audiences ultimately invested in, rejected, etc. Whatever the direction, the repetition of the leitmotif brings the audience back and leaves little room for interpretation as to what the they should take away, watching Harold walk away from the cliff's edge, plucking the tune on his banjo before Stevens' voice takes over the tune for the end credits.

Refusing to stay in the orchestra pit, the song jumps in and out of the world of Harold and Maude. Maude's rendition of the song halfway through the film entices Harold out of his shell to sing along. The reappearance of the leitmotif throughout the rest of the film both diegetically and non-diegetically pushes the viewer to succinctly create an investment not only in the individuals, but also in the developing, unconventional love story. As Larsen states in *Film Music*, "Music is used to characterize the agents in the narrative with the aid of leitmotifs that are not only connected to the characters as formal signals but can also sometimes be understood as statements about them, their personal qualities, their role in the plot, etc." (210).

Even if some of the negative reviews showcased before may attest to the inability of people to stomach the relationship, Stevens' music is employed as a bridge to quickly push people into a line of acceptance that helps to digest the visual taboo on the screen, and to possibly create meaningful relationships with each character. A little over an hour into the film, in the learning to love montage, the song comes back in full non-diegetic form. Amid shots of the two frolicking in green fields, and in rare appearance, blue skies, the song blares loudly the universal sentiment of acceptance in challenging times. The connection between friendship and love is connected with the song that was so previously disarming, helping us to understand their friendship first. Pushed to the extreme, the song attempts to weave in our preconditioned response to the music, to either be encouraged further as the song continues to reappear, or to be left in the dust for those overwhelmed by or disdainful of what they have viewed so far and will bear witness to in the rest of the film.

As the final scene of the film suggests, the music of Stevens is worthy not only of the audience's attention, but it also soothes and directs our protagonist after his catastrophic loss of Maude. The spectator is treated, much as in many other spots in the rest of the film, to a scene of disbelief as Harold drives his iconic car off the edge of the cliff. Amid the growl of a determined engine, a horrific silence, and then the crash of the car below, the audience is jilted from shock to the humble tune of a banjo picking out "If You Want to Sing Out, Sing Out" by Harold standing safely distanced from the ledge. The music again has been taken from the realm of the viewer, where it has been solely constructed by Stevens for the audience's use and guidance, and has aptly transcended to Harold, a person like us that can use of a lot of help in gaining perspective on the world around oneself.

Not formally produced at the time, due to the prevalence of Stevens' work for the soundtrack being available on prior recordings, the soundtrack, like the film, refused to die. As Stevens/Islam stated in his Criterion interview, there was an immediate chorus of voices asking for a soundtrack for the film. Inevitably, this want further increased demand for *Mona Bone Jakon* and *Tea for the Tillerman*, but it left some consumers frustrated in not being able to obtain the complete work, including those two new songs recorded for the film itself.

In a piece done for *Variety*, Phil Gallo shares that the demand was overwhelming for a domestic limited edition of the soundtrack put together by Cameron Crowe decades later, the first time all of Stevens' tracks had been compiled into an official release in the United States. The small run of 2,500 reflected the coming together of the bits and pieces of Stevens' work that composed the film's soundtrack. According to Light in the Attic Records, which stocked the LP:

> There's been a hole in the fabric of the film/music world for many, many, many years: late-great director Hal Ashby's bizarre, romantic masterpiece *Harold and Maude* was blessed with a Cat Steven's [sic] soundtrack (one that featured two songs written specifically for the film) that never truly saw the light of day. Yes, "Don't Be Shy" and "If You Want to Sing Out, Sing Out" were released on the *Footsteps in the Dark* compilation in '84, but besides that the original sound track of the film has gone unreleased ["We Have"].

The LPs quickly became a commodity, fetching $100–$150. On the same site, fans commented that for years they had been creating their own versions of the soundtrack on cassette and for later fans on CD and MP3s, due to the lack of an official release. With such a limited run, many fans would still be relegated to the do-it-yourself method.

The enthusiasm and inevitable disappointment for fans with such a limited run showed up on Light in the Attic's site even further, where one disappointed individual lamented that their handmade soundtrack was still their only route to capturing the music of the film, "This has been my emotional go-to move since ... forever. Glad this LP was made ... sad that I missed out. Back to my pieced together playlist." A comment posted two years later was a bit more direct with the following comment: "come on cameron!!! don't be a dick, be like maude and print some more!! i know you can't do the same package but another vinyl issue would be greatly appreciated" ("We Have"). Other fans have expressed similar sentiment such as a posting by "Jordaan Mason" on Mubi.com that expressed, "what's annoying, too, is that the vinyl release in 2007 toted itself as finally 'making available what had been rare for so long' and 'fulfilling film fanatatics' [sic] everywhere but only made 2,500 copies which sold out immediately. second pressing, people!" This could prove to be helpful to many appreciators of the soundtrack, as the price of the soundtrack version described above was going for approximately $900 on Amazon.com during the period of initial research for this chapter.

Part of the frustration for one reviewer on Amazon came from the fact that the diegetic versions of the song, which occupy such a central place within the film, are the most elusive to come by and are not easily quelled for do-it-yourself soundtrack makers:

> The people who have control over this are plainly stupid. When a film is still so popular almost forty YEARS after its release, perhaps these people should be relieved of their duties and fitted with diapers or straightjackets. Cat Stevens, now going by YUSUF ISLAM, placed his best music in this film, and to hear both his AND Ruth Gordon's versions of "IF YOU WANNA BE FREE BE FREE" is a musical joy [All You Need].

The soundtrack is no longer the primary domain of Stevens/Islam but has also been processed by this individual as a place for the voices of the films' players as well in claiming musical ownership. The limited edition soundtrack acknowledged this want by reportedly including Harold's banjo version on the soundtrack itself.

A complex production involving many talents, *Harold and Maude*, much as the opening credit sequence suggests, puts a great deal of influence on the voice of Cat Stevens in shaping the film and its conventional yet unconventional love story. In a concentrated form, showcasing the process of learning and love, *Harold and Maude* is a film that exemplifies the potentially powerful and lasting influence of using popular music in film. Through music's ability, as Chion argues in *Film, a Sound Art*, to manipulate "space and time, which it helps to expand, contract, freeze, and thaw at will" the soundtrack to *Harold and Maude* is a necessary part to creating a discernable and consumable whole. Though as Wierzbicki states that some may attest that popular music's role in film was born from "ignorance, bad taste, and crass commercialism" (192), we can see in the case of *Harold and Maude* a remarkably powerful narrative tool that was and still is able to resonate with filmgoers four decades later. Particularly efficient, Cat Stevens' work on *Harold and Maude* exemplifies the ability of music to shape not only the relationships of characters on screen, but also our relationship and investment in film.

The guiding light of "If You Want to Sing Out, Sing Out" was and is the central guiding force that linked the world of the viewer and the world of the characters themselves. Its simplicity was a continuous refrain that at times opened a sense of relation, legitimacy, and usability for audiences. It was also capable of becoming a simplistic sentiment for a movie that to some may speak of 1960s ethos triteness or even a dismissed part to a deplorable whole. As the "New Hollywood" would prove through a lasting body of work, no matter the effect, and no matter the intent, films like *Harold and Maude* would fundamentally change how people hear *and* experience film as a totality. A new level of centrality and commercial sensibility would intertwine film and the artists recruited to bring that world to life musically. Seemingly, if moving images were to be successfully encountered by audiences, it was best for a film's makers to have someone sing out to those in the theater's seats.

5. Space Is the Place: *Barbarella* and Hearing the Future

The 1968 cult film *Barbarella: Queen of the Galaxy* wastes no time establishing the nymphomaniacal realities of the future. Our protagonist, a galactic, barely-dressed diplomat of the Republic of Earth, is shown in the film's opening scenes encased in an aluminum foil-esque space suit. She begins an interstellar strip-tease as a hipster orchestra plays in the background. We are cued into the mysterious vastness and coldness of space as the camera focuses on a pulsating spaceship, yet we are then quickly warmed with the shag-covered interior of our strip-tease dancer's vessel. The presence of the tremolo of the strings and the isolated tings of a xylophone give way to a tambourine, hipster horns, and flowing woodwinds. The lounge for the space-age bachelor is created not only through the image of our space woman bearing all, but is sonically constructed, helping us to discern the weird and unknown, from the warm and sexual. Barbarella pulls us in from the cold of space, and is able (in zero-gravity no less!) to skillfully peel away each layer of clothing.

The entirety of *Barbarella* is made up of this dichotomy of the momentary unknown and the very human tour-de-force known as the sexual romp. Any fear or discomfort the viewer feels in the next hour and a half or so will be momentary, as peppy horns and lyrical celebrations of our "Barbarella Psychedelia" help the viewer get past the unknowns of distant worlds that are signified by more ominous uses of "primitive electronics and odd studio tricks" (Dusty Groove). In essence, the soundtrack is an essential part of the narrative and is a decoder for the visual arguments at hand. It may, according to several critical reviews, do more than the script does in telling the story of this odd, but ultimately familiar tale of the future "Other." It is thanks in large part to what some may call its "lounge" or "exotica" soundtrack, that *Barbarella* posits the future while remaining firmly planted in the post-war bachelor pad. Though set on distant worlds in space, the tale is an intrinsically human one. The music featured in the film acts as a central character, transporting the listener to the exotic, with an eye always on the timeless and familiar topic of sex.

The soundtrack to the film was a product of songwriter-producer-artist Bob Crewe and composer-producer Charles Fox (composer Michel Magne is also said to have worked on the film). Bob Crewe, by the time *Barbarella* was in production, had a long, storied life within popular music. Crewe, who had scored several hits in the 1950s, penning songs like "Silhouettes," found his greatest fame when he joined up with writing partner Bob Gaudio. The team was responsible for the Frankie Valli and the Four Seasons hits: "Sherry," "Big Girls Don't Cry," "Walk Like a Man," and numerous others. "The Bob Crewe Generation," an assemblage of studio musicians, was one of Crewe's many musical projects that came after this period, among other writing, producing, recording, and scouting projects. The Bob Crewe Generation's "Music to Watch Girls By" in 1967, "a prototypical easy listening/pop crossover instrumental with a '60s, party, go-go beat and Herb Alpert–like brass," as Richie Unterberger describes, became a hit ("Bob Crewe"). Crewe hoped to capitalize on the success that the Generation experienced, when he signed up to craft the soundtrack for *Barbarella*. Crewe, in addition to the Generation, brought in a New York State outfit, The Glitterhouse, one of his pet production projects, to provide some vocals.

Charles Fox, collaborator for the film's soundtrack, had already established some level of success in scoring the film *The Incident*, as well as penning TV scores including the *Wide World of Sports* theme ("Charles Fox"). Fox was pegged for the score after working with Crewe on an album by Ben Lanzarone, and then an album by the Bob Crewe Generation. His career would prolifically take off after *Barbarella* in film, popular music, and television. Fox's theme for *Happy Days*, his work on soundtracks like *Nine to Five*, and his composition, "Killing Me Softly with His Song" highlight a few of his more well-known works as a composer ("Charles Fox Biography").

The team was entrusted to create a sonic world for this campy, psychedelic interpretation of a French comic originally authored by Jean-Claude Forest. The answer for such a task came in the form of launching Crewe's contemporary bachelor pad into space. The approach taken in "Music to Watch Girls By" was jettisoned not only into an interstellar journey, but also into the inner journey of the psychedelic experience. As Fox reflects in his autobiography, *Killing Me Softly: My Life in Music*, the film "clearly needed to have a fun and futuristic approach to it, with sixties music sensibility" (143). The unknown corners of the galaxy and of the inner mind provided enough of a sense of dissonance and playful potential that the music became a new, to borrow a phrase, bachelor "Music to Watch Space Girls By" (this actually being the title of a Leonard Nimoy take on the song). Crewe and Fox would collaborate on the main title song "and four other songs that we would use in a scoring sense, over the action, as commentary on the film" (143). The songs and along with the other parts of the project created a space-age interpretation of "exotica" music, bringing an experience of "the Other" from the hi-fi systems of the post-war leisure nation to a new generation of listeners. This musical form would provide the cornerstone as well as a bridge to the worlds of the future that were sonically constructed within the film. As Fox shares, the film needed to have a certain playfulness to it, due to the fact that it "was a science fiction spoof very much in a campy, psychedelic, sixties style" (143). Hence, the mysterious, the familiar, and the funny were all to be sonically important themes within the finished product, where an "Other" was created.

In his *Mondo Exotica: Sounds, Visions, Obsessions of the Cocktail Generation*, Francesco Adinolfi describes "exotica" music or commonly referred to—to some critics and fans' chagrin—"lounge" or "cocktail" music, as one that was born out of a fascination with "the Other." Originally seen in the rise of the post-war tiki culture fad within popular culture, the "dream of escape and sexual liberation" was connected to this "adults only" affection for the strange (2 & xii). Such music and other associated products of popular culture in the jet-set age produced representations of life far removed from the banality of the 1950s culture-scape. This could mean a trip to the South Pacific on an album, or in the case of *Barbarella* in the late 1960s, it could mean a journey into the last great uncharted territory: space.

The subset of lounge known as space-age bachelor pad music was born to "invoke visions of machines, outer space, and the unknown" (Goldsmith 1072). It was the ultimate "Other" put into musical form. The music was created to both celebrate and anxiously deal with the "postwar obsession with the future and all that was associated with it: the atom, space, and science and technology more generally" (Taylor 73). Through the consumption of technology, one could perhaps more easily face any such fears of the unknown.

Adinolfi contends that the rise of lounge music in popular culture and its subsets, like space-age bachelor pad music, were directly tied to the notion of recreation. The so-called "swinging bachelor" was the undisputed king of the land. He was the colonizer consumer of the unknown, both terrestrially and beyond. "Plenty of disposable income" meant a healthy appetite for stereo equipment, a subscription to *Playboy*, a wealth of ingredients for cocktails, and a comparatively (for the time) low-key attitude towards sexuality (8–9). The bachelor could grab a cocktail, place the needle in the groove, and be transported to distant lands and worlds: a place to free himself from the suit and tie realities of the everyday. This was an environment in which he was ultimately in control and could have all he desired, through consumption.

The Rise of the Bachelor

Thanks to such celebration of the label within the pages of *Playboy*, in popular music, and in everyday life, the bachelor, as Howard P. Chudacoff explains in his *The Age of the Bachelor: Creating an American Subculture*, became a much different entity than it once was. Our modern conceptualizations of this social identity, although often looked down upon in the past, were shaped into a potentially romantic ideal during the end of the 19th century and beginning of the 20th. As men took more control of their careers and education, and moved to the city, a re-examination of the term occurred that ascribed the bachelor as the very definition of unadulterated masculinity (6–7). In the mid part of the century, "a newer, more assertive image of bachelorhood came to dominate American styles, and that image emerged from the pages of *Playboy* magazine" (260–261). This was an assertive argument of pride in the bachelor lifestyle that had not been seen by previous generations.

No longer seen as a result of selfishness or a mental illness, as it may have been considered in earlier times, the image of the bachelor was unashamedly adopted. It put the experience of the immediate and the pleasurable at the center of life. "Bachelorhood" was a life that could be obtained with consumption; it was the unabashed search for pleasure where "seductive and available young women constituted the reward for sophisticated consumerism" (262). Like their art, their music, and their living space, women were a source of cultural capital to be consumed for the bachelor. Chudacoff asserts that *Playboy* "elevated the bachelor life to a desirability, perhaps even a respectability, it had never before experienced. It also reinforced a common bachelor attitude that divided women into three categories: nuisances to be avoided, namely wives and women in search of marriage; objects of sentiment, mostly mothers and sisters; and sexual playthings—all the rest" (263).

Women as subject of this music, that celebrated and that was created for the consumption of the bachelor, were focused on as the latter, as sexual playthings. The bachelor's hi-fi was a place to play a musical product that was meant be a form of recreation, including music "To Watch Girls By." The music took the search for the primitive and the sexually-unabated from distant islands to the cosmos (Taylor 92). In terms of this genre-heavy discussion of "lounge," "space-age bachelor pad music," "exotica" etc., these were meant to be an experience of transcendence and escape from other geographical locations and other mores: sexuality included. All of this was to be tested on one's hi-fi: a bastion of technological innovation in the post-war period that Timothy Taylor refers to as "commodity scientism" (79). The hi-fis "do not simply occupy the space in the living room; music can fill a room like nothing else—

men and their hi-fis could colonize the entire living room and beyond" (Taylor 80). Through music, the strange and the unknown could be conquered through the consumption of new technological forms. Women, primordially fixated on sex, along with all of these other great unknowns, could be colonized too. Thanks to this march towards progress that was brought into the living room, the bachelor just simply had to embrace the notion of expendable income and surety in unsure times.

The Bachelor Swings into the 1960s

It is within this space of the unknown, that *Barbarella* fits so aptly. Even while pulling in supposedly a new generation of influence in the psychedelic and in the counterculture, the message remained the same as the one communicated in the post-war bachelor pad. Somehow the square-ness of the 1950s was partnered with the swinging sexual mores of the bachelor pad, and carried into the sexual revolution of the 1960s. The music, like the film, although kitsch, was also communicating an inherent zeitgeist of a social movement of the time into a vision of the future. Thanks to the film, the pre-AIDS world of the sexual revolution was finding a comfortable home on shag-carpeted spaceships of the future. Like other space-age bachelor pad music, the music for the film was meant to "bring together the bachelor, his stereo system, and his martini" (Goldsmith 1072).

In the case of *Barbarella* however, one can see that these intended targets were linked in earnest with more contemporary visions of hedonism via the march of the counterculture. Psychedelic blob patterns and musical texts that look to explore the uncharted spaces within the mind are married into these earlier musical visions of the unknown. By the time the film was made, the psychedelic movement was much less of a concentrated social experiment, and more so a popular fad within popular culture. The use of LSD and later the idea or culture of psychedelia promised a potential for escape. As Martin A. Lee and Bruce Shlain in their *Acid Dreams: The Complete Social History of LSD: The C.I.A., the Sixties, and Beyond* describe it, "LSD was a means of exciting consciousness and provoking visions, a kind of hurried magic enabling youthful seekers to recapture the resonance of life that society had denied. Drugs were a passport to an uncharted landscape of risk and sensation" (131). LSD became a chemical means to experience the authentic, the exotic, "the Other." Put together with the promise of the same destinations through the bachelor lounge and the surging power of hi-fi systems, a potent combination could be formed.

Much as exotica wanted to transport the post-war bachelor, psychedelia was promising a journey into some kind of authentic unknown as well. It is useful to point out here that such allusions could be referring to the actual drug experience, as well as the more general stylistic fad of psychedelia. One did not need to take the drug to partake in popular culture products that were meant to mirror the experience stylistically, whether visually or sonically. "Psychedelic" texts represented a vast spectrum of products from concert posters to lunchboxes. Though separated in time, exotica and psychedelia were a perfect match, as they both were part of the industry of escape from the everyday, from the ruled, and from the known. Like the path to freedom through consumption of "the lounge," the psychedelic "experience" was also a concentrated and consumed mode of escape that could be used as recreation. If looked at in the right light, both could also be considered challenges to dominant social and cultural life, though both re-emphasize the systems they attempt to escape through the consumptive habits built around them.

The space-age bachelor pad music used in the film showcased a variety of styles that incorporated a plethora of influences to create a sound of the future, including fuzz-driven guitars and other tropes a la psychedelia. The psychedelic, the aforementioned peppy horn sections, along with twangs, beeps, and electronic noise, came together to form the postmodern sound of space and distant lands. As Adinolfi describes such "space-age bachelor music":

> The music had to be surprising, and yet at the same time entertaining, passing from honey-sweet sounds to strikingly rhythmic compositions, rife with unusual noises and bizarre instruments like the theremin, together with a stream of marimbas, xylophones, timpani, bongos, electric organs, big band–style wind sections, guitars, and animal cries [122].

Barbarella uses these collections of cues to take the listener beyond their stereo and into the film-going experience. Odd animal cries created by electronic dissonance, psychedelic guitar effects, and Adinolfi's cited musical practices noted above become the greatest indicators of the distant and primal in the film. The controlled psychedelic and the film's juxtaposed easy listening motifs counter this sense of anxiety and bring us back to Earth. The music of the film eases the film-goer into comfortable spaces that act as a binary to the mysterious, uncharted lands our protagonist discovers. As one reviewer put it, the soundtrack incorporates a "mad mix of styles that blends 1960s adult easy with spacier themes—using primitive electronics and odd studio tricks to capture the cartoony space landscape of Jane Fonda's world in the move [sic]." The same reviewer continues on, describing the soundtrack as a "sonic film" (Dusty Groove). With sparse dialogue and sometimes confounding imagery, the music is able to tell much of the tale.

When one looks at *Barbarella* with such considerations in mind, it is interesting to see how the very real, and one could argue sexist traditions of the bachelor, help the viewer of the film to experience "the Other" or the unknown through the futuristic sounds of space-age pop and visions of the psychedelic. Conversely, a part is played by the more traditional role of "easy" or "lounge" music to reaffirm the very real and terrestrial sexism of the time period in which the music was produced. No matter how far into the future, or how far outside of Earth's orbit we got, the conventions of female sexuality were apparent in the visual and aural form.

This developing theme of importance placed on the music to further the narrative, and to create audience understanding, potentially offers a challenge to the canonized perspectives that focus on the absoluteness of the visual in studying, consuming, and interpreting cinema. Craig Sinclair in his "Audition: Making Sense of/in the Cinema" deals with this challenge specifically, taking issue with the focus taken by scholars such as Laura Mulvey: "Audition serves to undermine the very hegemony that Mulvey posits in the visuals and in doing so appeals to 'other' elements of the audience from those who choose to merely gaze at the screen" (21). Indeed, the lasting presence of film scores and soundtracks in popular culture showcases a definitive appeal and possible alternative sense of narrative and meaning to a film. Sinclair continues, "Sound challenges the assumed power, the assumed superiority and supremacy of the image, and thus challenges the perception of the experiencer." He adds, "This may not necessarily promote agency" but it does "position the experiencer as the producer of meaning, while the viewer was a mere passive recipient" (24). One can only imagine the gaps left in *Barbarella* and in the viewer's mind without the guidance of the music.

In *Film Music*, Peter Larsen discusses that there is a fundamental need to use the music to establish a sense of context and direction. Larsen, as quoted in the last chapter, contends that in its simplest use, a film-maker utilizes music within a film to "support and structure the narrative" (206) in predictable ways. The music "sets boundaries, it measures out and rounds off the individual narrative event." He continues, "With the aid of its own structure, the music structures the events on the screen, separates them from each other or links them, points out connections and transitions, closes sections off and opens new ones" (208). However, music, along with the other sensory stimuli involved in film, allow not only the producers of the film to communicate a message and narrative, but it also provides the raw materials for audiences to do the same: "When music, images and dialogue are coordinated and appear as a perceptual whole, we automatically expect there to be an underlying intention. We search for a meaning, and we find it—no matter whether the coordination was actually intentional or not" (205).

An extreme example of audiences creating such a coordination between the visual and music is exemplified in the great dorm room or urban myth experiment of watching *The Wizard of Oz*, while listening to Pink Floyd's *Dark Side of the Moon*. Though the band contends that no relation exists, listeners have sometimes vehemently linked the album to the film, saying that the musical-visual links are too numerous to ignore. The power of Larsen's contention is especially on display in that, in this instance, the audience is doing all of the creation. The producers of the texts have been left behind. Music and the visual are being used to create a certain sense of narrative or meaning.

The music, like the film *Barbarella* itself, is a hodge-podge of mixed messages about sex, space, the unknown, and the familiar. Ultimately, it is the viewer who is left to make sense of the trippy narrative. Whatever message is taken, though, is linked inherently to the sonic cues that alert us to this binary. There is a give and take with the film and its soundtrack that creates an ability to keep the film in two musical worlds: the lounge and the psychedelic. These divergent messages bring about a variance of audience interpretations. Above all though, a spectrum of audiences could probably agree that the main target of the film was the topic of sex. Yet, what this spotlight on sex meant for the film's audiences, and how the music aided in creating the narrative, seemed to be up for grabs in this time of social, political, and cultural upheaval.

Variety did not see any liberatory possibilities of the film upon its release: "Jane Fonda stars in the title role, and comes across as an ice-cold, antiseptic, wide-eyed girl who just can't say no. Fonda's abilities are stretched to the breaking point along with her clothes" (Variety Staff). Louette Harding, mirroring such concerns, claimed in a more recent article that for Roger Vadim (Fonda's director and husband at the time) Fonda "turned herself into the film sex doll *Barbarella*, and became one privately, too. He told her fidelity was bourgeois and pressured her to join the swinging 1960s by participating in threesomes, on three occasions with prostitutes" (26). Such contextual information supports those viewing *Barbarella* as being represented as object versus subject. Fonda, in such perspectives, was a representation of the timeless consumption of women as a sort of cultural capital, regardless of the social, political, filmic, or musical prognosis of the times added to the mix.

The film has and continues to also solicit comments from critics that see a sense of potential empowerment through countercultural embracement of sexual taboo within the text. Susan McLeland in "Barbarella Goes Radical: Hanoi Jane and the American Popular Press" offers, "Fonda as *Barbarella* was both symbol and product of a 'revolution' that capitalized on free love and sexual pleasure as shocking and therefore resistant." She continues in a discussion of images of Fonda as *Barbarella* that Fonda is "challenging the viewer to possess Fonda and constructing Fonda's body as the repository of a healthy, liberated, utopian sexuality that promises a host of once-forbidden pleasures." Yet, the "effect is not indifference to the objectifying gaze but open provocation of it" (233–234). Such discussions continue in other critical work on the film. Pauline Kael from *The New Yorker* remarked how Barbarella "is playfully and deliciously aware of the naughtiness of what she's doing" (qtd. in Fonda 178). Such readings allow us to bear witness to the fact that the film, with its dependence on music to support the narrative, creates seemingly archaic as well as combative messages about sexuality and women's roles in the late 1960s. The act of consuming the sights and sounds of a film can yield and support these divergent views. Reception ignites meaning and use for the viewer. As Peter Larsen contends, watching a film is an activity, an interpretive act:

> We are constantly interpreting the information presented to us. We classify it, we assess it in relation to other information, we scan it against our own background knowledge, and we contemplate how it is to be understood and positioned in relation to the narrative and its narrators. This is also what we do with musical information [200].

When combining these forms, the plethora of raw materials in a film such as *Barbarella*, can enliven debates from those who see Barbarella as a feminist icon and those who see her as an intergalactic tramp.

Andrew Keech discusses in his liner notes for the 2004 *Barbarella* CD release how "Ski Ride" leads "into the attack of 'Hungry Dolls' and the wonderful vocal romp 'Love, Love, Love Drags Me Down' sung by Mike Gale, lead singer of Glitterhouse as Barbarella and Mark Hand practice the old-fashioned method." The development of these tracks reflects a use of electronic shrills and screams that is eventually replaced with the safety of a tuba and then horns and upbeat electric guitar when they travel on the Catchman's ship. From dissonance and the unknown, Barbarella eventually finds something more terrestrial. By the time the viewer gets to "Love, Love..." they are hearing what sounds like Herb Alpert meeting the Strawberry Alarm Clock in an orchestration of climax.

A new woman, Barbarella prepares to debark from the ship in bliss. She is now experienced in physical love-making, versus the supposedly more efficient and logical pill-induced equivalent featured in Earth's future society. Any oddness or feeling of discomfort created by the visual and the soundtrack depicting strange worlds up to this point is alleviated with a new soothing string arrangement that is joined by a vocal, sweetly delivering the next song's thesis of "I Love All of the Love in You." Flesh-eating dolls, and pills that take the place of sex be damned, the traditional cues of the afterglow are sweetly delivered to the film-goer.

Soon after, Barbarella is saved again. This time she falls into the arms of Pygar, the arch-angel of The Labyrinth. The oddness of the place, the destitute nature of its inhabitants, which include Marcel Marceau as a whimsical professor, includes a complementary soundscape of the future unknown. There is a continuous chiming of bells, and occasional stabs from a heavily overdriven guitar. The music alerts us, along with the visual, that this isn't a safe or normal place. It is at this point that the music pushes the viewer into "the Other" with electronic whirls and screams indicating that the evil forces (the Tyrant's Guard) nearby. After some tense moments we can see things are going to be okay. Pygar saves her from the guards and brings some humanity into this cold, unfeeling world for both Barbarella and for the audience along for the ride. Of course once she is safe, such a thoughtful deed demands another sexual encounter, this time in Pygar's large nest home.

Barbarella is next shown enjoying the spoils of such nest-making, where another swirl and crescendo of horns and winds create a sense of dawning. Physical contact has assured everyone's happiness and redemption. We hear Pygar explain, "I've regained the will to fly." The professor, as he sees the arch-angel fly remarks, "Interesting therapy." Again, a confusing and surreal vision of the future is quickly brought back to contemporary contexts of sex and space-age bachelor music. Either Barbarella is the agent or the object (or something between), depending on the viewer's mindset.

Psychedelia is a partial indicator of "the Other," but is overwhelmingly held at bay by the comfort of the post-war lounge, and is even used to communicate, in part, along with more traditional fare, the sexual act. It thusly is employed as a creator of dissonance, as well as peppering in its influence on the music of redemption, through sex and the body. Somewhere between the ill-feelings created in a world of machines, and the comfortable world of a peppy horn section, psychedelic music is used as a sort of bridge in the narrative, sometimes erring towards either binary, depending on the context.

For example, earlier in the film when Barbarella is first traveling to these distant lands, this bridge is created in "Spaceship Out of Control," where the space between complete dissonance and familiar musical forms is actively engaged via the use of psychedelic musical stylings, along with semiotic indicators of the same. Barbarella embarks on a journey through "temporal space" in the scene. She lays down on her see-through bed, chest first, for a long pill-induced nap. This occurs amidst the lullaby of beeps and bops, and dreamlike, whispering brass lines. The viewer is invited to lay beneath the girl in intergalactic lingerie. Our protagonist is awoken, with only a few minutes to wipe the sleep out of her eyes, when an alarm of electronic organs and shrill, psychedelic guitar chords pierces the calm rumpus room. Add to this the visuals of "space" that Barbarella sees in front of her: liquid-projected patterns of colors, bubbles, and electric collage. Simply put, space seems to be the sonic and visual equivalent of a Moby Grape concert at the Fillmore or Avalon Ballroom in late 1960s San Francisco.

The music, representing not only a strange new generational "Other" musically but also culturally, fits perfectly into the realm of the unknown. Taylor, when discussing space-age pop, describes that "different" was enough to distinguish an interchangeable range of music in indicating its "Otherness":

> That all these different sounds from different (sub)styles and/or (sub)genres were used points to how interchangeable all of these categories were. *Exotic* could mean Hawaiian, "Latin," Indian, Middle Eastern—it was a single musical sign system to which electronic instruments such as the theremin were added to signify "space." Others were others, and you have to travel to get to them, or they to you, either by jet or spaceship [92].

Who needs a spaceship though or even a jet-set frequent-flyer membership card, when a small tab of LSD can take a person on his own trip into the unknown? Luckily, no matter the journey, we are constantly brought "back to earth" by the sex-capades of our protagonist and familiar sounds.

The only real exception to the practice of sex as relief and recognition for the viewer musically and visually comes in Barbarella's run-in with the leader of the resistance. It is at this point that the sound of a militaristic march combines with psychedelic musical cues to showcase the now, in Barbarella's mind, soulless and ridiculously efficient practice of sex through pill form: the exultation transference pill process. Begrudgingly, Barbarella agrees to take the pill as a thank you to Dildano for saving her life. Relegating the level of intimacy to simply touching a single hand to each other, the scene is the antithesis to all the viewer has known so far. Devoid of sensuality, the worst fears of the future come true for the bachelor. A zealous horn section, and the newly technologically engaged psychedelic sound, including overdrive, distortion, etc., are employed together to showcase the ridiculous in the unknown: sex through efficiency, and without physical intimacy.

Just when one thinks our protagonist may be onto something a bit more redemptive, Durand Durand, the evil antagonist of the film, traps Barbarella in his Excessive Machine. The examination of the machine by the camera is joined by a fuzz-driven guitar, string tremolo, and various plinks and plonks. Here "the Other" is created. Thankfully, the viewer-listener quickly learns Durand Durand uses the machine to kill via pleasure. A slew of strings and horns indicate the playfulness. Suddenly as he describes her forthcoming death via the machine, the musical score bounces between horns, guitars, and furious cadences as the machine does its best to kill our hero. The horns retake the center stage though as Barbarella shamelessly challenges the machine, soaking in all of its excessiveness. Again comfort is sounded, and finally in a psychedelic crescendo mixed with whirls, wheezes, and of course horns, any sense of oddity or unfamiliarity created through the music and the visual of the machine is trumped as climax is blaringly indicated on Barbarella's face. The viewer/listener is comfortable that any threat has been neutralized and what we are hearing is the sound of the peak of sexual experience. Thanks to the score that bridges a generational hipster divide, the promiscuity and hipness of the 1950s lounge or bachelor pad is met with the psychedelic vision of hipness and its complementary perspectives on the role of the sexual being.

Dissonance, created through primitive electronica, tech-driven sounds of the psychedelic, and other accompanying whirls and beeps create a sense of the unknown, of the primal, or even of the feared. It is in the familiar sounds of the lounge that all of this is taken away. Oftentimes momentary, these important sonic cues provide a space of relief and familiarity in an unfamiliar world. Combining the two can bring visions of the inner self, of excess, and climax. No matter whether it is the psychedelic or the lounge, sex is intrinsically related to the sound. It is within this theme that the two styles share a basic meta-narrative; no matter "the Other" to be explored, the experience whether in distant cultures on Earth or in the massive "Otherness" of space is always related to a sense of primal sexuality. Sex trumps time, space, and technology. Perhaps the generational divide between the swinging bachelor of the 1950s and the psychedelic, sexual celebration in 1960s popular culture was not too far apart.

Sex as repression or sex as empowerment can not only be seen but also heard in *Barbarella*. In this version of space-age pop, the sounds of the lounge and the sounds of the psychedelic combine into a polysemic and polysonic orchestration that delivers mixed messages at best. Are we seeing and hearing an empowered sexual being or are we seeing and hearing the continued exoticization of other places and the primitive sexual mores that supposedly exist in such places? The music of the film and the history of "lounge" or "exotica" would seemingly point to the latter. In essence, from tiki to the planet Lythion (the setting for most of the film), a changing same exists. Regardless of its countercultural context, the lineage of the music continues a practice of sonic and voyeuristic representation and imagination: it is music to *watch girls by*.

Still, the ability of audiences to use the combined elements of music and the visual to create meaning is a prolific one. Time and context shape texts like *Barbarella* into raw materials that can be embraced or rejected as challenges to dominant societal norms. Due to its connection to the time, the social milieu, the visual cues, the film's camp humor, and the musical cues,

Barbarella occupies numerous ideological potentialities. Though the musical legacy present in the film and the conventions of musically interpreting the future represent a terrestrial consumption of women, the cues given by the film, including its amalgamated sound, seemingly provide enough raw materials to construct a potential challenge to this consumption. Under the guise of the sexual revolution, or empowerment, these cues, with their countercultural signification, are enough to challenge the idea that this is another conventional playboy exercise.

The score/soundtrack, like the film, leaves some gray area in terms of giving the receiver a definitive message. These mixed messages, including the sonic cues, create a film which some can see as empowering and some as regressive. As stated, the divide can be significant and the debate elongated when focusing on the messages of the film and its role as a supposedly countercultural text. Such sentiments need to be seriously considered and weighed against each other when trying to make sense of the text, and the usability that audiences demonstrate with the text. However history continues to deal with the film, including possible remakes on the horizon, a central place should be reserved for the narrative created by the film's music. How we hear the film and how we make sense of sonic narrative in cultural and historical terms can do a great deal in terms of placing how far, for example, we have come or, in the case of *Barbarella*, how much we have possibly remained in the bachelor pad of the 1950s.

6. Did the Soundtrack Also Blow It?: Using Rock to Capture Counterculture Generational Identity

Introduction

Released in 1969, *Easy Rider* is an iconic countercultural film. Characterized for its "postwar American experimental and avant-garde" roots, it is a "counterculture classic" with pounding rock music (Calavita 18). The film's stars, Peter Fonda and Dennis Hopper, along with Terry Southern wrote the film addressing social issues at the time including drug use, the hippie movement, the idea of freedom and patriotism, and untraditional commune-style living arrangements. Fonda acts as Wyatt, nicknamed "Captain America." His motorcycling partner, Billy, is played by Hopper. The film was produced with an estimated budget of approximately $400,000 ("Easy Rider" IMDb; Scharres 25). Emily Burnham writes that *Easy Rider* was "made for a really, really low budget [but] made a huge, huge profit." Despite this limited budget, *Easy Rider* made over $41 million in the U.S. and about $60 million worldwide ("Easy Rider" IMDb). Vincent Canby attributes this success to the film's "[capturing] the spirit of the times as it woke Hollywood up to the power of young audiences and socially relevant movies." The film, both visually and aurally, addressed the conflict between the established social norms and attempts to challenge them by the participants of counterculture.

The film received a handful of awards. Although many of the early films that heavily relied on rock music tended not to be successful at the box office, it was not the case with this 1969 film (Kornbluth). Dennis Hopper won the Best First Work at the Cannes Film Festival in 1969. Jack Nicholson won the Best Supporting Actor Award at the Kansas City Film Critics Circle Awards.

For the Academy Awards in 1970, the film was also nominated for Best Actor in a Supporting Role for Jack Nicholson and Best Writing, Story and Screenplay Based on Materials Not Previously Published or Produced for Peter Fonda, Dennis Hopper, and Terry Southern. The film was also nominated for the Best Drama Written Directly for the Screen at the Writers Guild of America in the same year ("Easy Rider: Awards"). The list of accolades continues.

As Canby discusses, *Easy Rider* reflects "the increasingly violent Vietnam-era split between the counterculture and the repressive Establishment." Additionally, to this day, the film continues to be relevant to many contemporary viewers "for its trailblazing legacy and its sharply perceptive portrait of its chaotic times" (Canby). One could say that the value of the film is partially evident from the ways in which fans reacted to the auction in 2007 when Fonda decided to sell his memorabilia from the film. Many of the items had an estimated value of thousands of dollars or more. The American flag that was on Fonda's jacket was thought to be worth $50,000, eventually being sold for $89,625. His Department of Defense pin on the jacket was valued at $15,000. Fonda's gold record for the film's soundtrack was estimated at $2,000. The prototype Rolex watch Fonda wore in the film was sold for over $33,000 (Young; "Fonda Auctions"). This is just a story that shows the lasting impact of the film in the context of the twenty-first century.

The plot of the film is simple. Wyatt and Billy are hippie motorcyclists. Wyatt wears a helmet with the design of American flag and a jacket with the aforementioned $90,000 flag sewn to it on the back. He is friendlier than Billy. Wyatt welcomes others while Billy, wearing a leather fringe, tends to be suspicious of and even antagonistic to others. The story begins as they smuggle cocaine from Mexico to the U.S. They sell it and fill Wyatt's motorcycle fuel tank with money stashed in a plastic tube. They plan to travel east, eventually to New Orleans for Mardi Gras.

The film is mostly about the journey of the two characters. This is why, despite Fonda's later comment—"it wasn't a biker movie at all. It was a Western. I wore spurs"—the film is usually characterized as a road movie (Young). Throughout the trip, Wyatt and Billy experience a rancher's simple lifestyle, meet a hitch-hiker, witness free love, and get arrested after riding along with a parade. George Hanson (Jack Nicholson) joins them after being released from the jail with Wyatt and Billy. All of them, aspiring to live a free lifestyle, soon experience resistance from a local conservative community. When they go to a restaurant, the local clientele stares at them curiously. As strangers, they leave the restaurant without being served. George comments that even though the country was supposed to stand for freedom, in reality, it refuses those who actually practice it. The locals were not just resistant to these passers-by. They find the three in the middle of the night and kill George while Wyatt and Billy narrowly escape. Counterculture may have been a part of American culture at the time, but it was clear that there was a cultural clash between the traditional and new values.

In spite of the loss of their new friend, Wyatt and Billy make it to New Orleans. They decide to visit a brothel which George had planned to go to. In Billy's mind, the trip to find their American dream was a success. They hit a jackpot with drug dealing. They are ready to retire. Wyatt, however, disagrees and utters one of the most famous lines of the film, "We blew it." The morning after, Wyatt and Billy continue their eastbound trip, now to Florida, their ideal retirement location, with the money still hidden in the fuel tank. At this point, a passenger of a truck shoots both with a shotgun. Billy is covered with blood. Wyatt, attempting to seek help, is also shot at. The bullet hits Wyatt's motorcycle's fuel tank, leading it to explode violently.

While the film chronicles two characters' eastbound motorcycle ride, the music often becomes a focal point of the viewer's experience. David Shumway writes, "The music in *Easy Rider* often becomes the focus of attention. For long stretches of the ride east from California to violent death someplace between New Orleans and Florida, *Easy Rider* presents the two motorcyclists riding against the background of a changing landscape and songs that comment on their adventure [*sic*]" (38). Drake Stutesman, on the other hand, claims that the music becomes a central part of the film because the film was "all about the camera following ... people who don't do anything." He says that he found such cinematic practice "boring like hell" (Price and Stuteman 48). But the music is still an integral part of the movie because it neatly frames the counterculture as a part of the story. Al Auster and Leonard Quart say "The trip is enhanced by the film's existing use of landscape, space, movement, and sound (especially the contemporary rock music of Jimi Hendrix, The Byrds, Steppenwolf and others)" (12). Shumway continues to explain that the soundtrack was "the first multi-artist record of its kind to become a significant sales success" (38).

Choosing Music for the Soundtrack

An interesting paradox of the film is that despite *Easy Rider*'s significant use of music, it was not recommended for any music-related awards. The soundtrack had a successful sales record. Damaso Reyes calls the soundtrack "a work of genius." Elaine M. Bapis writes that the film's music has become "its own legend" (*Camera*, 92) and praises that the film "[celebrates] ... popular rock music by The Byrds, Steppenwolf, Jimi Hendrix, Roger McGuinn, and other music celebrities" ("*Easy Rider*," 157). Nonetheless, it seems to have escaped the minds of those in charge of giving awards. Without formal accolades, however, the significance of music in *Easy Rider* is immense without question.

Phil Powrie and Robynn Stilwell explain that the use of pre-existing music in a film "can be compared to geological strata." It reveals "a kind of archaeology of the undertone, historically and materially bound, that aims to work through the layers of connotations to reach the affects lying under the concretions of time." They continue, "There lies too the seismic potential of the soundtrack to disrupt the placid surface, to erupt unpredictably or create subterranean tremors that resonate throughout a film; and the shock waves never run deeper than when an 'inappropriate artefact' ... turns out to be appropriate in ways we might never before have imagined" (xix).

Easy Rider's use of existing music could very well be read as an attempt to take advantage of the layers of meanings that Powrie and Stilwell discuss. But it is also true that the film was created in haste. Peter Bart claims that the film was made without a final cast or script. It was produced with a crew gathered in five weeks. From this perspective, the use of unoriginal music could very well be a reflection of Hopper's practical choice as the director. Either way, Mark Evan's characterization that the film "emphasized pop record albums and commercial sounds instead of dramatic underscoring" is accurate (203). Additionally, Peter Larsen correctly observed that *Easy Rider* is one of the "first examples of modern film-makers returning to the practice of the silent film era of using compilations of already existing music as an accompaniment" (151).

This practice of using existing music might come as a surprise to some contemporary film fans. A lot of blockbusters today indeed take advantage of an original score, especially when it comes to the main theme song. From *Star Wars* to numerous Disney films, composers are hired to create a theme song unique and original to a movie. Exceptions, of course, exist. But *Easy Rider*, along with some other films included in this volume, returned to the old practice and utilized existing works. By the early 1970s, many films began to use existing music, leading "many decorated and venerated Hollywood composers into an early and unwanted retirement" (Hubbert 180). Such a practice could be interpreted as an early example of creative mash-ups bringing musical and visual cues together to create a new meaning.

Easy Rider's use of existing music, Shumway explains, should not be interpreted as an attempt "to create nostalgia" (38). In other words, it is not intended to remind viewers of the good old days. After all, Wyatt and Billy are escaping from the past, without any reason to reminisce about the good old days. Hubbert concurs by stating "to hear only the nostalgia in [*Easy Rider*] is to miss the vérité in their music" (201). Rather, Shumway argues that it brings a "strong sense of generational identity" (38). This, in part, contributes to the characterization of the movie by Elaine Bapis who wrote, "*Easy Rider* touched a generational nerve by gathering together essential realities of the 1960s and ensured it would be widely revered in popular culture" (*Camera*, 79). When viewers identify themselves with Wyatt and Billy, it is not just through visual cues but also through music that they feel a sense of belonging.

Use Value of Rock Music

The list of musicians whose recordings are used in *Easy Rider* consists of rock musicians such as The Byrds, Jimi Hendrix, and others. Because the film features America's beautiful scenery, it is completely justifiable to characterize it as a travelogue or a road movie. However, it is also a "rock video." Furthermore, Kevin Michael Grace argues that it was "the first rock video" (36). Choosing rock as the genre of music for the film was a meaningful one. Any category of music could carry a message. But rock, in the context of the film, occupies a special space. Jesse Kornbluth writes, "The soundtrack is always rock because, however badly it has been hyped, packaged, turned into the hippiest of Muzak, rock is still able to communicate something, and 'now' films—which generally have nothing to say to anybody about anything—need all the support their producers can purchase."

The "something" that Kornbluth mentions is a countercultural frontier. Similar to the eastward journey that Joe Buck took in *Midnight Cowboy* (1969), Wyatt and Billy venture east, from California to New Orleans, and eventually to head to Florida. This advancement of a personal and cultural frontier is contradictory to the history of the westward American frontier. However, the resistance to the past and even the reversal of a historic shift are prime examples of countering the normative culture. In her analysis of *Easy Rider*, Bapis explains that the movie established the countercultural generation identity by characterizing the counterculture as a legitimate response by the youth to "oppression and struggles with their own establishment" ("*Easy Rider*," 170). She elsewhere notes that the film contains a "gesture of solidarity" within the counterculture generation (*Camera*, 88). To seek an alternative to the establishment, Wyatt and Billy embark on a journey.

The journey on the road is that of the counterculture. A substantial part of the story happens while the protagonists are on their motorcycles. As Michael Allen characterizes, there is a parallel between *Easy Rider* and Jack Kerouac's *On the Road* (292). Wyatt and Billy get on the road because the freedom their predecessors found in the West was no longer appealing to them.

They will not follow the footsteps of the previous generations. Therefore the movie's choice of songs such as "Wasn't Born to Follow" by the Byrds or "If 6 was 9" by Jimi Hendrix makes sense.

Both songs have the theme of "individualism, bravery, and wanderlust" (Allen 289). While the Byrds create a dreamy world where they would "rather go," they ultimately recognize that the things they have learned would not have any value. Similarly, Jimi Hendrix does not worry about others. His lyrics suggest that he has his own world and that he does not care what might happen in the world. Rock music enabled this countercultural identity to permeate within the film.

Easy Rider's music helps generate the imagery of mobility and resistance. From the motorcycle rides to Wyatt and Billy's strong assertions of values, the story is about how to find a new type of American dream appropriate for the social and cultural contexts at the time. The westward mobility that contradicts the eastward historical trends, seeking individual freedom and detachment of the establishment, exploration of new lifestyles, and others are all ingredients of a countercultural journey. The filmmakers used motorcyclists' rock music, especially heavy metal as will be explained below, as an important identifier of their culture. Furthermore, as Kornbluth writes, once the film became a success, it affirmed the meaning of rock music.

Steppenwolf in Easy Rider

The American rock band Steppenwolf produced two significant songs that were adopted in the film: "Born to Be Wild" (1968) and "The Pusher" (1968). John Kay (vocalist), Goldy McJohn (keyboardist), and Jerry Edmonton (drummer) started the band in 1967 and added Michael Monarch (guitarist) and Rushton Moreve (bassist) later. Although the band continues to perform to this day, its prime lasted only until the mid–1970s. Nonetheless, Steppenwolf offered numerous hit songs to the rock fans in the U.S. In addition to the two aforementioned songs, the band released other popular works such as "Magic Carpet Ride" (1968), "Rock Me" (1969), and "Move Over" (1969) to name a few. The band's total record sales were over $25 million. More than fifty movies adopted their songs. Over ten singles by Steppenwolf made it to the Billboard Hot 100 chart, with "Magic Carpet Ride" ranked at number three at its peak and "Born to Be Wild" at number two (Dahl; Tolzmann).

Steppenwolf is often considered to be one of the pioneers of heavy metal. Robert Gross explains,

> Some music historians prefer to credit the band Steppenwolf with the invention of the heavy metal music form. In 1967 they recorded "Born to be Wild," a tune

that not only features many criteria that fit the modern day definition of heavy metal, but the words, "heavy metal thunder" actually appear in the second verse of the song [120].

Of course, "heavy metal" in the lyrics refers to the motorcycle, and not a musical genre which was still at its relative infancy. However, the reference to "heavy metal" reflects the countercultural nature of the musical genre, that of the heavy metal motorcyclist culture, and the general counterculture of the mid–twentieth century. John Kay is quoted in *German Life* stating, "Our philosophy was hit 'em hard, make your point and move on" (Tolzmann).

The first song by Steppenwolf to be heard in *Easy Rider* is "The Pusher." The song was written by Hoyt Axton and released the year before the launch of the film. The song begins during the opening scene of the drug deal. Wyatt and Billy sell drugs and Wyatt stuffs bills into his motorcycle's fuel tank. The lyrics of the song are a window to countercultural attitudes toward drugs which tend to be oversimplified by many as they reminisce, remember, or recount the 1960s.

Commonly and over-simplistically, the 1960s or the counterculture period is considered to be the era of drugs. A Wikipedia entry on "Counterculture of the 1960s" offers that the 1960s saw "a subculture that extolled the mystical and religious symbolism often engendered by the drug's powerful effects" as it discusses "casual LSD users." Similarly, *Cliffsnotes* characterizes the decade by explaining that hippies "embraced sexual promiscuity and recreational drugs, including marijuana and the hallucinogenic LSD. The sex and drug culture were reflected in the rock music of the time by such groups as Jefferson Airplane and the Grateful Dead and performers like Jim Morrison and Janis Joplin" ("The Counterculture of the 1960s"). Even Donald Wesson at University of California, Los Angeles, writing in the *Journal of Psychoactive Drugs*, stated, "Mainstream culture and a psychedelic drug-using counterculture shared a belief in 'better living through chemistry'" (153). The 1960s, therefore, is a decade of drugs, sex, and an anti-war movement, at least according to many popular sources.

The reality of the counterculture was much more complex. Drugs were not treated equally. Just as music provides vehicles to understand the complexity of intertwined perspectives on sexuality, the Vietnam War, and other social issues, it enables listeners and critics to understand how Americans in the mid-century looked at drugs as a component of "alternative life styles" (Robinson, Pilskaln, and Hirsch, 125). Surveying fans of protest rock music, Robinson, Pilskaln, and Hirsch argue that there was a distinction between hard drugs and soft drugs, namely heroin being out of the sight and minds of many (130). John Markert agrees with this observation. He argues, "Popular music has been generally hostile toward hard drugs (heroin and cocaine)" (214).

"The Pusher" affirms the findings of these studies. The pusher is contrasted to the dealer in the lyrics. The dealer is the type of people with whom Wyatt and Billy had worked. They deal so-called soft drugs, or in the words of Steppenwolf, "grass" and "pills." The dealer is also "a man." To the contrary, the pusher is someone that can kill the spirit of his clients. Furthermore, the pushers are indifferent to whether or not you are alive. The pusher is not a man, but a monster, Steppenwolf describes.

"The Pusher" also reflects a conflict in values during the counterculture period. The song can be interpreted as anti-drug, at least anti-hard drug. But the song was nonetheless banned by the authorities in Winston-Salem, NC, where Steppenwolf was scheduled to perform. The decision to eliminate this anti-drug song took place because it repeatedly said, "god damn." The authorities' censorship raised concerns particularly among strong advocates for the freedom of speech. However, Steppenwolf obliged and decided not to sing the line in question. Regardless, John Kay explains that he urged his fans to sing the line for them, and indeed, "thousands of fans at the concert shouted out the chorus themselves" (Taylor).

Although "The Pusher" resonated well with countercultural sentiments, it was not the only song by Steppenwolf to do so. "Born to Be Wild" is another example of musical representation of countercultural lifestyles. Written by Mars Bonfire and released in 1968, the song is still "considered to be an anthem to a variety of heavy metal fans, especially motorcycle clubs" (Gross 120). Lindsey Millar further adds that that the song "quickly became an anthem for the steadily emerging counterculture," even before it was used in the film, but especially after it was included in the movie's soundtrack (Millar; Grace 36).

"Born to Be Wild" is the second song to be heard in the movie. After "The Pusher" disappears, the song begins with the opening credits while Wyatt and Billy ride their motorcycles. Used in one of the pioneer biker road movies, "Born to Be Wild" set a standard for other similar movies. When a camera follows motorcycles, audiences might find it monotonous. For example, *Easy Rider* features a series of scenes that shows only the moving background scenery just with two motorcycles at the front stage. Not much changes aside from the background. There is no conversation between characters. As mentioned earlier, this is partly why Stutesman called such segments "boring" (Price and Stutesman 48). But music, including "Born to be Wild," keeps the film going. Mervyn Cooke writes that the motorcycles "seem propelled onwards by Steppenwolf's repetitive and hard-driving rhythms, strong bass line and powerful sonorities" (413). The use of such music in road films was not unique to *Easy Rider*. Cooke continues to explain that "music with these ingredients continued to feature heavily in the genre of the road movie" (413).

Steppenwolf's music highlights the contrast between the ugliness of people and the beauty of the scenery. On the one hand, Wyatt and Billy, as well as other characters, experience a clash of values. They may be refused service at a restaurant. But Billy is not the one to trust others easily. Personal interests and ideals create complex human relations. Steppenwolf's music justifies the ugliness of human lives. On the other hand, throughout the film, audiences are given opportunities to appreciate the magnificent scenic background of the American countryside. The nostalgic and consistent view almost suggests the unchanging nature of society in general. Countercultural and social resistance may exist, but ultimately, society is slow to change.

Compared to the use of existing instrumental music such as Beethoven in *A Clockwork Orange* or the James Bond theme in *Deep Throat* as examined later in this volume, Steppenwolf's music, along with that of others used in *Easy Rider*, allows its audience to experience the film while listening to the lyrics, as well. Cooke speculates that "the lyrics of pop songs made them uniquely suited to promoting both audience distanciation or personal involvement, for exploiting emotional and situational anempathy, or for unequivocally underlining unspoken aspects of character and motivation" (413). This is a significant difference in audience experience from using well-known instrumental or classical music which runs the "danger that once recognized a song might distract a viewer's attention from the intended dramatic function owing to his or her personal feelings about it ... and even a snatch of a familiar melody can call up a paradigmatic memory of an entire song and its associations" (Cooke 413).

A natural question to follow, then, is how *Easy Rider* attempts to take advantage of "a unique opportunity to editorialize and to focus audience attention" that the lyrics of "Born to Be Wild" provide (Altman 26). What is important to remember is that "Born to Be Wild" does not attempt to describe the characters' personalities. Shumway argues that "the most important effect of the music is not to provide commentary" (38). Even without the help of the song, visual cues are clear about the countercultural nature of Wyatt and Billy. As the audience follows the story, their values and beliefs in the counterculture become even clearer. There is no need for Steppenwolf's song to retell the story. The music accompanies the film, instead, to "foster generational solidarity" (Shumway 38). The generational identity that "Born to Be Wild" portrays enables viewers of the movie to associate themselves with the protagonists of the film. Both those that partake in the counterculture and those who one day hope to can reaffirm their identity as a part of the countercultural generation that was "born to be wild."

The countercultural generational identity that "Born to Be Wild" framed is not only a strategic move to appeal to young audiences (Hickman 383), but also is reflective of the social atmosphere that led to the three-day-long gathering in Bethel, New York, in August 1969, or the Woodstock Festival. Rodman writes that the film "used a pastiche of popular songs to portray youth culture" (Rodman 123). Ronald Helfrich explains, "By the 1960s, the village of Woodstock had become the site of generational cultural warfare" (222). The village's establishment made sure that the planned festivity would not happen in the village, leading it to take place in Bethel, a town about fifty miles away. Although Steppenwolf was not one of the artists to appear at the festival, its song symbolizes the sentiment of countercultural youth whose culture Hopper and Fonda tried to capture.

Of course, Wyatt and Billy were far from being the youth in the film. Hippies living in the commune that they visit were more appropriate as countercultural youth. As grown-ups, Wyatt and Billy still participate in youthful countercultural norms. To borrow the words of Barbara Scharres, they are "thirty-year-old adolescents" (27). Steppenwolf's music offered a means though which the audience and the participants of counterculture could identify themselves with these two characters in the film, as well as their values and lifestyles. This is why Shumway wrote that the music did not exist to provide commentary or nostalgia (38). Music was a significant vehicle for the film producers to establish a generational and countercultural solidarity.

Conclusion

When Kornbluth wrote that "the rock soundtrack has become a set form, a *rite de passage*, for the now filmmaker," he was absolutely right. The success of *Easy Rider*, not simply defined by its disproportionality between its budget and box office sales, but also by its status as a road film, a western film, and a rock film, made it almost impossible for any movie directors and producers to ignore the power of rock music. But the popularity came with a price.

The irony of *Easy Rider* as a countercultural film exists in its popularity. The film would have to balance between the film being countercultural—or anti-establishment—and being a part of the mainstream, if it were to remain truly countercultural. In its production process, *Easy Rider* was an epitome of counterculture. Bart explains:

> *Easy Rider* was conceived in a marijuana haze. Though countless young people in the '60s came up with, like, wow, really "heavy" ideas while stoned, Peter Fonda actually followed through on his inspiration. On a budget of only $360,000, *Easy Rider* began filming with 16mm cameras, no final cast, no final script, and a crew that had been assembled in five weeks. Dennis Hopper was a first-time director, who, as Fonda wrote in his 1998 book, *Don't Tell Dad*, began the first day of shooting with a two-hour rant to the crew that began, "This is *my* fucking movie and *nobody* is going to take it away from me!" (emphasis in original) [150].

He advances the idea that it "remains the ultimate example of zeitgeist cinema: it not only reflected the moment, but galvanized it" (150). Once the film became popular and an icon of a particular cultural movement, however, it was also turned into a commodity. It became an object of consumption. Leerom Medovoi analyzes that the film was turned into a "[product] of the culture industry itself" (180). This is why John Gorman fears that *Easy Rider* put counterculture at risk. He writes, "The counterculture would soon be threatened with extermination in the form of mass re-enactment of *Easy Rider, Joe*, and *Z*" (391).

The same was true with music. Hubbert writes, "By encouraging the use of pop and rock music in film, studios were reaping enormous profits not just from movie ticket sales but also from the sales of record albums that featured the new soundtracks" (181). Some musicians declined to have their music used in a film for one reason or another. Bob Dylan, for example, "refused to let Peter Fonda use 'It's All Right, Ma' at the end of [the film]" because he did not believe it was the optimal choice. The music ended up appearing in the film, however, thanks to Roger McGuinn of the Byrds, whose performance of the song was utilized in the film.

Easy Rider begins with hope and aspiration. It is adorned by Steppenwolf's music of mobility and resistance. The main characters explore their options in life while experiencing countercultural alternative lifestyles. In the process, ominously, they ride by cemeteries across the country. The audience is, however, assured that they are headed to New Orleans, and later to Florida where Wyatt and Billy's dream could come true. Billy is hopeful that they have made it. Wyatt does not agree. Not only is he pessimistic, he is convinced that they blew it. The "it" is, of course, their countercultural dream. It is the dream that is "haunted by the American past, which echoes only death." Wyatt and Billy "continually pass graveyards; they sit and expand their own current consciousness on an old mount of Indian bones; a final stop in their trip is a bad trip in a graveyard just outside a slave market" (Costello 189). The reality and the correctness of Wyatt's assessment are confirmed soon after with his and Billy's deaths.

If Wyatt and Billy "blew it," then did their music blow it, too? On the one hand, the film's soundtrack made an immense contribution to the movie industry. It established rock as a significant musical genre at the time while it was still relatively young. It was also one of the movies to stimulate the discussion about the value of using existing music. Furthermore, as Bapis writes, "The musical score cemented identity to activism and brought the 1960s revolutionary onto the screen in a lasting way. The legendary odyssey highlighted nostalgic desires for untrammeled freedom, landscapes of grandeur, and rock music as the liberating truth" (*Camera*, 92). But it also meant that the countercultural identity that the music tried to portray became a part of the Hollywood mainstream. Costello offers that Wyatt's words are "a warning for a counterculture that can't really be counter if it accepts the values of the dominant culture into which it enslaves itself" (190). In other words, popularizing and mainstreaming counterculture contradicts its raison d'etre. Facing this difficult conundrum, both the music and the film became a part of the canonical artistic works of the counterculture period. But it continues to maintain its original countercultural identity in the minds of scholars, film critics, and fans.

7. Setting the Escapist Scene with Music: Sex and Comedy in an Exotic World

Introduction

With Robert Altman as the director, Ingo Preminger as the producer, and Ring Lardner, Jr., as the screenplay writer, *MASH* (1970), also known as *M*A*S*H*, was one of the most successful films by 20th Century-Fox in the early 1970s. Based on Richard Hooker's novel entitled, *MASH: A Novel about Three Army Doctors*, the film generally followed its original literary version's plot. Its popularity also generated the television adaptation *M*A*S*H* on air from 1972 to 1983. With an estimated $3.5 million budget, the film grossed over $81 million in the U.S. alone ("MASH"). In addition to the Palme d'Or awarded at the Cannes Film Festival in 1970, *MASH* was nominated for five Academy Awards: Best Picture, Best Director, Best Film Editing, and Best Screenplay, as well as Best Supporting Actress for Sally Kellerman. The film won the Oscars for Lardner's screenplay. It also won the Golden Globe for Best Motion Picture in Musical and Comedy in 1971. Aside from these international accolades, the movie has been selected as one of the classic comedies by various popular culture outlets including Bravo, or even by the Library of Congress as it listed *MASH* to be preserved in the U.S. National Film Registry.

The story of the film takes place primarily in Asia, namely South Korea and Tokyo, during the period of the Korean War. The comedy begins as two new army surgeons are assigned to the 4077th Mobile Army Surgical Hospital (or MASH). Captain Pierce, also known as Hawkeye, and Captain Forrest, or Duke, are both skilled and talented surgeons, although they are rebellious, free-willed, and flirtatious. Starring Donald Sutherland and Elliott Gould for these roles, the film touched on what was considered a taboo subject in Hollywood at the time. Writing for *The Observer*, Philip French wrote "[*MASH*] captured the mood of the time. Set during the Korean War, it was actually about the madness of the Vietnam War ... and the combustible mixture of anarchy and suppression in Richard Nixon's America." Hawkeye and Duke are also joined by a third surgeon, Captain McIntyre, or Trapper, as the story develops. For two hours, a series of comedic episodes surround these three main characters as well as Lieutenant Colonel Blake, Major Houlihan, dentist "Painless Pole" Waldowski, and others.

In this film, two distinct types of notable sounds exist, in addition to dialogue. One is the series of announcements overheard on the PA system. The announcements are often silly, if not downright confusing and probably even stupid. But they add to the comedic nature of the film. For example, the PA system refers to war movies such as *When Willie Comes Marching Home* (1950), a World War II comedy film by John Ford with Dan Daily and Corinne Calvet, and *Halls of Montezuma*, another World War II film from 1951, directed by Lewis Milestone, starring Richard Widmark. These films treat war efforts more seriously. They portray war actions as heroic acts, completely opposite from how *MASH* portrayed them. Cooke suggests that

> since the end of the 1960s, both individual pop songs and historically resonant compilation scores have come to redefine the genre of the war movie for the post-Vietnam age, helping it move beyond its traditional heroic and patriotic vein to far darker and disturbing messages of protest laced with bitter satire [412].

The other type of sound is its soundtrack. Some accompanying songs are original to the movie, whereas some others are Japanese renditions of popular American music. Both of these categories of music create an escapist sentiment and a tacit anti-war message throughout the film.

Life of Johnny Mandel

Much of the music heard in the film is composed by Johnny Mandel. Born on November 23, 1925, he composed popular music and jazz, as well as film music. In 1999, he was awarded the Alumnus of Distinction Award by the New York Military Academy ("Alumni of Distinction"). His compositions have included "Emily," "Time for Love," and "The Shadow of Your Smile," a winner of an Oscar and a Grammy in 1965. He has also composed scores for over thirty films. Reflecting on his own life, in an interview, Mandel explained that his father was in the garment business. His mother was an aspiring singer. But being successful as a singer in the early twentieth century, he stated, was very difficult. Mandel surmised that, "back then, in order to make it in the music business, you had to sleep with the producer. [My mother] grew up in a Victorian era when nice girls just didn't do that. So she gave up her ambition of becoming a professional singer." He explains that it was because of his mother's abandoned dream that she was so supportive of him when he decided to pursue his career in music ("Interview: Johnny Mandel (Part 1)").

The turning point in Mandel's life, however, came when his father passed away in 1937 when Mandel was only 11. The family was no exception in experiencing the economic downturn of the Great Depression. They decided to move out of New York to California after Mandel's father closed his business and retired. After his retirement, his father did not last long. The day after his death, Mandel met a cousin who he had never met or even knew existed before. It was Mel Rosenbach. Rosenbach explained to Mandel that he was soon leaving for a tour with Harry Reser, a musical partner. Mandel remembers, "I asked why he was doing that. Mel said he was a drummer. I said, 'You mean you're a drummer all the time?' He said, 'Yeah, I play with this band, and we play at different dances.' I said, 'Wow, is it fun?'" Mandel continues, "[Mel] said, 'Oh, yeah.' ... When Mel told me what he did with Reser, I wanted to become a musician, too. It sounded like they had a blast" ("Interview: Johnny Mandel (Part 1)").

Mandel admits that there was a bit of an ulterior motive to become a musician as he learned more about the world. He said, "I discovered that most band and jazz guys become musicians because they could get girls easily. And I was one of them. But that would come later" ("Interview: Johnny Mandel (Part 1)"). Simultaneously, though, he had been interested in music. Even though his mother had given up on her dream to become a professional singer, she was nonetheless interested in music and their house was filled with music. Once the immediate reaction to the Great Depression had subsided, the music industry slowly took on, allowing the popularity of radio and band music to come back.

Once the family moved back to New York after his father's death, Mandel further explored his interests in music. He met Marshall Robbins, a son of Jack Robbins. Robbins ran a large music publisher, Robbins Music. Thanks to the fact that the Robbins family lived in the same building, Mandel was able to see many different bands perform. Eventually he attended New York State Military Academy on a band scholarship. He learned how to march and play and started arranging for its dance band ("Interview: Johnny Mandel (Part 1)"). Mandel particularly does not believe that his obsession with music was unique. "In those days, I was like any other kid. You grew up glued to the radio. I know I wanted to become a musician. There were bands everywhere, and the cheapest form of entertainment was listening to live remotes of the different bands from the big hotels. Everything sounded so exciting, especially live from those hotels" ("Interview: Johnny Mandel (Part 2)"). In the late 1930s to early 1940s when Mandel was under various musical influences in New York, he was still a teenager. However, he was beginning to show his unique interest in songs, and not only in bands. He remembers, "I was captivated by the songs as much as the bands." He was intrigued to explore how "melodies were interpreted by different band arrangers" ("Interview: Johnny Mandel (Part 2)").

As he examined the music and its messages, he continued to play the trumpet and the trombone. But his focus shifted toward arranging and composing for big bands in the mid- to late 1940s. His music could be often heard on the radio during this period. When the popularity of television expanded in the 1950s, his music was often on TV, as well. Shifting from one media outlet to another was a smooth transition. So was the move to films, with his first score composition for a film, *I Want to Live* (1958). Six years later, he wrote his first song for *The Americanization of Emily* (1964). Although Mandel had written instrumentals, it was his first with lyrics ("Interview: Johnny Mandel (Part 3)").

Exploring new types of music and different experiences in composition and arrangement, Mandel had established himself as a composer. One of the projects at the end of the 1960s was *That Cold Day in the Park* (1969) with Robert Altman. Featuring Sandy Dennis, this drama allowed Altman and Mandel to get to know each other well, leading to their collaboration for *MASH* a year later. Mandel explains, "I was brought in before the movie was even shot, which was highly unusual. In most cases, you're the last one in the line to see the film when scoring it. So Bob and I were sitting around getting rather ripped one night. Bob said to me, 'You know, I need a song for the film" ("Interview: Johnny Mandel[Part 5]"). This is the origin of what Robert T. Self called "a complex and cacophonous range of aural discourse" (155).

Stupidity, Escapism, and Demythicization through "Suicide Is Painless"

The most iconic music of *MASH* is undoubtedly "Suicide Is Painless." Before Mandel composed its music, its lyrics had been written by Mike Altman, the son of the film's director, Robert Altman. The director had one of the film's iconic scenes in mind. It was the depiction of the Last Supper after which Captain Painless, or Captain Waldowski, would commit a fake suicide by taking a sleeping pill. For this scene, Altman knew that the accompanying song had to be "the stupidest song that was ever written." He tried to write the song himself, but his creativity did not bear fruit. Mandel remembers that once Altman realized that he needed someone else to write "the stupidest song," he admitted to Mandel, "I can't get anything nearly as stupid as I need.... But all is not lost. I have this kid who is a total idiot. He'll run through this thing like a dose of salts" (Bates 15).

This "total idiot" was Michael Altman, fourteen years old at the time. Michael Altman remembers that in his childhood, he would write much poetry. This encouraged his father to tell him to write a song entitled "Suicide Is Painless." Bates explains that "after some false starts, the son wrote the lyrics 'in about ten minutes'" (15). It is well known that Michael ended up making more money writing the lyrics than his father did directing the film. He received $500 and 50 percent of the song profit. Once the TV version of *MASH* started with his song as the theme, he began to see a flow of income. Michael remembers, "I got another check for, like 26 bucks. And then the second check was like $130.... And the next check was like $26,000.... I think I ended up making close to $2 million. And [Robert Altman] had gotten paid $75,000 to direct the movie and no points" (Bates 15; Legge 68). After all, Robert had nothing to do with its television version ("Obituary"). It was thanks to *MASH* that Altman eventually became an eminent movie director. But until 1970, he was not a known director who could expect high pay to direct a film.

This substantial success by a teenager is just an example of how impactful the song was. "Suicide Is Painless" was adapted to the television version, and attracted various cover versions. Marilyn Manson's version compiled in *Books of Shadows: Blair Witch 2* (2000) is one. The song unexpectedly appeared in *Stewie Griffin: The Untold Story* (2005) as *Family Guy*'s character, Stewie, sat at a bar table with his canine companion, Brian. Over forty years after the film's premiere, artists both in the U.S. and outside continue to cover the song and feature it in their albums.

Once the lyrics were written, it was time for the music. Altman talked to Mandel and told him that he needed a song. He said, "It's the Last Supper scene, after the guy says he's going to do himself with a pill because his life is over, because couldn't get it up with the WAC the night before." Mandel was taken aback by this proposition. Altman continued, "Yeah, that Last Supper scene where the guy climbs into the casket and everybody walks around the box dropping in things like scotch, *Playboy*, and other stuff to see him into the next world. There's just dead air there" ("Interview: Johnny Mandel (Part 5)"). As previously noted, Altman tried to write the lyrics himself but failed. His son ended up writing it. In the meantime, Mandel thought, "I can do stupid" ("Interview: Johnny Mandel (Part 5)"). This is how what a critic called "an outrageous theme song" came to the world (French 12).

As Altman stated outright, the film's theme song was designed to be the "stupidest song" ever written. He appreciated what his son and Mandel created. When Mandel shared his work with Altman, he liked it so much that he tried playing it over the title credits. "You guys are crazy. It doesn't fit," Mandel remembers telling Altman. He explains, "You have these army medic helicopters flying in a war zone with this soft melody playing. It felt odd. But I wasn't about to get into a fight over it. So I left the screening room. Sure enough, when I saw the film, the song was used over the opening credits. Then it was used on the TV series in 1972" ("Interview: Johnny Mandel [Part 5]"). This sense of disconnect that Mandel immediately noticed opens the film with a comedic disjunction. Film scenes showing battles and soldiers are not usually accompanied by such a soft tune. Its instrumental version aurally adorns heroic acts by military personnel at the beginning of the film. The gap is immense.

The gap between Mandel's peaceful tune and images of a battle is not only counterintuitive and comedic, or "stupid," but also thought-provoking. As the screen shows numerous human bodies maimed in combats, the film repeats the idea of suicide. Although *MASH* does not provide a clear answer to the implication of engaging in a war, it leaves its audience wondering if participating in a war is a suicidal act. While the story of the film took place in South Korea, the film itself spoke to the ongoing war in Vietnam. The Navy Department's statistics show that out of 8,744,000 that served in the Vietnam Conflict, 58,209 lost their lives (Fisher). This is a death rate of roughly 0.6 percent, higher than leukemia, cervical cancer, and other common diseases, or double the average death rate at war (World Health Organization). Even without these statistical figures, the increasing death toll and the stagnation in Asia fueled antiwar sentiment within the U.S. in the late 1960s. Mitchell K. Hall wrote that the public opposition to America's continuing involvement in Vietnam became "one of the largest social movements in the nation's history" (13). In this context, the implicit message that "Suicide Is Painless" seemed to question the behavior of military personnel willing to risk their lives, even for a noble cause.

In other words, the song perhaps portrays wartime death, typically interpreted as a heroic act and symbolic of one's patriotism as well as national civic values, as a matter of poor personal judgment. This anti-war sentiment is consistent with the contrast that the PA system makes via its reference to war films. This representation of human loss is unique. The film handled a taboo subject. What is more significant is that the film's message could have easily been interpreted, because of its theme music, as being critical of not just the military or its high echelon staff, but also common soldiers who were usually heroicized in public discourse.

After "Suicide Is Painless" creates an interesting binary at the beginning of the film, it comes back during the very scene for which the music was made, the scene of the Last Supper. As noted earlier, the scene depicts Captain Painless committing suicide with a pill. His suicide is metaphorical. He plans to simply fall deep asleep and expects to wake up the following morning. The silliness of this idea well matches the tone of the accompanying music. From the recreation of Leonardo da Vinci's famous Last Supper scene under a military medical tent to the series of items that Painless receives in his casket which included a copy of *Playboy*, the scene is filled with silly comedic ideas. William Johnson wrote "the fake suicide sequence is … considerably less comic than the rest of the film. At first viewing, one's interest is held by the preposterousness of the incidents; but at a second viewing the sequence seems hollow and contrived" (39). The scene is shallow. But as Hickman states, "the biting criticism of the war is presented within a prevailing comic mood" (15).

The suicide scene, however, cannot be judged solely as a comedy. Captain Painless decides to take a pill because he was unable to perform sexually with a visiting nurse and was consequently convinced that he might be homosexual. A lack of performance one night is significant for him, because of his sexual prowess hinted to by the fact that he is engaged to three women to whom he tries to be faithful. "I'm a fairy, a victim of latent homosexuality. I've turned into a fairy," Painless confides to Hawkeye. "I can't face it," he says. This is the reason for his suicidal plan. This is a very escapist message. Altman's lyrics hint that suicide can change the world. Suicide will also allow Captain Painless to "take" the status quo or "leave" his trouble behind. Altman expresses that in order to win what you want, you have to "cheat" and lie down before losing. Christof Decker also states that the film's "depiction of suicide lacks the emotional intensity of individual suffering and desperation." Suicide, in other words, is shown as a "means of … ridicule" (76).

The Last Supper scene begins with violinists playing "Taps." It sets the scene for the Last Supper. From St. Thomas' finger pointing upwards to the controversial crew of three—Judas, Peter and John (or Mary, depending on the viewer's perspective)—the scene recreates the famous supper scene. "Suicide Is Painless" during the suicide scene is guitar-based. It starts with a sorrowful tone while Painless walks to his casket. Painless takes a pill in front of his coworkers. But once they start offering mementos, the tone of the song begins to pick up, to the extent that it is even somewhat cheery. The song ends with Painless holding a bottle of alcohol between his left arm and his body, and a copy of *Playboy* resting on his lap.

This combination of escapist imagery and lyrics also suggest the demythicization of authority and religion. On the one hand, the film makes fun of the military. There is no doubt that *MASH* is an antiwar and antimilitary comedic satire. From the perspective of the antiwar message, it is similar to *Catch-22* (1970) by Mike Nichols. As Johnson accurately noted, most of its characters do not have any respect for the military. As a satire, the only combat they willingly engage themselves in is a football game against another unit in which they win thousands of dollars (38). One of the things that successfully make this antimilitary satire into a comedy in addition to the PA system messages is its soundtrack.

Those that are supposed to be heroic individuals, soldiers and those who take care of them as medical personnel, are not presented as brave and courageous protectors of American liberty and freedom. Even the divine power cannot escape from being a subject of comedy as Major Burns prays and his colleagues ridicule him. Therefore there is no surprise when the film treats suicide so lightly and the lyrics of "Suicide Is Painless" invites others to "do the same" when they face difficulties in life.

The anti-war sentiment of the film is evident in other songs, as well. When "The Lights Go On Again" is sung when the light goes off in the operation room, it is a tactful double entendre. On one level, this song directly references the obvious power outage that happened while soldiers were on operating tables. On another level, though, is that the song written in 1942 is a response to Edward Grey's famous remark, "The lamps are going out all over Europe, we shall not see them lit again in our time," made the night before World War I. Through this allusion, Altman strategically underscores the popular perception about the war in Vietnam and calls for its termination so that, as the song goes, a kiss is not for farewell but welcome.

"Hail to the Chief" is not a presidential anthem in this film. A group of medical staff sings the song in honor of the best war surgeon. But they do not sing the song to pay respect for his honorable duty. Just as the Last Supper scene negated authority and religion, they sing the song to emphasize the sexual urges that must be met by having female staff around him. The chief at the medical camp is no longer the commander in chief, back in Washington, D.C. It is Hawkeye, whose behaviors do not match that of traditional militarism.

The PA System as Soundtrack

The general scarcity of music does not mean that sound affects the film little. In reality, sound is a major factor in this film. Announcements through the public announcement system are major auditory cues in the film. The PA system almost invades the cinematographic space. Johnson states that "the PA system continually breaks in with an odd announcement" (39). Self writes that "sound contributes to.... The viewer's sense ... of story situation, place, time, point of view, action, or character." He lists dialogue, sound effects, and music as three components of aural input (142). The PA announcements are similar to the film's soundtrack. When the PA announcer says, "Attention. Captain Bandini is now performing a femoral po- a popli- a p, a femoral P, O, P, L, I, T, E, R, A, L, artery expl, explo, exploration and possible graft," he paints a comedic scene for the audience. Similarly, the PA system announces, "All base members must report for a drug test for marij, marijua, disregard last transmission." This comedic feature parallels with three categories of sound input that Self listed. Just like the gap that exists between the war scene and the tone of "Suicide Is Painless," there is a discrepancy between a scene at a war camp and unrealistic announcements overheard by the audience.

What is heard from the PA system is not just out-of-place announcements. There are multiple Japanese songs in this film. On one level, the dominance of Japanese music is confusing considering the film takes place in South Korea within the context of anti–Vietnam War sentiment. Marvyn Cooke explains that the film "deliberately cultivated the look of the Vietnam war to strike a chord with audiences disaffected by the ongoing conflict in South East Asia: the implications were so obvious that the studio forced the director to insert a 'Korea' title card at the beginning of the film" (412). Hawkeye and Trapper may take a trip to Kokura, Japan, to operate on the son of a U.S. congressman, or more truthfully to play golf. The introduction of Japanese music, though, well precedes this development of the story.

Japanese Music in Relation to Korea and Vietnam

In many instances, when Japanese music is heard on the PA system or on the radio, it signals something sexual is about to happen or end. For example, Teruko Akatsuki's "Tokyo Shoe Shine Boy" is the first Japanese song to appear in the film. Akatsuki's hit song from 1951 is repeated twice in the film. But the very first time it is heard in the film is after Hawkeye was interrupted during his attempt to sleep with Lieutenant Dish by Ho-Jon who told him that there was a new chest cutter. The lyrics are about a boy who polishes shoes for living and who has a crush on a young woman. The song is not about love, sex, or relationships. The protagonist of the song is waiting for his crush to come with her red shoes. Akatsuki sings that she is not there yet. But the shoe polisher enjoys his work and he can make anyone's shoes shine even after a raining day or a windy day.

Furthermore, "Tokyo Shoe Shine Boy" was a symbolic song that reflected the upbeat recovery from World War II. Especially after a series of aerial bombings using incendiary ammunition between March and May 1945, particularly the one on March 10, 1945, that led to the deaths of over 100,000 residents of Tokyo, wiping out over 40 square kilometers of the downtown area. Hewitt states that about 2,000 tons of incendiaries set buildings on fire. The population density at the time was about 103,000 to 135,000 per square mile. He writes, "Though some 300 fire engines were quickly on the scene, their efforts were useless. It took 25 days to dig out the dead. Large areas were simply abandoned as survivors left the city, and maintenance workers saw no point in trying to restore services" (273). The recovery from this devastation took time. By 1951, though, there were many signs of hope. The song talks about the young lady shopping in the Ginza district, an upper-scale shopping area. This sense of optimism was what Akatsuki's song represented. This is a clear contrast against the situation in the Korean Peninsula during the war.

Nobody knows how Akatsuki would have reacted to the adoption of her song in the film. On the one hand, the aforementioned gap between the social context within which the Japanese enjoyed her music in the early 1950s and that in South Korea is clear. On the other hand, the song sends the message to remain positive even during a difficult time. There is an overlap between those who suffered in Tokyo in the early- to mid-1940s and Altman's characters in Korea. Akatsuki, however, was not there to comment. Born in 1921, she debuted as a child actor at age twelve. She was 28 when she released her first song, "Minami no Koiuta." Just two years later, two of her most representative songs, "Egg Seller in Minnesota" and "Tokyo Shoe Shine Boy," were released. In 1962, at age 41, Akatsuki suffered from a heart attack and passed away 8 years before the release of *MASH*.

Other songs sung in Japanese include, "My Blue Heaven," "The Darktown Strutters' Ball," "Hi-Lili, Hi-Lo," "Happy Days Are Here Again," and "Chattanooga Choo Choo." "My Blue Heaven" was composed by Walter Donaldson with lyrics by George Whiting in 1927. Its Japanese version was translated by Keizo Horiuchi. While the English version depicts a happy family getting together in comfortable room in a house, the Japanese version is about a person walking home thinking about seeing his or her family again, even though the house may be very small. This image of a happy family also offers an effective contrast in the film. The music is first played right before Major Houlihan and Major Burns' sexual encounter begins. The music is silenced for a while as Major Burns makes his move to Major Houlihan, who undoes her pajama top by saying, "His will be done." The music comes back as soon as Houlihan pushes Burns out of her room.

When two surgeons arrive in Kokura, Johnny Mandel's "To Japan" welcomes the audience. This instrumental music features traditional Japanese music. What is comical, especially after so many Japanese renditions of music in the film, is that Trapper and Hawkeye pretend to speak Japanese but in reality they speak nothing better than nonsensical gibberish. Furthermore, once they arrive at the hospital and open the door to the building, the act is accompanied by the sound of a gong, a non–Japanese instrument which is nonetheless associated with Asian music generally. This confusion about the national origin of sounds is not surprising after South Korea repeatedly plays Japanese music and the film never features a Korean song.

The second time "Tokyo Shoe Shine Boy" is heard is near the very end of the film. Hawkeye rushes to Duke who is operating on a patient and tells him that they could go back home. The aforementioned optimism about recovery from a difficult time that this song carried to the mind of the Japanese in the 1950s might be relevant to soldiers stationed in South Korea. From the lyrical perspective, "My Blue Heaven" that talks about the sentiment of missing home and looking forward to being home is more apt. The hopefulness of Akatsuki's music, however, is consistent with the escapist attitude that the film has portrayed. American surgeons can flee the devastated region and go back to the American way of life. Americans, despite the social instability of the late 1960s and the early 1970s in the U.S., could leave the chaotic war and its consequences behind. Akatsuki's cheerfulness resonates with the escapist depiction of the world that "Suicide Is Painless" contained.

Conclusion

M*A*S*H is undoubtedly a countercultural film. On one level, it resonates with the social and cultural sentiments of the time. Albeit indirectly, it talks about and criticizes American engagement in the Vietnam War. It challenges established hierarchy such as the military structure or an organized religion. On another level, it also tries to depart from the status quo. The departure from the reality may be escapist. It may involve suicide. Or it may simply be moving away to another country. Regardless of the choice, it is a countercultural theme that resists the society as it is and aspires to seek an alternative.

In order to create this countercultural theme, the film relies on visual cues, dialogues, and music. Sound—the combination of the soundtrack and PA announcements in the case of *M*A*S*H*—serves to set up a scene. This chapter looked at Altman's canonical film from 1970 as a work of sound art. The art's comedic messages were conveyed via sound. PA announcements were nonsensical. Publicly airing the sound of sex via the PA system may be an overkill, but is nevertheless comical. "Suicide Is Painless" was, and probably continues to be, one of the "stupidest" songs ever written. Simultaneously, the film's soundtrack helped advance its political message, namely its anti-war and anti-military sentiment. Through music, the film makes fun of the military structure. It questions the value of the war in Vietnam. It also reflected American ignorance about the Far East and Asia. Through sound and music, in addition to other cinematic tools, Altman created a unique world in which he challenged the establishment.

8. Generational Genocide: Selling Youth Rebellion in Roger Corman's *Gas-s-s-s*

Released in 1970, Roger Corman's *Gas-s-s-s* (subtitled: *It Became Necessary to Destroy the World in Order to Save it*) did not especially entrench its feet into the canon of classic countercultural film and the New Hollywood. It had a lot going for it when the film applied for inclusion though. The film was directed by Roger Corman, the famous "exploitation" filmmaker responsible for the release of films like *The Wild Angels* and *The Trip*. Corman was also well-known for his abilities to launch and perpetuate many careers in Hollywood. Key figures in the "New Hollywood" such as Jack Nicholson, Peter Fonda, Francis Ford Coppola, Peter Bogdanovich, and Dennis Hopper all had previously worked for Corman. Additionally, the film featured a performance by Country Joe and the Fish, and a soundtrack that included, among other tracks by Joy of Cooking (as "The Gourmet's Delight"), seven songs penned and produced by Barry "The Fish" Melton of Country Joe and the Fish. The film starred Robert Corff, a cast member of the LA *Hair* cast, Elaine Giftos, Cindy Williams, Ben Vereen, as well as an actor that shows up in a few other films in this book, Bud Cort.

Despite such associations, the tank was generally only seen as half full by audiences at the time. Though not in the public eye after its unsuccessful initial run, interest in Corman in the past several years has breathed a new life into the film. Its rerelease in several Corman collections allowed *Gas-s-s-s* to rise a bit more into the public eye. Even in its marginality, the film proves to be a useful historical document when framing the counterculture and the New Hollywood.

For the purposes of this text, the film, much like several other titles, is not the subject of inquiry due to impressive box office receipts. What the film does, like many of its brethren in this book, is to successfully pull into the fray a definitive theme of countercultural life. It does so not only due to the visuals seen and the words spoken, but also because of the music utilized to encode these messages. *Gas-s-s-s* is a visual, narrative, and musical relentless assault of youth and youthful rebellion. Taken on in an outright (and according to some, a bit too heavy-handed) way the film is the filmic equivalent of the mantra of: "Don't trust anyone over thirty." Thanks to its (sometimes quite literally) cartoonish, humorous take on that status quo and boomer or youth rebellion, the film is home to both youthful idealism and the cynical exploitation of a still youthful but aging cohort facing a new decade. Linking the concepts like the counterculture, the baby boom, and even the "hippie," youthful rebellion was an empowering and marketed theme apparent in many films of the time. The overt message in the film is made even more so thanks to the importance placed on music to drive the point home.

The onslaught of age was a difficult for a generation that had its youth so formally catered to by commercial, governmental, and cultural interests. To fully understand how youth was addressed and packaged in *Gas-s-s-s*, and why it was so heavily played to as the main theme, some detail is needed in chronicling the rise to power of youth rebellion as a marketing strategy and a cultural institution. Postwar America simultaneously entrenched a culture of moral panic directed at youth and a celebration of this vast consumer target market.

Of course, a delineation of "youth" was nothing new in the postwar period. A focus of discussion in the post-war period was on the American "teenager." Even though this formally defined and powerful market segment came into the public mindset, J. W. Macquarrie reminds us in "The Teenager: A By-Product of Industrialism,": "In the strict chronological sense, teenagers are as old as the human species." It was the Industrial Revolution that initially created this byproduct that separated children and adults (Macquarrie 17). With the rise of mass mediation and numerous other factors, the notion of youth had to be updated to meet the economic and cultural milieu of the 20th century.

Jon Savage in his *Teenage: The Creation of Youth Culture* contends that a certain formalization of youth culture came to fruition in 1944 and 1945, reflected, for instance, in the rise of *Seventeen*. Claiming that the magazine "pulled together the strands of democracy, national identity, peer culture, target marketing, and youth consumerism into an irresistible package," it was poised to take on "this still virtually untapped market" of youth. This market was an ideal one, as "American youth had an estimated spending capacity of $750 million" (448). Under the umbrella of consumption and the many years of tending to the soils of "youth," one especially potent theme connected to youth would rise to the surface of the public mindset: rebellion.

The concept of rebellion and its connection to the youth or teenager following World War II brought economic opportunity, parental and societal concern, and an identity to appropriate and fulfill. When looked at from an authoritative perspective, youth rebellion was a threat to social order and something to be combated. Joshua Garrison in "The Teenage Terror in the Schools" offers that in the 1950s, "There is little doubt, then, that adults feared that a radically changing social context, coupled with a distinctly youth-centered culture (which was frequently regarded as tasteless and corrupt)" was at play (8). To put it a little more overtly, a *New York Times* article in 1945 postulated, "Defining young persons as 'teen-agers,' that is, not ready for the serious matters of adulthood, invites their absorption in the frivolous matters of 'teen-age culture,' and the leisure and the unprecedented affluence of teenagers predispose them to accept the invitation" (qtd. in Savage 462).

Popular culture was one of the battlegrounds in which youth could be saved or lost and in which identity could be formed. In films shown in schools chronicling the effects of too much rebellion (Garrison 6) all the way to major motion pictures like *Blackboard Jungle* and *Rebel Without a Cause*, youth were often portrayed as hedonistic fools, ready to trade a bright tomorrow for some teenage kicks today. The rise of rock music also attracted significant concern from parents, religious leaders, etc., as well as providing another outlet for youth to find common ground and experience.

Blackboard Jungle, in a very deliberate way, represented a coming together of the sound and the vision of youth rebellion to audiences fearing the worst, or hoping for more. Often cited as the first film to utilize a rock song, *Blackboard Jungle* harnessed the power of moral panic and teenage youth rebellion to create a polysemic vision and sound of a quickly formalizing market. Seeing the financial power of the "untapped market," film studios knew featuring the right music allowed for focused encodings for the youth market. Additionally they knew how to speak to parents, eager for some easy answers.

Like *Blackboard Jungle*, *Gas-s-s-s* focused on the generational divide and discord. Both films did so through arguments of a generational binary. Such absolutisms are easy to come by when discussing generational difference and would be the case too of baby-boomers labeling their parents. Those *potentially* aiming to bridge the gap, or at least blur the line dividing generations, simply were not profitable, compared to such absolutisms. Benjamin Spock, in a 1966 article for *Redbook*, cautioned parents of aging boomers: "Rebelliousness against parents is a natural, built-in aspect of adolescents. It assists them in giving up the comforts and security of home and achieving real independence" (qtd. in Klein 305). Voices like Spock's were sometimes not heard over the din of youth and teenage rebellion messages in the media, from both generations. Instead of being seen as a facet of human development, it appeared that the gap widened between the generations as the media, violence, war, racial strife, etc., added to the rhetoric of both camps (and even those between).

Baby-boomers, many with an excitement and dedication to the early rock music of the 1950s; images seen in film, television, and in school; and the idea of youth and rebellion charged into the '60s and were about to share several events as a community of viewers and listeners. Many took with them a growing sense of self, impertinence, and cynicism. Leonard Steinhorn argues in *The Greater Generation: In Defense of the Baby Boom Legacy* that this ability to openly question authority and to find a voice of dissent was due to several reasons including: fallout from the Red Scare and the attack on free speech; the denial of the American Dream to African Americans and their subjugation; hypocrisy due to the drug and alcohol culture of their parents; corporate greed; violence; and doubt in leaders. In regards to the last two, Steinhorn argues: "It wasn't that Boomers saw all leaders as hypocrites—but it seemed as if those who stood for something good were gunned down, and all the rest seemed soaked in malfeasance and duplicity" (69).

For many invested boomers, the identity that came in youthful or teenage rebellion had already effectively been established as a marketable category and as a target of moral panic thanks to the factors offered by Steinhorn above. This is not to say all members of this generational cohort universally experienced life and the creation of ideologies in the same way. What they all did share were events like the assassination of John F. Kennedy, the escalation of the Vietnam War, and the shootings at Kent State University. They also shared a common background, in terms of being the target of a market both lauding and damning the power of youth.

As Sherman B. Chickering in "How We Got That Way" argues, such commonalities were a powerful force: "We have our own America, our own bag. We all participate to a greater or lesser extent in a common youth culture. The culture is homogeneous, integral and pervasive. We are part of it because we were born into it. We differ only in how much we identify with it, not whether" (qtd. in Klein 196). Along with such sentiments, the marketplace (affluence), and "The Bomb," Chickering cites, "The most important, and most multidimensional, of these forces shaping youth culture was mass communications" (qtd. in Klein 199), which to him provided a sense of a global village (McLuhan would be a featured character in *Gas-s-s-s*), and "made hypocrites, squares, finks and nerds of the world's big shots, and made hippies and swingers of us little boys" (qtd. in Klein 201).

Regardless of place, or as Chickering describes, participation "to a greater or lesser extent in a common youth culture," mass media created a common space for interpreting and understanding the world around many Boomers.

From the television, theaters, record players, and transistor radios, common experiences and potential ideological frameworks could be marketed, rejected, accepted, etc., by those audiences. The concept of youth or teenage rebellion resonated with many that could find outlets both inside and outside of dominant systems of capital and ideological control.

Even though these mediums were taking on new ideas, challenges, concerns, fears, and possibilities, as the '60s progressed, the dependence on isolating youth as a demographic in cultural terms was the key to launching the revolution in which those over thirty could not be trusted. Roger Corman's *Gas-s-s-s* utilized youth or teenage rebellion as the backbone for a narrative looking to measure exactly what would happen if challenging social, political, and cultural structures became the norm. The results are mixed in the film, but the demographic can be visualized *and* heard, as the young become the torchbearers for all of humanity. For a generation nursed on mass media, the notion of gaining control of those same mediums was an enticing notion, with great potential power coming in the manipulation of those forms. Like so many other products of the time, *Gas-s-s-s* would be judged worthy of inclusion or exclusion by audiences as part of a body of works aiming to identify, reflect, frame, question, and potentially, in some cases, be looked to lead this "counterculture" fueled by youth rebellion.

The film pulled no punches in its narrative, characters, dialogue, and music to communicate the counterculturalness of the film. Roger Corman, a director associated with the "exploitation film" or "B-movie," if trying to "exploit" anything, was trying to capitalize on the counterculture of the time and a national fascination with and fear of youth rebellion. At the same time, he was also a trusted source by many in the New Hollywood movement. As mentioned earlier, Corman launched or furthered the careers of many associated icons within the counterculture film lexicon. In his book, *How I Made a Hundred Movies in Hollywood and Never Lost a Dime*, Corman asserts: "Because of my notoriety as an 'outlaw,' a new generation of filmmakers, educated in the 1960s counterculture, saw me as an uncompromised artist/entrepreneur who got his own movies made outside the Establishment." He continues by saying, "A Corman credit in the 'minors' was their fastest path to the majors" (viii).

According to some of his protégés, Corman was right. Francis Ford Coppola shares that "if Roger Corman were running one of the major film studios and specifically gave new people the kind of opportunities to work on films a lot of people would go on to do more ambitious things and would find their own talent." He said, "And the fact that he was giving us a chance primarily so he could make money was fine" (qtd. in di Franco 27). Though there was concern and criticism at times regarding how far this system did deviate from major Hollywood production, there also seemed to be a sense of respect, due to authenticity, for Corman's work.

Even though the idea of exploitation was attached, and money was unashamedly the first order of business, a connection by several of his protégés was made to authenticity. Peter Bogdanovich sees a spirit of adventure in Corman's film that was seen in the early film industry: "He's still getting a bunch of people, talented or not, and saying, 'Here's some film and a camera, go out and shoot something. You don't know about the 180-degree line? Well, I'll show you.'" He continues, "That spirit of adventure is what the movies were born in and what they have lost to a great degree" (qtd. di Franco 45).

Yet, this connection to profit was also a turn-off among a contingent of filmmakers and other counterculture interests. Later, in Chapter 13, Country Joe McDonald, who was featured in *Gas-s-s-s*, recalls, "Obviously he just wanted to do something to cash in on the youth culture, because he wasn't a hippie or anything like that." Corman, because of this utilitarian style of filmmaking was viewed in some circles as disingenuous and opportunistic, themes that could be off-putting in the search for the real among the noise. Corman does not seem to argue with any claims concerning making money: "We live in a compromised society, and I would think of myself as something of a compromised artist. I think one of the great things about motion pictures is that it is a compromised art form. So, much as I work on the basis of what I want to put into a film and the reaction I want from the audience, at the same time I want my films to make money" (qtd. in di Franco 67)"

Gas-s-s-s did not leave any doubt that youth culture was the focus, and it used several methods to draw attention to this fact. The pitch was overt and the want to cash in on youth culture was a targeted and overt one. To do so, the film would use a plot where everyone over twenty-five, thanks to a gas created by the American government, would die. It would also utilize a soundtrack commenting often overtly on youth culture and the pathos of rebellion successfully tied to it. All of this can be clearly seen, to begin, in promotional materials for the film's release.

The press book from American International features publicity pieces that overtly sell the ethos of youth and youth rebellion. To come back to Corman momentarily, one piece identifies him as "One of the so-called 'new generation' of Hollywood's creators, his films have been marked by their direction toward the tastes of youth audiences" (3). Corman, in fact, had been directing or producing films since the mid–1950s and created a long lineage of exploitation films like *Teenage Doll* (1957), *A Bucket of Blood* (1959), and *The Trip* (1967), that used youth and often a sense of moral panic to take on the world of the teenager and young adults. For instance, the tagline for *Teenage Doll* reads, "too young to be careful ... too tough to care ... now it's too late to say

'NO.'" In another film building on youthful rebellion and generic perceptions of the counterculture, the poster for *The Wild Angels*, a film about a Hells Angels–like group, warns: "Their credo is violence.... Their God is hate ... and they call themselves 'The Wild Angels.'" Corman, like so many other purveyors of popular culture in the 1950s and 1960s, created texts propped up by themes of generational divide, autonomy, the "Otherness" of youth, and the potential effects of rebellion.

Gas-s-s-s, although a celebration of youth rebellion, also acts as a cautionary tale of where the counterculture could take us. One publicity piece proposes that the film provides "a sure-fire method of eliminating the 'generation gap.'... Eliminate a generation." After describing the plot, the piece offers: "The remaining youngsters who prematurely inherit the earth then provide the film's action as they go about creating a society more suited to their tastes" (3). As the viewer will bear witness to in the film there are many pathways possible for youth to inherit the earth, from becoming fascists to reinvigorating "the clutches of the rampant middle class" (*Gas-s-s-s* 2).

Music is also featured prominently in promotional materials as a signifier of youth rebellion and the counterculture. Country Joe and the Fish appear in one scene in the film but are given top billing on most posters and ads, along with the two main stars, Robert Corff and Elaine Giftos. The band plays "World That We All Dreamed Of" and Country Joe McDonald has a brief speaking part as "F.M. Radio." The appearance is short but adds counterculture credibility with the inclusion of one of Woodstock's own. One ad refers to "Robert Corff 'Star of Hair,' and to a "Special Guest Appearance [by] Country Joe & The Fish Stars of 'Woodstock'" (7). One piece of promotional material describes the band's role in the film as such: "Their audience in the film are the young 'liberated ones,' set free to prematurely inherit the earth" (*Gas-s-s-s* 3).

Such focus on the band and its role in shaping the "Woodstock Generation" might create the appearance of an organic placement and strategized move by the filmmakers to attract the youthful counterculture of the time. According to Corman, music did appear to be a planned contingent, but Country Joe and the Fish were not. Citing an especially difficult shooting, in terms of the overall project, Corman explains that music was part of the mess. He recalls that the Grateful Dead was originally pegged for the appearance: "In Albuquerque they were supposed to play a concert in a drive-in for the film. At the last minute they demanded a huge increase in money. We got Country Joe and the Fish instead" (Corman 164). The haphazard musical issues were apparent to some audiences and to Country Joe himself when his performance and vocals of the song were not included. Those tracks were replaced with versions featuring the voice of Robert Corff. Barry "The Fish" Melton from the group produced and wrote seven songs, "and the band performing five numbers under the pseudonym Johnny & The Tornados" ("Liner Notes").

The totality of incorporating the Joy of Cooking (as mentioned, playing under the name of Gourmet's Delight), Melton's compositions and productions, the work of Johnny & the Tornados, and the high billing of Country Joe and the Fish, produced a sometimes confusing but very potent signifier of the important role of music, especially the San Francisco scene, in addressing and selling to their targeted markets of the young and the counterculture. Corman perhaps was not able to land the initial band he had in mind for the film, but he was aware of the importance of music in creating a vision of the counterculture, a movement entrenched and sold through its association with youthful rebellion. Finding another artist associated with the San Francisco scene, and even better, one popularly associated with Woodstock, brought an essential element to the film representing the counterculture.

In the film, music drives the theme of youthful rebellion and the counterculture from the onset. After its animated opening, Coel (Corff) is seen running through a college campus, with the authorities chasing closely behind. The Barry Melton–composed "Don't Chase Me Around" frames the protagonist from the get-go feeling oppressed by rules, and brought down by a relationship. Soon, many of the oppressive forces of straight society confronting Coel will die off when the aforementioned government-sponsored toxic gas mistakenly escapes and manages to kill everyone over 25. Eventually Coel and Cilla escape the young, though still conservative Texas population, heading west in an Edsel. Their flight is featured along with "Got to Get Movin,'" another Melton composition expressing a need to leave behind one's "scene" and to take to the road to escape the shackles of an oppressive world. The two characters find some travel companions in a record store that will join them for the trip. Marissa (Cindy Williams) at this juncture reminds the group of the importance of music in everyday life. She states, "From Motown to Liverpool from Woodstock to Memphis, it was music that rocked the '60s!"

Along the route to finding their hippie utopia they run into characters like Billy the Kid and the Nomads, a fascist group, and the "clutches of the rampant middle class, led by Marshall McLuhan (LOU PROCOPIO)" who represent "that many of the kids are simply repeating the patterns, prejudices and madness of the old world" (*Gas-s-s-s* 2). Music propels the travelers from the lamenting "I'm Looking for a World" of peace, "day glow colors," and a way to get away to a world "different from mine," to the new world presented in "This is the Beginning" (both penned by Melton). Finding one's way among the clutches and sins of the baby-boomers' parents is the prerogative, where a generation can "make it better."

The message is one that is further driven home in the musical crescendo of the film, with Country Joe and the Fish performing "World That We All Dreamed Of" at a drive-in movie theater that the travelers come across. The song mentions how the older generation wanted the boomers to die, how older Americans fixated on "war and hate," and ultimately how the young, the counterculture are the ones with heads on their shoulders who possess a potential of creating a new utopian society.

The musical voice speaking to rebellion and countercultural values to propel the narrative forward might be argued as a glue that holds a disparate "*Mad* magazine kind of world" together (*New York*). Possibly, taking on the entire generation and any associated rebellious impulses, or even the notion of the counterculture was too much, but they could at least be kept at bay by these musical cues. As *Variety* stated in a review, "Corman, in trying to 'put down' the present way of life has tackled too many targets" (Robe). Naturally, it is possible to argue that with its "us versus them" mentality, the music was also part of too wide a net cast in the hopes of capturing the massive target of the counterculture and youthful rebellion.

At least in terms of reviews, the music was generally regarded better than other aspects of the film. The perceived heavy-handedness of the focus on youth and the counterculture appeared to be at the center of several critics' reviews. *New York Magazine* called the film "cult entertainment for the young with the major music supplied by Country Joe and the Fish." The piece continues: "It is fascinating for adults as an indication of how politically and socially conscious the so-called bikini-beach-party kind of movie has become over the past few years." The quote, referring to Corman's other youth-focused films, connects Corman to the youth market, indeed calling it "Corman's forte" to give insight into the world of teenage or youth rebellion (Untitled).

A review in *Variety* called the cast "an assortment of unproven talent, with the possible exception of the rock group, Country Joe and the Fish." Any reverence for the group was overshadowed by the remainder of the musical experience for the writer. The author states, "The music, which will probably appeal to under 25s, is almost continual, even during quiet scenes where it jars on the nerves." "Obviously aimed at the youth market," the review contended, "it will take some very tolerant youngsters to sit through this poorest of the Corman films" (Robe).

The known and necessary signifier of music to communicate the ethos of the counterculture, as was so apparent in the publicity materials, overstepped its boundaries for the reviewer. Such reviews may have been of concern as the music, including the billing of Country Joe and the Fish, was supposed to act as a successful draw for the counterculture crowd. Publicity materials highlight this marketing focus. It is recommended that theaters should play "the original motion picture sound track album in your theatre prior to your engagement, as well as during the engagement" and to not "OVERLOOK TIE-INS WITH RECORD AND BOOK STORES [referring to the paperback version adapted from the George Armitage-penned script]" (*Gas-s-s-s* 14). Getting the sights and very importantly the sounds of the film would "create and arouse the interest of the 'NOW GENERATION' members of your community" (14). The soundtrack was further pushed in the materials with even more aggressive use of capital letters: "AND BE SURE TO SERVICE YOUR LOCAL D.J.'S WITH COPIES OF THE ALBUM." (*Gas-s-s-s* 16).

The desire of those responsible for the film to take on "too many targets" and to build on a generality of youth rebellion so present in the market and so in-focus via the counterculture of the '60s and early '70s created a pastiche of youthful rebellion that splintered in its want to bottle the cultural milieu of the time. Looking back at publicity materials highlights a heavy-handed (even for exploitation films) aim to sum up and sell the counterculture.

The musical experience described as "jarring" in the *Variety* review counters other reviews that comment favorably on the music included. In several reviews, both negative and positive when it comes to the film, the music is separated from the totality as being a redemptive quality of the film that ultimately could, especially with hindsight in mind, act as one of the essentializing pulls of the film to communicate and make more palatable its thesis. For example, a 1981 ad for an upcoming showing of the film at the Denver Cinema Center calls *Gas-s-s-s*, along with *The Giant Spider Invasion*, "Thanksgiving Turkeys: Two of the worst films of all times." One certainly does not expect too much with such a headline, and the included *New York Times* review by Vincent Canby attached to the piece certainly doesn't do much for the film. However, Canby creates a caveat, saying that among other aspects of the failed experiment, the film featured a "soundtrack score by Country Joe and the Fish that's not bad at all" ("Thanksgiving Turkeys"). A similar focus on music was used to sell the film for a showing at the Berkeley Art Museum, touting "Special guest: Country Joe McDonald" ("PFA at the BAM").

It also should be mentioned that film was not universally panned nor was music included and referred to as a sole redeeming quality in every treatise on the film. Positive reviews, namely ones written years after the film's release, are occasionally much more complimentary. For instance, a 1974 review for *Films & Filming* pointed to the film's "lightness of touch and controlled wit rarely encountered in U.S. parodies" and its "quick-fire action of the film, almost entirely composed of inverted *clichés*, they are hilarious" (Elley).

Perhaps what is seen here is affection for the film coming from *Gas-s-s-s*'s attempt to take on numerous targets, and the film's use of a soundtrack filled with countercultural references to rebellion and generational divide. A film that takes on dissent, generational rebellion, war, peace, style, ethos, and music offers an even overwhelming taste of the time and the zeitgeist. To have so many cues operating within the same text, for good or ill, creates a potential hypertext of the times. Demand for the film and especially for Corman's work has led the film to be packaged with other counterculture focused films such as the 2005 release of a *Wild in the Streets–Gas-s-s-s* double "Midnite Movies" feature, or sharing disc space with *The Trip* in the *Roger Corman Collection*.

Coupling these films appears to be a means of nostalgically looking into the "hippie exploitation" film and its ability to frame the time period and the generational rebellion that propped up the counterculture. Their bundling also helps to reaffirm a sub-genre that encouraged and formalized the use of popular music as a narrative trope and definitive formulaic part of signifying rebellion in their time period. The releases also act as living texts from which future generations could and can judge and make sense of the time and the undercurrent of rebellion that linked a vast population domestically and abroad.

In such texts, the legacy of the '60s, the counterculture, and various other concerns become fodder for debate for those partaking in the discussion, with music playing a key role in the decoding. One can browse Amazon reviews, for instance, to see how audiences continue the debate concerning the film's merits, weaknesses, authenticity, shamelessness, etc. Soundtracks are a reoccurring topic in many reviews of films such as *Gas-s-s-s*, *The Trip*, and *Wild in the Streets*, and are a factor in whether the film itself is liked or loathed. Though it was part of the totality of the piece itself, the music, as it was initially marketed, did become a link, or a promissory note commenting on youthful rebellion and the counterculture. Ultimately it was a force that in some cases, isolated from other aspects of the movie, may well be considered by some as a more suitable or authentic reflection of the times and the zeitgeist. To have artists like Country Joe McDonald, Barry Melton, The Electric Flag (*The Trip*), or the stylings of a fictitious psychedelic band like Max Frost and the Troopers in *Wild in the Streets* warning us of the "Shape of Things to Come," was an essential key for these exploitation films to signify the madness and power of youthful rebellion. As contended elsewhere in this book, the sound of films, both in scores and in popular soundtrack selections, critically lauded and dismissed, tapped into an essential medium to sell an ethos of the times. The times themselves were built upon the back of a successful campaign of self-assertion and moral panic aimed at identifying and marketing of youth rebellion in the post-war world; a soundtrack helped sell it.

Gas-s-s-s, despite being a relatively unpopular film, is now a part of canon that can be isolated via time, theme, or focus, no matter its critical reception. In part due to films like *Gas-s-s-s*, the very notions of identity connected to youth rebellion, the counterculture, and to baby boomers were hashed out in the public eye and in personal consumption. Film, music, and other popular culture texts ensured there would be markers, whether they be perceived as authentic or inauthentic, to situate and signify youth and rebellion to baby boomers and to situate those looking in from the outside. Exploitive and critically received films each contributed to this series of markers, making sure in the process, that one could hear the counterculture.

9. African American Artists in Hollywood: Isaac Hayes' Contribution to *Shaft*

Introduction

Directed by Gordon Parks and produced by Joel Freeman, *Shaft* (1971) is a film about John Shaft, a private detective played by Richard Roundtree. Despite its status today as a classic work of the period, the film was originally not expected to be a major hit. Its success was imagined to be somewhat limited for a few reasons. One of the reasons was that at the time of *Shaft*'s release, an African American main character in a film was a relatively new idea. It was even rare to have a heroic main character who was African American. But this same reason enabled Shaft to become a hero for many African Americans. Samuel L. Jackson, who would play Shaft in a remake in 2000, remembers that when he first saw the movie while in college, he felt it was "pretty awesome." He states: "It was the first time I actually saw someone who looked like me, sounded like me, dressed the way I always wanted to dress and played a hero. He was our first real hero. It was all about Black Pride, and he was very proud. He was strong; he was smart; he was unafraid. He had the power and even the ego that we all wanted to have" ("Cover Story" 61). The film's appeal was widely appreciated by a diverse audience, including both blacks and whites. By the end of the year, *Shaft* became the twelfth most successful movie of 1971 (Briggs 27).

The popularity of the film was welcomed by the MGM movie studio. In the early 1970s, the film production company was suffering from a serious financial slump and was making some investments with limited budgets. *Shaft* was one of them. Robert Gordon describes that MGM "was willing to take inexpensive gambles, such as throwing half a million dollars at a movie that could wring a few bucks from the neglected African American audience"

(254). The gamble turned out to be a smart move. Donald Bogle illuminates that *Shaft* made "some $12 million within a year in North American alone—and single-handedly saved MGM from financial ruin" (*Toms, Coons* 238).

The film that saved the studio has a storyline based on the literary work by Ernest Tidyman, and is rather simple. At the beginning of the film, Police Lieutenant Vic Androzzi tells Shaft that two gangsters are after him. Immediately after the conversation, Shaft finds them and engages in a fight that leads to the death of one of the gang members. Shaft's investigation then leads to the leader of these gangsters, Bumpy. He tells Shaft that his daughter has been kidnapped and needed his help to find her. During his rescue operation, Shaft becomes targeted in a shooting and witnesses the rising tensions in the neighborhood. Despite being shot in his shoulder in an exchange of fire, Shaft, a detective hero, successfully rescues Bumpy's daughter.

For this film focusing on an African American private detective, Isaac Hayes (1942–2008) provided the score. As will be discussed shortly, his soundtrack was an immediate hit with remarkable sales and a series of international awards. In *The Sacramento Observer*, Herb Kole, vice president of merchandising for Stax Records, is quoted as saying, "We've never seen an album explode in sales like this before.... It's the fastest-breaking album we've ever had. Our distributors tell us 'Shaft' is selling like a single. They've even offered to send their own trucks to the pressing plants to pick up more copies" ("Soundtrack Hits"). The article continues to explain that the soundtrack record became a million dollar album in a matter of only two weeks.

As far as the storyline is concerned, Parks' story in itself is not particularly unique. However, what adds value to the film as a canonical counterculture work of the mid-twentieth century is Hayes' involvement in the film and his music. In other words, Isaac Hayes played a significant role in framing *Shaft* as an important counterculture film, even though he did not appear in the film. His legacy is still pertinent in the way counterculture is remembered today. Hayes and the film provide a window to the counterculture and its surrounding environment in two different ways.

First, Hayes' success with his soundtrack represented an increasing African American influence in the general music industry of the mid-twentieth century in the U.S. It was different from the conditions of the earlier half of the century when art of various kinds created by African Americans was placed aside of the so-called mainstream American art. Hayes' creative pieces were more widely accepted including outside of the African American community. The difference is clear when the wider reception of Hayes' work is compared to the musical, literary, and other art works that were produced by African Americans during so-called renaissance periods such as the Harlem Renaissance and the Chicago Renaissance. Hayes' success, therefore, can be read as a testament to the progress that the American society had made during the civil rights era.

Second, the film's music represents Shaft as a clichéd Blaxploitation character. Hayes' music, especially "Theme from *Shaft*," characterizes him through African American stereotypes. From this perspective, not much was different from the pre–civil rights era treatment of African Americans. *Shaft* can be read as a piece in which strong racial tensions and prejudices continued to exist, even in the post–civil rights era U.S. The complexity of the period is well reflected in the way Shaft's character is constructed and represented both visually and aurally.

Isaac Hayes' Success

The success of *Shaft* and Isaac Hayes cannot be separated. During the second half of the twentieth century and almost the first full decade of the twenty-first century until his death, Hayes took advantage of his various gifts and appeared in different kinds of entertainment. He appeared in TV programs and movies including *Dr. Dolittle 2*, *That '70s Show*, and *Soul Men* (released posthumously), just to name a few. But he is most renowned as a singer-songwriter and a music producer. Eventually known as "one of the most bankable composers in the [music] business," he started his career in recording and producing music in the 1960s.

By 1971, Hayes was already a well-known cultural icon. In the 1960s, he had produced a hit album, *Hot Buttered Soul*, and singles such as "Walk On By" and "By the Time I Get to Phoenix." His popularity helped the movie, and the movie helped him in return. Hayes' score for *Shaft* was a major success partly because the film by itself was a success. But it was also true that his score attracted many fans because of Hayes' existing reputation. A newspaper article from 1971 even states that "the phenomenal success of the soundtrack album can only be attributed to the great popularity of Isaac Hayes. His three previous albums, all multimillion sellers, and his appearances at the nation's top concert halls have built a huge following for the multitalented Hayes" ("Soundtrack Hits"). Clearly, Hayes did not become popular because of *Shaft*. He was already a well-known artist. However, it is fair to say that *Shaft* enabled him to become one of the most renowned music producers of the period.

Despite the inseparable connection between the film and the composer, Hayes' original intension was not to produce the score for the film. First, Hayes hoped that he would be able to play the role of Shaft. This is why Hayes requested a screen audition as a condition for writing the theme song for the film (Gordon 259). In reality, however, Parks had already chosen Roundtree for the main character role (Bowman 229–233). When the movie was being produced, Hayes was better known than Roundtree. As stated above, although Hayes was not an actor, he was a very popular musician. On the contrary, Roundtree had only had a minor role in a film. Roundtree remembers working on the film. He says, "I had no concept of what starring in a film was about.... I was thrown into the water and just started swimming. And then to have it explode like that—it caught me totally off guard" ("Covers Story" 61). Joe Bob Briggs explains that Parks chose Roundtree because he wanted to avoid making a rather rational choice of actors. For example, Jim Brown and Raymond St. Jacques were two names that Parks considered to be "more obvious choices" (24–25). This is why Roundtree was chosen for the role for $12,500 (Briggs 28).

Of course, critics and fans today can only wonder how Hayes's career might have developed differently if he had been chosen for the role over Roundtree. On the same token, the film might be remembered differently today. Either way, Burlingame explains that the movie "launched an acting career for Hayes, who not only scored but starred in *Three Tough Guys* (1974) and *Truck Turner* (1974) and later made memorable appearances in films like *Escape from New York* (1981) and *I'm Gonna Git You Sucka* (1988)" (90). What is clear is that *Shaft* pushed Hayes to the forefront of the film music recording industry. Burlingame also explains that Hayes' album "helped to sell the movie and vice versa, and today the score is better remembered than the film that inspired it" (90).

Although Hayes was disappointed in the news that he would not be Shaft, he nonetheless was willing to fulfill his commitment to offer the music for the film. So a few weeks later, Parks shared some footage of the film with Hayes to see if he could compose the score for the film. Hayes knew that nothing was promised. Although it was not called a test, it was indeed a test. Gordon writes that Hayes was well aware that "if he didn't get it right, the job would vanish" (259). Hayes remembers that "Gordon Parks knew I'd never done a soundtrack so they handled me with kid gloves" (Gordon 259).

To respond to Parks' request, Hayes gathered his team including Al Bell (record producer), Willie Hall (drummer), and Lester Snell (keyboardist). They played the clips that Parks had shared with Hayes. The wah-wah guitar sound that is well known for "Theme from *Shaft*" was made by accident, Gordon explains. Charles Skip Pitts, the guitarist, comments that "When I play rhythm, I will put a lot of drum beats with it.... I was checking my pedals. I tested my overdrive, my reverb, the Maestro box, and then I started in with the wah-wah. Isaac stopped everything and said, 'Skip, what is that you're playing?' I said, 'I'm just tuning up.' He said, 'Keep playing that G octave'" (260). After this fortunate accident that led to the most iconic feature of the theme song, the creative process came smoothly. Hayes says, "Within two hours we had the arrangement for the main title." Even the second and third pieces came just within a matter of hours. The outcome of the work was "Theme from *Shaft*," "Soulsville," and "Ellie's Love Theme." Hayes took the music recorded on tapes to Parks' apartment. The production team was satisfied with Hayes' compositions. Parks said to Hayes, "Okay, you can go to Hollywood now and start on the film" (Gordon 260). Parks commissioned Hayes and his team to compose the rest of the soundtrack.

Despite the quality of Hayes' work, he was "an unlikely Oscar winner to the old-guard music community of Hollywood" (Burlingame 90). Within a matter of a few years, however, Hayes won an Academy Award, a Golden Globe Award, and a Grammy Award thanks to his involvement with the film. The album stayed at the top of the Top R&B Albums chart for a few months. "Theme from *Shaft*" was ranked at number one for two weeks on the Billboard Hot 100 chart, as well ("Legendary"). In a matter of weeks after the release of the soundtrack, Hayes made $2 million. The soundtrack went platinum. Ed Guerrero writes that "the *Shaft* theme became so popular that it was heard everywhere, from nightclubs to half-time at football games" (97).

Hayes' winning of the awards is historically and culturally significant. When he won the Academy Award for Best Original Song in 1972 for "Theme from *Shaft*," he became the third African American to win an Academy Award from the Academy of Motion Picture Arts and Sciences. Only Sidney Poitier and Hattie McDaniel had won awards previously. Although by 1971, a few years after the civil rights struggles were fought to lead to the Civil Rights Act of 1964 and the Voting Rights Act of 1965, African Americans suffered from continuing *de facto* racism. The end of the 1960s and the early 1970s, also known as the Black Power Era, often created a sense of fear among whites. Therefore, it was a significant cultural event for an African American artist to win such a prestigious award. Furthermore, the film did not just have an African American music producer. Its protagonist was black. So was Gordon Parks. Much of the audience was black, as well. The success of *Shaft* not just at the box office but also at the Academy Award ceremony was a testament that the entertainment industry might be changing.

Yet, America's racial landscape did not seem as promising to Hayes, a firm voice in unsure times. He was not a conformist. Francesca D'Amico explains his supportive view on Black Power by referring to an incident that happened in 1968. Hayes learned about the assassination of Dr. Martin Luther King, Jr., in his ride to a studio. Originally, he was "unaware of the degree to which King's death would change his consciousness as an artist and an African American." But later Hayes stated that just like other African American artists, he was "artistically paralyzed for an entire year with bitterness and anger over

American race relations and the assassination of one of black America's foremost civil rights leaders." D'Amico writes that "by the turn of the 1970s, [Hayes] would become re-inspired, energetically constructing his artistry as a vehicle for activism, consciousness, and resistance" (185–186). Hayes did not intend to produce music just to appeal to a wider—or white—audience. He was outwardly different from Sidney Poitier. He embodied black pride.

In addition, the fact that he won awards for *Shaft* is significant. As discussed later in this chapter, it is a Blaxploitation film. Although this genre category, in essence, is a bridge between black and white audiences, the film nonetheless features urban decay, gang activities, and other social issues that were similar to the concerns that many whites felt after urban rebellions of the 1960s and the rise of the Black Power Movement. Despite the assumed social changes that the U.S. had witnessed during the civil rights era, American racism did not disappear quickly. For the Academy to appreciate and celebrate a film that dealt with topics that would cause moral panics was a meaningful event.

Hayes' success through *Shaft* is a significant story of the counterculture era. Larry Neal writes that "a main tenet of Black Power is the necessity for Black people to define the world in their own terms." Both Roundtree's character and Isaac Hayes believed in this tenet, and still won the popularity of the larger American audience. As will be discussed below, the fact that the cultural product that was so heavily enmeshed with the signs of Black Power and black agency received such wide popularity attests to the social complexity at the time.

Black Sexuality, Stereotypes, and Counterculture

Shaft is a Blaxploitation film. As Briggs correctly identifies, despite some common misconceptions, it was not the first film of the genre (24). But Parks' work indeed matches the description of the cinematic genre that Guerrero characterizes as "the films that are usually associated with the production of the sixty or so Hollywood films that centered on black narratives, featured black casts playing out various action-adventures in the ghetto, and were released roughly between 1969 and 1974" (69). Hayes explains in *The Black Chord* that "Blaxploitation was the first time we ever had a Black hero on the screen, instead of just playing a subservient role, like butlers or chauffeurs" (Goldman 114). Shaft, as a private detective, embodied a departure from such stereotypical roles that African American actors played in Hollywood films.

The rise of Blaxploitation movies at the end of the 1960s reflected the changing social and political environment of the U.S. In other words, "these films were made possible by the rising political and social consciousness of black people ... which translated into a large black audience thirsting to see their full humanity depicted on the commercial cinema screen" (69). This is to say that African Americans were more vocal about their dissatisfaction about Hollywood's lack of African American representations. Few movies prior to this period featured African American characters. When they were portrayed in a film, Hollywood would degrade black characters. The post–civil rights era witnessed a huge surge in the expressions of African American interests in media contents that positively represented African American characters.

Although this new cinematic genre increased the number of African American characters appearing on a screen and improved the depiction of those black characters, the Blaxploitation movie, as the naming of the genre derived from "exploitation" clearly suggests, had its own shortcomings. After all, Briggs comments that "the films that were initially conceived as an antidote to racism became ... racist" (28). Hayes concurs by saying, "You had a Black guy that was a hero, so whatever he did, people loved it. Some critics became concerned that it was giving the wrong image to the Black community" (Goldman 114). At first, it was refreshing for many black viewers to see African Americans on television and movie screens. But soon after, they began to notice that these films had their own problems.

One of the problems of the Blaxploitation film came from Hollywood's priority for profit generation over social or racial justice. Although Hollywood in the post–civil rights era saw African Americans as viable consumers of their entertainment product, it did not mean that the movie industry was engaged in a social project. Instead, Hollywood was interested in cashing in from the rising disposable income of African Americans. The white flight, their fear about African Americans in general and also Black Power specifically, all contributed to this trend. But it was not willing to risk profits generated through a white audience. The purpose of Hollywood movies, therefore, was "harmless entertainment."

Produced in the same year as *Shaft*, *Sweet Sweetback's Baadasssss Song* (1971) had a clear anti-authority and anti-establishment message. *Shaft* had its messages toned down. On the one hand, Melvin Van Peebles' work was independently produced. But *Shaft* was produced by a major film production company. So *Shaft* took a safer option by "[coming] across as less stridently antiwhite" (92). This success was partially possible because the white audience accepted the film. Bogle also writes that "this film in later years has proven far more acceptable to the large white audience than such features as *Sweet Sweetback's Baadasssss Song* and *Super Fly* (neither of which has ever had a television network showing as did *Shaft*, both of which have true underground, outlaw heroes, free of traditional bourgeois values). Later *Shaft* was even turned into a routine television private eye series" (*Blacks* 186). Guerrero analyzes that "although the film was carried to smash-hit status by black audiences, it was able to cross over and play well with whites also. This is why *Shaft* "was generally applauded by the critics, both black and white, as being a breakthrough production in terms of expanding black representation in commercial cinema" (92–93). For many African Americans, these conformist attitudes were troubling. Although appealing to both white and black audiences made financial and business sense, it did not allow blacks to tell their own story on their own terms.

In the film, Shaft clearly reflected this complex racial dynamism in the movie industry. As the lyrics of "Theme from *Shaft*" say, Shaft is a complex person. He lived with Black Pride. But he was also subject to black stereotypes. He was not only an African American protagonist but also a private detective hero. He would not easily give in to his white contact on the police force. He may experience name-calling, but he remains calm, or answers right back as he did in the coffee scene. However, Shaft was portrayed as a hypersexual African American stereotype. He was not Sidney Poitier who was shown with elegance and without such sexual urgency. He was different from Bill Cosby from *The Cosby Show* of the following decade whose sexuality was stripped with the producer's shrewd decision to make him an OB/GYN doctor to make him an African American whose sexual interests were left behind in the interests of medicine (Kiuchi 27). In the case of Shaft, his masculinity and sexuality were placed at the forefront of the movie.

One of the ways in which the movie sexualizes Shaft is Hayes' "Theme from *Shaft*." Having a theme song "as an anthem dedicated either to the hero or to the plot in general" was a common practice with Blaxploitation films. The practice, started with *Sweetback*'s "Sweetback's Theme" that functioned "as a sonic backdrop for Sweetback's flight from the police," allowed Hayes' music to celebrate Shaft (Demers 46). The music is heard in the opening credit scene in which Shaft aggressively crosses a street in New York City. Demers describes that

> as the song plays, Richard Roundtree ... walks calmly through Manhattan, dressed fashionably in corduroy and leather. His nonchalance seems utterly oblivious to Hayes' laudatory song; as if Shaft were too cool to notice his own sophistication. This sequence cleverly divides responsibilities between the actor and the composer, allowing the actor to avoid emoting while letting the music tell the audience what to think. The stylized combination of opening images and theme music rendered *Shaft* an archetype of Blaxploitation films [46].

The scene, shot with a camera on top of a Times Square building without closing the street, not only introduced the hero to the audience but also glorifies him (Briggs 24; Demers 46).

In Hayes' "Theme from *Shaft*," the lyrics first morph Shaft into a sexual organ. Then the song calls him a "sex machine" for any woman. This portrayal of an African American character is consistent with the sexualization of blacks in American history and in American popular culture. African American males have historically been characterized as hypersexual and as having uncontrollable sexual desires. Such a prejudice justified the beating of black slaves after they were found to be sexually engaged with white women, castration of African American victims of lynching, and even the tragedy of Emmett Till.

The song was written with a specific guidance by Parks. In an interview with Bill DeMain, Hayes explains that Parks had said to him, "All you have to do [is] to zero in on the character." Hayes characterizes Shaft as "a relentless guy" who "was always in pursuit ... [and] on the move." Gordon Parks shared, "That's what your main theme should denote." To Robert Gordon, Hayes explained, "[Gordon said,] Shaft is always revolving, always moving. Your music should depict that—something to capture his personality. His being. He's a cool dude, too. But he's tough. You got to pull all that in your music" (250). Interestingly enough, Hayes felt like he had to make it audience friendlier. In the interview with DeMain, he also explains that he had to censor some parts of the lyrics for fear that "somebody would [tell] me to shut my mouth" (43).

The lyrics of this stereotype-ridden theme song and the scene in which the song is heard do not match up well. Demers explains that in this scene, "the well-dressed main character [is] walking the streets of Manhattan. His actions display his cool lack of regard for authority: he jaywalks, and 'gives the finger' to a taxi that threatens to run him over" (49). But the theme song actually compliments who Shaft is. In addition to the sexualization of Shaft, Hayes continues to characterize him as someone who would not back out even if there is a danger and who would risk his own life to help his friends. Nonetheless, one of the reasons why Shaft was a safe and harmless character that could be accepted by the white audience was that he avoided violence unless it was absolutely necessary (Demers 49). Hayes' lyrics reflect the character's "charisma and intelligence" (49).

The theme song truly reflects the intricacy of Shaft. Both visually and musically, Shaft is exploited through sexualization. He is seen having sex with females in the film. These scenes are not necessarily essential to solving the kidnapping mystery. But the sex scenes help the movie develop Shaft's character. However, he is also portrayed as a talented and dedicated detective. He is a hero who saves a young girl. Nonetheless, he is seen breaking laws and not following the order of his boss. Violence is not his first choice of action, though. This is how the character is complex. The same happens with music.

A part of the music is about Shaft's sexual prowess. But the lyrics also tell how loyal and brave he could be. The film shows both sides of Shaft.

The complexity that *Shaft* presents both through its main character and its theme song reflects the complexity of the countercultural period. Especially in relation to racial politics, the counterculture period was chaotic. The promise of racial justice seemed to have been fulfilled with federal acts of the mid–1960s. But such optimism was overshadowed by the assassinations of two African American leaders. They had many differences but also many similarities. Commonly, they are remembered as opposites, but the reality is not as simple. This complexity of the period is well reflected in the film. *De facto* racism was still visible in many, if not all, facets of American society. It included the film industry. When Hattie McDaniel became the first African American to win an Academy Award, she did so by playing the mammy role. When Sidney Poitier became the second African American to win an Academy Award, he did so by playing a safe African American male identity. Hayes, the third African American to win an Academy Award, did so with his complex music that both defied and underscored African American stereotypes, heroicized a black character, and glorified a character that embodied the Black Power movement. Achievements by these African Americans all reflect the social and political environment of each period. For Isaac Hayes, the award was a recognition about the complexity of American society that was well reflected in his score for the movie.

Conclusion: Hayes' Lasting Legacy

Hayes' influence continues to survive to this day. In many ways, until his death in 2008, he remained pertinent to America's popular culture through his appearance in movies and TV programs. Between 1997 and 2006, he was the voice of the chef in *South Park*. Three movies were released after his death. But Hayes' composition for *Shaft* resonates decades later. Nelson George, for example, explains:

> The final, and perhaps, most crucial link between '70s pulp movies and late '90s youth culture is Blaxploitation soundtracks. No one can dispute the enduring quality of Isaac Hayes's *Shaft* and Curtis Mayfield's *Superfly*. Both soundtracks, the products of '60s soul producer-writers using movie scoring to expand the sonic scope of their work, are jammed with wahwah guitars, sensuous Latin percussion, blaring horns, supple flutes, and vocal choruses that still inspire current music makers [106].

DeMain also notes,

"Theme from *Shaft*" along with many of Isaac's other songs are now R&B staples, and have been sampled by over 140 artists, including Dr. Dre, Snoop Dogg, Destiny's Child, and TLC. Beyond Isaac's writing and performing, his Afrocentric styles and political activism have set standards for black artists over the past thirty years. As director John Singleton (who did 2001's remake of *Shaft*) says, "Isaac Hayes changed the way black men saw themselves" [40].

But it is not just the legacy of Hayes that is still around us. Nostalgia about counterculture still surrounds us. Although the racial tensions and prejudices may be more subtle than what they were in the 1970s, the U.S. is far from being post-racial. Various forms of injustices and inequalities continue to exist. In this social environment, a culture of resistance and an exploration for a new social identity occur frequently to this day. At many political rallies, for example, a witness can observe a counterculture-like atmosphere. The Occupy movement, the LGBTQ rights issues, and many other similar topics show the need and want of the contemporary society for justice and equality. In this social sentiment, the memories of the counterculture are still relevant. *Shaft* is a part of such memories. Although it is consumed in a vastly different social and political context today compared to 1971, *Shaft* connects the social instability and complexity between the 1970s and 2010s.

10. I'm Watching It for Its Music: *Deep Throat* and Its Soundtrack

Introduction

Arguably, one of the most controversial films of the American countercultural era of the 1960s and 1970s is Jerry Gerard's pornographic film *Deep Throat*. Written and directed by Gerard (Gerard Damiano), an experienced pornographic director, and produced by Lou Perry (Louis Peraino), the film was released in June 1972, starring Linda Lovelace, Harry Reems, and Dolly Sharp. The film's popular cultural impact is evident to this day as its title continues to be used to refer to Mark Felt, former associate director of the Federal Bureau of Investigation, and, of course, to a form of oral sex. Furthermore, the name "deep throat" and its variations have appeared in popular television shows such as *The X-Files* and *Family Guy*, while a Trojan horse computer virus is also called as such. Despite America's usual public aversion to pornography, it is clear that the film has become a significant part of its history and culture. Although critics considered the movie as a prototypical symptom of the social malaise associated with the counterculture at the time, the film's success and impacts are irrefutable.

A simple and measurable way to understand the success of the film is examining the ratio between the cost of production and the profit. *Deep Throat* had a budget of $25,000 and hired "a handful of $75-to-$100-a-day actors and actresses." After its release on June 12, 1972, the film grossed over $3 million within the first half year (Blumenthal). Although the film's overall revenue figure varies among different sources, IMDb, for example, indicates the film grossed approximately $45 million ("Deep Throat" IMDb). Writing for the *Los Angeles Times*, Michael Hilzik discusses that the estimated revenue is as large as $600 million. However, he continues to analyze that although

$100 million might be an underestimate, a more realistic figure lies somewhere between $300 and $600 million. Despite these variances in estimates and exaggeration of popularity by the studio, the film, nonetheless, was financially successful especially as a pornographic film.

The film truly stirred the American public. For the first time in American history, a pornographic film broke into the mainstream. In *A History of X*, Luke Ford explains, "*Deep Throat* brought hardcore into popular culture, earning at least twice as much money as any other porno in history." The film was hugely popular. David Vandor, an official for the Mayor's Office of Midtown Planning and Development in New York at the time, is quoted in the *New York Times* saying, "*Deep Throat* is an excellent film. It is better than most situation comedies or grade C comedies." Blumenthal wrote, "There is no harm or shame in indulging their curiosity—and perhaps even their frankly prurient interest—by going to see *Deep Throat*.... Some French United Nations diplomats went and insisted on paying with traveler's checks. Some off-duty policemen went and became the objects of search in the theater by fellow officers." The film even started the so-called "porn chic" trend (Blumenthal). Simultaneously, the film was a focal point of contestation. On one level, America's Victorian civic values collided with those of the counterculture. In 1973, Judge Joel J. Tyler called the film "this feast of carrion and squalor," "a nadir of decadence," and "a Sodom and Gomorrah gone wild before the fire." He continued, "The alleged story lines are the façade, the sheer negligee through which clearly shines the producer's and the defendant's true and only purpose, that is, the presentation of unmistakably hard-core pornography" (Weber, "Joel").

On another level, the allegations came from within. Although Linda Lovelace once said, "I wasn't paid much but now I'm known, so it's OK," about only making $1,200 from the film, she later claimed that she was forced into the pornographic industry (Leonard). The reason behind this change in attitude toward pornography is unclear. It is highly possible that Lovelace finally felt safe enough, ten years after the production of the film, to be honest about her difficulties and struggles in life. Or she might have realized, as she got older and wiser, the implications of her past career and the industry. However, writing for the *Daily Mail*, Tom Leonard is skeptical that the change in her attitude was sincere. He wrote, "In 1980, with feminists increasingly attacking pornography as demeaning to women, Lovelace found a new opportunity to grab the limelight." Either way, by the mid–1980s, she was a strong advocate for anti-pornography activism. Testifying in front of the Meese Commission that investigated pornography in the U.S., she stated, "When you see the movie *Deep Throat*, you are watching me being raped.... It is a crime that the movie is still showing. There was a gun to my head the entire time" (Leonard).

Deep Throat is first and foremost pornography. Both its title and its depictions of sexual acts support such genre identification. It is, however, also a comedy film. Explicit portrayals of oral and penetrative sex are just a part of the plot. The premise of the story—Linda Lovelace's inability to reach an orgasm because she was born with her clitoris in her throat—is unrealistic and comical. From here, the film takes its audience through Lovelace's sexual exploration. Initially, being aware of her problem, her friend hosts a sex party, only to learn that Lovelace's problem might need medical attention. Her doctor, Dr. Young, then figures out that her clitoris existed in her throat and she would be able to achieve an orgasm through oral sex. Dr. Young and Lovelace continue to have oral sex while he is also sexually engaged with his nurse. Once Lovelace expresses her wish to marry Dr. Young, he advises her to have oral sex with other men to find the right man. The rest of the film is a series of sexual acts between Lovelace and her patients or clients, and between Dr. Young and his nurse, leading Linda eventually to find a partner to marry.

This comedic storyline locates the film well in the context of the counterculture movement. Barry Reay, for example, characterizes the mid-century as a period of "casual sex" (2). Ira Reiss and Albert Ellis also called this new tradition "body-centered" and sex "without affection" (1). On one level, casual sex and openness about sex through pornography signaled American cultural departure from its early twentieth-century value systems. On another level, connecting a topic such as sexuality that was supposed to be discussed in a very limited environment—between married couples, at church, in a doctor's office, to name a few—to popular comedy is also an example of detachment from previous cultural beliefs. In this film, sex is both an obsession and an afterthought. Actors and actresses continuously have sex. But they also do so sometimes on the side, as is the case with Dr. Young who engages himself in sex while recording his patient's information.

Music and Deep Throat

What is often forgotten about the film because of its popularity or notoriety is its soundtrack. Music, for example, often helps the film portray sex as something purely for fun. Most of the scholarly and popular books on films in the 1970s do not discuss the music used in *Deep Throat*. The soundtrack, however, is a rich source of counterculture values. Ralph Blumenthal wrote, "The sound track, too, is sprightly and haunting, so much so that when Herman Tarnow, an attorney serving with the Police Department, returned home one day after viewing the film preliminary to a bust, he caught himself absentmindedly humming the theme song." An American pornography actor,

Ron Jeremy, explains that the music of *Deep Throat* was "campy and adorable" ("Deep Throat," *Fused*). The film's soundtrack was much different from that of its predecessors—not just aural accompaniment of the visual work.

One of the most significant differences between the soundtrack of *Deep Throat* and that of other pornographic films before is that *Deep Throat* did not rely on traditional pornographic music. This is another example of clashing values and expectations. Ron Jeremy explains, "Porn films always had that boom-chicka-boom-chicka-boom music, but Gerard Damiano ... always had the desire to go straight, so he put in music that was unlike typical porn music. Not just bouncy stuff, but more fun-goofy-crazy music" ("Deep Throat," *Fused*). If the "bouncy" music represented the hidden and taboo nature of pornography, *Deep Throat*'s use of more mainstream music reflected "the relative frankness" of the counterculture period (Tincknell 143).

The film's music is mysterious in many ways. Except for a few, most songs lack any information about composers or singers. Their identities are hidden partially for fear that the U.S. government's witch-hunt as the police of American morality would endanger them. The mystery, however, does not end here. In numerous instances, the music does not match the visual images on the screen. While pornography viewers might expect music to enhance their sexual anticipation, the music sometimes is overly calm or soothing. On the one hand, it betrays the convention of a pornographic film. On the other hand, it treats sex as a mere means for personal sexual pleasure, expression, and freedom, a widely shared thought of the counterculture era.

Mismatching Music

Deep Throat is filled with musical cues that are not truly helpful. Peter Larsen asks, "What [is film music] used for, how [does] it [function] within the context of the film?" (7). In many instances in this film, the audience is left with these questions unanswered. The level of mismatch is so much that the use of particular music or a theme does not seem to make much sense but simply challenges those who try to understand the reasons behind such music selection. Conventional reasoning does not help viewers understand the film's music selection.

For example, elements of surprise exist with *Deep Throat*'s use of Beethoven's work and the James Bond theme music. The film begins with a view of a river in Florida by which Linda Lovelace walks to her parked blue convertible. Once she gets in the car, a somewhat bouncy, relatively typical mid–twentieth century pornographic soundtrack tunes in. But it is not a typical porn groove with an organ and drums. The bouncy music soon turns into the last movement of Beethoven's Ninth Symphony, "Ode to Joy." It is a pornographic interpretation of the nineteenth century masterpiece. The film repeats its first segment several times. Although the music is not accompanied by words or vocals and is purely instrumental, with the memorable tune of the symphony, the audience may be reminded of the original poem by Frederich Schiller which reads in English translation as:

> Joy, thou beauteous godly lighting,
> Daughter of Elysium,
> Fire drunken we are ent'ring
> Heavenly, thy holy home
> [Schiller Institute].

The message of the poem that celebrates the unity of mankind as attested by the fact that the European Union uses it as the anthem of Europe does not match the film genre within which *Deep Throat* was produced and consumed. The music is adapted completely out of its original scope, just like another counterculture film also discussed in this book, *A Clockwork Orange*, did only a year prior. Nevertheless, Beethoven's joyous tune provides an upbeat atmosphere. It is a pleasurable musical accompaniment but does not seem to generate any significant meaning.

While Beethoven's symphony is played, the open credits run and Lovelace continues to drive to a residential area. She parks her car in front of a house. It appears to be a typical suburban one-story home in Florida. It has a two-car garage. It has green grass. Behind the house are a few palm trees. Soon, the audience learns that it is the house where Linda and her friend, Helen, performed by Dolly Sharp, live together. Helen is a divorced woman who lives on her alimony. Linda receives money from her "old man." This is when the music fades out as Lovelace's car door opens. Through this entire segment with Beethoven, the film does not look anything like pornography.

It was not just the German classic composer whose work was adopted in *Deep Throat*. James Bond-related themes, a film series that started in 1962 with *Dr. No*, make several appearances. In addition to the name of the doctor, Dr. Young, whose last name is the same as Terence Young, the director of some of the James Bond movies, and the fact that Dr. Young refers to one of his patient cases as "Case 007," a small segment of the movie's theme song appears in the film, as well.

Deep Throat uses the theme of James Bond just as a motif but nothing more. The use of this music is less apparent than that of Beethoven's symphony. The theme of the secret agent movie series starts as a male perpetrator covering most of his face with a handkerchief enters Linda's house near the end of the film. She is in the bathroom shaving herself. This male character is nothing like James Bond, though. He does not look confident. He looks uncertain how to advance in the situation. His uncertainty is only enhanced when he realizes Linda is sitting on the water tank of her toilet with her legs wide spread to shave her genital area. The music continues to have a hint of James Bond. It sounds mysterious and tense.

Once she is done shaving and leaves the bathroom, she finds the perpetrator. However, she does not look too scared. She asks him to take whatever he wants to but not to hurt her. When he says he will rape her, she quickly obliges to his wants, as long as he will not hurt her. After this low-quality conversation scene, the perpetrator takes his mask off. Linda calls him Wilbert. Clearly, they know each other. This entire scene is accompanied by the continuation of the James Bond–inspired music. Unlike the tense but cool images of James Bond, the conversation to follow between Linda and Wilbert is corny, at best. The mismatch of music and the tone of the story is evident.

To make the situation even more awkward, Wilbert asks Linda to marry him. She refuses. The silliness of the situation is not only that Wilbert asks her to marry him right after he has broken into her house and threatened to rob or rape her, but also that Linda's reason to not marry him is because the man has to have at least a nine-inch-long penis for her to marry. In order to fill this four-inch gap that Wilbert faces, Linda recommends that he call Dr. Young in case he might be able to operate on him.

Neither of these adaptations of existing popular music truly matches the general story of the film. On the surface level, the joyful tune by Beethoven and the suspenseful tune from James Bond films seem to carry proper messages. However, the love of mankind described in "Ode to Joy" is not what the movie tries to present. The conversation between Linda and Wilbert is far from more refined interactions seen in Terence Young's film. If these adaptations are read as a refusal and re-interpretation of the original work, the film's intent is more understandable. As discussed later in this volume, *A Clockwork Orange* did something similar with Beethoven's compositions. Both films challenge their viewers to consider who owns the proper interpretation of artistic works.

The examples of these questionable choices of music are not limited to the aforementioned two. They also include the way music discusses the kind of sex Linda is having. Needless to say, pornography's intent is not in teaching the value of meaningful sex. The image of casual sex is a frequent theme of any pornographic film. In *Deep Throat*, the idea that sex is for fun, is something casual, and is something inconsequential is also conveyed through its music use. For example, when Linda reveals to Helen that she does not enjoy sex as much and they discuss how to solve the problem, the accompanying music is very light and calm. The music does not match the seriousness of Linda's medical condition which might very well be causing emotional pains.

Linda explains that sex makes her "feel tingly all over," but nothing follows after. She says, "There should be bells ringing, dams busting, bombs going off." Helen wonders if Linda might be doing something wrong. Linda might have to try something else. Acknowledging the intricacy of sexual pleasure, Helen says sex is more than just "bam-bam-thank-you-ma'am." In order to try various options for Linda, Helen proposes to invite multiple male friends of hers as Linda's potential sex partners in order to try to solve the problem. Linda agrees to "try anything" with a hint of smile on her face. Interestingly, this entire conversation again takes place with quiet soothing music in the background. This polyamorous conversation is far from the innocence that the music carries. It is true that Linda might feel better once she could sort out her problem. But the music masks the gravity of Helen's promiscuous idea to have an orgy party.

A similar light treatment of sex by music happens after the orgy. Linda admits to Helen that despite the efforts by fourteen men that showed up, Linda was unable to achieve an orgasm. There still were no "bells ringing, dams busting, bombs going off." Helen refers Linda to Dr. Young, a psychiatrist played by Harry Reems. Similar to Helen, Dr. Young inquires if there was any traumatic experience in Linda's life that might prevent her from an orgasm. Soon after, a very playful tune begins. Linda begins to explain that she indeed enjoys sex. She states that she would not mind spending the rest of her life "getting laid." However, unlike the happy-sounding music that is audible in this scene, Linda is unsatisfied with the lack of orgasm in her sex life. Dr. Young speculates that her problem might be physical, rather than psychological. When asked if she has had an internal check-up, Linda admits that she has not. Dr. Young takes Linda to his examination room, which turns out to have a bed, rather than an examination table.

Dr. Young examines Linda's genitals. He says, "Miss Lovelace, you don't have one." Linda responds, "I'm a woman; I'm not supposed to have one." This corny joke is the undercurrent of this film combining comedy and pornography. Dr. Young tells Linda that she does not have a clitoris. He says, "No wonder you hear no bells, you have no tinkler." The atmosphere of the scene is optimistic, though, assisted with the happy tune that continues, even though Linda is almost in tears.

These musical features, as well as the one from Helen's cunnilingus scene, portray sex as a soothing tool. When Helen is first seen receiving oral sex, it is not for romance. As the accompanying music explains it is simply to "ease [her own] pain" with oral sex. Sex is merely a tool to break away from the tedious day-to-day activities. Similarly, having sex with multiple partners is just a means for Linda to find "right" one. Even when Linda learns her physical abnormality, the psychological pain is ignored by the music. The music simply plays a playful tune because now Linda would be able to experience orgasm. Soothing and playful music, in various scenes, portrays sex as a pure means for self-pleasure.

Two Iconic Songs of the Film

Deep Throat includes two particularly memorable musical compositions. The first is "Love Is Strange," an American R&B song by Mickey & Sylvia. The duo of Mickey Baker and Sylvia Robinson released "Love Is Strange" in 1956.

The song sold over a million copies and became a gold disc winner (Murrells 84). *Billboard* characterized the music as such: "Some cute repartee adds interest to this insinuating effort. More good guitar here" ("Reviews of New R&B Records" 48). The music was used later in other movies including *Dirty Dancing* (1987) and *Casino* (1995) (Russell).

Baker himself had an interesting journey until he had his recording hit in the mid–1950s. Born in Louisville, Kentucky, in 1925, he spent much of his youth in institutions. One day, he ran away to go to New York where he worked as a pool-hall hustler until at age nineteen he decided to become a jazz musician. After "Love Is Strange," he opened a nightclub and a publishing house (Russel; Weber, "Mickey"). As for Robinson, she had several hits with Baker but also as a solo singer, including "Pillow Talk." She went on to establish a label, All Platinum, only to soon lose money in the late 1970s. However, she is now most known as the "mother of hip hop" for her work in recording what was at the time a little known musical genre referred to as "rapping" ("Sylvia Robinson").

When the song starts, two men who had received an invitation from Helen to the sex trial party arrive at the house. Helen gives numbers eleven and twelve to those men. At least twelve men have come to have intercourse with Linda. Linda is already with a man, or Man Number 10. "Love Is Strange" begins as the camera shows Linda's face pressed against a couch on the side. Her mouth opens several times. She even looks into the camera for a brief second and smiles. The view changes to show Linda's back and her face. Soon, the camera moves to show the man's perspective that is behind Linda who lies on all fours on a couch. Linda is visibly more and more aroused. Her eyes are now closed. Soon after, the camera shows a penetration from behind.

As "Love Is Strange" continues and Linda carries on having sex, the music's famous segment appears. It is the part that is probably most known today thanks to various adaptations in popular culture, including in Nationwide Insurance's commercial. Once the vocals begin, the audience realizes that Linda was not having vaginal sex, but actually anal sex. While she manually stimulates her clitoral area, it is evident that Linda is, once again, having tingly feelings. The man ejaculates, but Linda only smiles and does not reach a climax. As the song goes, "Love," or probably simply sex, "is strange." In a film in which sex is supposed to be as simple as a source of pleasure, *Deep Throat* defies the conventional story line of pornography.

The second iconic song in the film is "Deep Throat." Unlike previously mentioned uses of Beethoven, James Bond's music and others, "Deep Throat" is indeed the driver of the storyline. The music advances the story not just as an accessory to visual cues, but rather as audible cues. In other words, the music instructs actors and actresses what to do, rather than simply adding a layer to an independent story. In the use of "Deep Throat," the tie between the music and the story is extremely close.

Before "Deep Throat" appears in the film, the story is advanced by comedic conversation between Linda and her newly found doctor, Dr. Young. After the aforementioned mismatched light music fades away in the midst of the conversation between Linda and Dr. Young as they discuss Linda's problem, Dr. Young asks what part of sexual intercourse Lovelace enjoyed the most. Her answer is simple: "Giving head." She points at her own throat to say, "I get excited here." Linda continues to cry while Dr. Young says, "Let me have a look at that," as he laughs at this unexpected news. He finds Linda's clitoris deep in her throat and consoles her that having it in the throat is better than "not having one at all." Dr. Young says they need to find a solution now that they have located the problem. After thinking for a moment, he asks, "Have you ever taken a penis all the way down to the bottom of your throat?" Linda says she has, only to choke. Dr. Young gives some advice and Linda quickly says "What have I got to lose?" As Kenneth Turan and Stephen F. Zito sarcastically explain, Dr. Young "[volunteers] his body to the cause of science" and "has Linda perform fellatio ... in order to test his strange hypothesis" (141).

As soon as Dr. Young takes his pants down and Linda starts giving him fellatio, "Deep Throat" fills the scene. It is an extremely cheesy song. The lyrics primarily repeat the advice given by Dr. Young. The male singer's voice tells Linda to relax her muscle, do all she can, and try to hit her newly found clitoris. As much as Dr. Young is shown amazed by Linda's skills, she is also portrayed to be enjoying the experience. Turan and Zito characterize Dr. Young as "a generously endowed man" (141). Linda follows the song and the song takes her to the sensation that she has not experienced before. The song is no longer in the background. It is at the forefront of the story narrative. It guides Linda to achieve her first orgasm and describes her new technique, deep throat. As the music continues, she does not look like she would stop at any time soon.

As soon as "Deep Throat" moves to the background, Dr. Young's shocked face appears on the screen briefly, only to be followed by the sound of a large ringing bell. The ring continues. "Deep Throat" comes back. Linda continues with her action. Then there is no more music. It is a cacophony with ringing bells and the bursting noise of fireworks. Slowly, the music comes back in the background, but it no longer helps the story move forward unlike it did only a minute ago. It is now the sound effect combination of bells and fireworks that are at the front stage. Eventually, the screen goes back and forth between Linda's deep throat and a rocket. The rocket takes off slowly as Linda's oral sex intensifies. The noise of the rocket culminates to the chaos of explosions, bells, and fireworks. Linda's mouth is now covered with Dr. Young's semen, but she does not seem to care. She continues to give oral sex to Dr. Young.

"Deep Throat" is now much more upbeat and fast. There are no more corny lyrics. It is more dance music than a porn groove. The music suggests that the worry is gone in Linda's mind and the solution to her problem has been found. Linda is seen smiling with continuing images of fireworks here and there. It is clear that it was not just tingly feelings. She says, "I'm a fulfilled woman." She asks Dr. Young to marry her, but he tells her his nurse will not allow it to happen. Instead, he decides to employ her as a physiotherapist to make house calls. Dr. Young explains that she could start working immediately because she was born with all the equipment she would need as his physiotherapist.

Later in the film, "Deep Throat" comes back again to conclude this 1972 movie. As noted earlier, Linda's friend, Wilbert, asks her to marry. But she rejects him because his penis is too short. Probably, "Love Is Strange" was properly used in this film. If Linda's definition of love corresponds to the size of a man's penis, it indeed is a strange concept. But Linda encourages Wilbert to call Dr. Young to ask if he could operate on him to solve the problem. Once he calls Dr. Young, Wilbert learns that he could have any size penis he wants. With this good news, he takes his penis out of his pants. Although he has yet to have an operation, Linda looks at it and says, "Oh, Wilbert." Unlike her reluctance and refusal to accept his proposal for marriage earlier, Linda immediately takes his penis into her mouth. This is when "Deep Throat" slowly comes back. The lyrics state that the song will describe how things should be.

The song is, once again, leading the story line. Linda has found her "tinkler." She knows that once Wilbert can reach as deep as nine inches into her throat, she will be satisfied. While Wilbert manually stimulates her vulva and the clitoral area, Linda is focused on oral sex. The bells start ringing, the rocket is ready to be launched, and fireworks explode.

Other Music Used in the Film

There is other music used in *Deep Throat* that creates an interesting cinematic atmosphere. One of the examples is a patriotic marching song. When Linda makes her first house visit, the background music is marching music with light drums. Wearing a nurse's outfit with a very short skirt, Linda is headed to a nice community of houses. Linda is almost a lone soldier on a mission. Although there is no visual message that suggest that the film is making light of America's military engagement abroad at the time like *M*A*S*H* did, the gap between what one would expect the military march to signify and Linda's quest does not follow the convention. However, as a new physiotherapist, she looks determined to cure the illness of her patient.

As soon as she enters the house, however, the music begins to be slightly mysterious, stimulating the viewer's curiosity as to what this new physiotherapist would do. Linda's patient is a middle-age man sitting by the dining room table. Once Linda shows up, he unbuckles his pants to take them off. Linda is equally quick to take her nurse's outfit off. He sits down on the table, and without exchanging any words, Linda starts to give him oral sex. It is now clear that Linda's role as a physiotherapist is nothing different from prostitution with oral sex.

A similar sense of mission is felt when the song comes back for the second time. Dr. Young is in his office and is speaking to a microphone, a common method he uses to keep track of his patients' statuses. This time, however, the patient is nobody but himself. As the marching music continues, he dramatically explains that he is "wounded in his line of duty, near death." Between the nurse and Linda, Dr. Young has been engaged in sex more than he can handle. But this is a new territory for him. As the music suggests, he is exploring a new venture. Once again, the slapstick character of the joke created by the gap between the marching music and Dr. Young's conquest is evident.

When the music comes back later in the film, however, it carries a very different significance. The third and last instance of the marching music to be heard is in Dr. Young's office. He and his original nurse are engaged in sex. The following minutes to come are a long period of sex-only shots. Oral and vaginal sex continues for several minutes. There is no conversation. It is just the background music—the continuation of the marching song—with acts of sex on the screen. Eventually, the audience can hear a bicycle bell ring, birds chirp, and whistle in the middle of the music. Unlike the first instance of the marching music, in this second instance, there is little explanation for its use. Especially with the added sound effects to represent orgasm, the version of the marching music almost sounds like that from a Disney film. Of course, the visual cues are completely different from Disney. It is far from porn grooves. It pictures sex as noncommittal fun daily activity.

There is also music of melancholy in the film. The sadness of the music reflects Dr. Young's condition. After having sex both with Linda and his nurse, Dr. Young has gotten sick. Linda is there to take care of him and brings medicine. But he does not look like the person who was enjoying intercourse with her earlier in the film. Dr. Young is clearly sick. Linda tries to give him a pill, but Dr. Young refuses. But the music shifts slightly as if to reflect Linda's caring attitude toward Dr. Young. The song is no longer just sad. There is a hint of care and thoughtfulness. He presses a bag of cold water against his groin. Linda tries to take a look, but he covers himself up. Linda tries, nonetheless. When she succeeds, she sees Dr. Young's penis has a white bandage on it. Indeed, it looks like an injured soldier from the field. She picks it up, plays with it, and removes the bandage.

Quotes and Bubbles as Soundtrack

Deep Throat's soundtrack includes not only music but also quotes from the film. For example, one of the most famous quotes of the film, "Mind if I smoke while you're eating?" is a part of the soundtrack. The statement is made during the first sex-related scene of the film. About six minutes into the film, Linda is seen carrying two white boxes into her house. Inside the house is Helen receiving cunnilingus. With the appearance of Linda, the anonymous male character looks awkward to be caught in the middle of an action. But Helen has him continue. She even asks Linda to pass her a cigarette. This is when Helen asks him, "Mind if I smoke while you're eating?" The music to follow this scene depicts Helen's pleasure. Linda is already out of the house. Helen continues to receive cunnilingus. As the lyrics go, Helen is "taking a break" from her monotonous life with sexual pleasure.

Similarly, a comical quote of Linda's patient appears in the soundtrack. This is from her second house visit which takes place at a motel. Back in his office, Dr. Young, while having sex with his nurse and recording his patient observation simultaneously, explains that the patient is a man who has not had sex for three years since his wife passed away. The sexual abstinence, according to Dr. Young, is causing some pain. Linda is sent to help the man to relieve the sexual stress. Unlike her first visit, she is wearing pants. She is assisted by very upbeat music. After the treatment is done, lying on the bed, the patient clearly looks satisfied. He even tells Linda she is an angel and inquires if he could get a similar "treatment" three times a week. Linda is willing, as long as he is able to afford it because it is "an expensive treatment." The soundtrack includes the man's response, "Look, I have Blue Cross."

The sound of blowing bubbles also plays a vital role in this film. The first time the blown bubbles are heard is at Helen and Linda's house. While Linda is undergoing her multiple-sex-partner party, Helen herself is also enjoying sex with men that she has originally invited for Linda. The main music is the continuation of "Love Is Strange" from the scene in Linda's bedroom. Once Linda and her partners experience intensified sexual pleasure, "Love Is Strange" adds a new layer of sound effect with blown bubbles. This sound does not seem to match the sound of a moan or a scream, but these blown bubble sounds signify a more heightened level of sexual pleasure. Helen's pleasure is visibly intensified with a man on her breast and another on her groin. When the camera shifts back to Linda on the other side of the wall, she is seen giving fellatio, which, later in the film, turns out to be Linda's favorite experience. Farther into the music, Linda is back to vaginal sex on her back. This long scene of sex continues until the music begins to fade away, and Linda is seen having penetrative sex on top. The blown bubble sound effect comes back and viewers are assured that Linda is enjoying her sexual encounter. However, the audience will also realize that the bubble sounds do not seem to be the code for an orgasm.

Linda similarly experiences the sound of bubbles in Dr. Young's office. During the unprofessional looking interview between him and Linda, Dr. Young sits on a table next to a television set and plays with bubbles. The sound effect of bubbles—not synched with the actual bubbles visible on the screen—come back, as if to hint upcoming sexual activities. Slightly flirtatious Linda even says, "You're all getting me all wet" to make him stop playing with bubbles. The sound of bubbles disappears when Linda and Dr. Young move to the examination room where they come to the realization that Linda lacks a normal clitoris. The sound effect that symbolizes sexual pleasure, of course, is absent in this scene of despair.

The bubble sound effect implies that Linda is willing to enjoy unconventional sex and that she is happy with the knowledge that she can finally achieve an orgasm. During the first house visit, Linda offers oral sex. But she and her patient soon engage in penetrative sex. The background music is somewhat mysterious but also upbeat and jazzy. Furthermore, the viewers are left to wonder why the male character tries to insert what looks like a small glass into Linda's vagina. As soon as he picks up a bottle of red wine and pours its contents into the glass that is now in Linda's vagina and out of view from the camera, the music changes to "I'd Like to Teach You All to Screw." This is a parody of Coca-Cola's famous advertisement music, "I'd Like to Teach the World to Sing." The man picks up a plastic tube to drink the wine. The bubble sound effect comes back. The man does not seem to enjoy the experience, though. So instead, he tries to use Coke. There is an interesting product placement—most likely unintended by Coca-Cola—here. This time, with Coke in the glass hidden in Linda's vagina, the bubble sound leads to the man's facial smile. He shares the tube with Linda so she can also drink possibly by-then lukewarm Coke. While the man and Linda share a Coke, the music accompaniment says that "it is the real thing." Linda may not be having an orgasm from oral sex at the moment, but she is nonetheless enjoying her sexual experience, knowing that as a physiotherapist she could have an orgasm if she wishes to.

Conclusion

Although there is no doubt that Jerry Gerard created the film primarily as pornography, the film's use of music is worthy of scholarly investigation. On one level, the film betrayed the conventional use of music in pornography. Not only did the film change the landscape of the pornographic film world, it redefined what music could do in adult films. While *Deep Throat* relies on and uses some stereotypical porn-groove, it also incorporates non-traditional pornographic music. Beethoven, first and foremost, is not a composer whose work one would expect to appear in an adult film. Similarly, James Bond, as much as his sexual prowess was evident in his films, is not a character whose theme music is expected in a film like this.

Musical representation of sex in *Deep Throat* also agrees with the way the counterculture period in general looked at sex. Although it is somewhat stereotypical to state that it was the period of casual sex and free sex, the film also suggests a more complex view on sex and sexuality. Micah L. Issitt writes that sex was "something to be celebrated rather than hidden, encouraged, rather than scorned" (19). He continues by stating that sexual behaviors at the time were often characterized as "indiscriminate, unhygienic, and irresponsible" or "revolutionary and profound" (24). *Deep Throat* shows sexuality more complex than Issitt's dualistic view. The film's music undervalues the seriousness of the sex-related concerns that Linda explains. The music never depicts her concerns as something serious. Rather, it creates an optimistic environment in which as soon as she can find a way to orgasm, she will be able to have a satisfied life. It also presents sex as a story. From outside, the story of the counterculture may make little sense. From the hippie culture to this pornographic film, many criticized. But many others celebrated the new cultural trend.

All of these examples show that music was indeed important in this film. It was actually so important that "Gerard Damiano edited the film to its music, so the actions would match and the beat would match ... like up and down strokes on the old shaft" ("Deep Throat," *Fused*). Gerard's interest in music led to elongated portrayals of sex in some instances. For example, Linda's sex with her Partner No. 10 is extremely extended. In a sense, music determined the visual composition of the film. This is a counterintuitive decision by the director. Pornography, first and foremost, is a visual medium. What audiences see and imagine thereafter creates sexual arousal. Damiano, however, allowed sound to control the visual, one of the most significant parts of pornography. The film's soundtrack, therefore, is not just an accessory to the iconic film.

Similarly, as stated earlier, Gerard was able to use some of his songs as instructions and guides. The lyrics of such songs instruct actors and actresses what to do, including relaxing muscles, or taking a penis deeper. From this perspective, music supplemented dialogues and conversations among actors and actresses. Characters in the film, in return, focused on sexual acts. Emotional, psychological, and romantic nuances embedded in conversations were eliminated. The film's focus on sexual acts parallels countercultural views on casual sex.

The general lack of discussion on music in *Deep Throat* is by no means because of music's insignificance in the film. The movie was controversial enough for its classification and social meanings to dominate what fans and critics have discussed in the 1970s and even to this date. Hidden behind Lovelace's testimonies, moral panics, a surprisingly large revenue for this genre of film, and other topics that newspapers and other mainstream media—including Randy Barbato and Fenton Bailey's documentary *Inside Deep Throat* (2005)—exists a meaningful use of film music that enabled one of the most controversial, but also socially and culturally reflective, movies to impact the American public of the early 1970s.

11. Challenging Normativity and Pushing Boundaries: *Midnight Cowboy* and Cultural Resistance

Introduction

Based on the 1965 novel by James Leo Harlihy, *Midnight Cowboy* (1969) depicts the life of Joe Buck (Jon Voight) in New York and his friendship with Enrico "Ratso" Rizzo (Dustin Hoffman). Directed by John Schlesinger and produced by Jerome Hellman, the film portrays the harsh realities of an urban life, the shattered hopes of a migrant from Texas, and a sex-obsessed underground lifestyle. It was a very successful film. Not only did it become the first X-rated film to win an Oscar for best picture, it made over $44 million with a budget of $3.5 million (Corkin 619). *Midnight Cowboy*, however, is not just about chaos or the lack of order. It showcases countercultural attempts to challenge normativity in two distinct ways. One is more symbolic through Joe's reversed cowboy narrative moving from west to east, rather than from east to west. The other is more culturally significant. He challenges heteronormativity and the dominant discourse on sexual politics at the time throughout the film.

In the depictions of social and cultural resistance, Harry Nilsson's cover of "Everybody's Talkin'," despite its catchy tune, captures the loneliness of Joe Buck as he moved away from home in Texas, to New York where rain seemed to pour every day, and then eventually to Florida with Ratso, seeking a place "where the sun keeps shining." Joe's resistance and the life of his friend, Ratso, are not always as upbeat as Nilsson's music. If this song, associated with but not written by Nilsson, helps create the dreamland of New York in the mind of Joe at the beginning of the story (and Miami as the dream world of Joe and

Ratso), their life in New York is characterized more by John Barry's melancholic theme song.

The film is commonly associated for its popularizing of Nilsson's cover. Barry's work on the film is often left behind in public memory, as he is most frequently characterized or referred to as the composer of the James Bond film series soundtracks, but Barry was a key figure in establishing the artistic quality of *Midnight Cowboy*. Born in York, England, in 1933, he served as the supervisor of music for the film and composed its theme music. He was also a prolific soundtrack composer. He won five Academy Awards, a Golden Globe Award, and a Grammy Award before his death in 2011. *Midnight Cowboy*, therefore, was a film in which two musical stars contributed to delicately picture a sense of hope, its betrayal, and solitude.

The film opens with a clear identification of Joe Buck as a 1960s cowboy. Joe is a young dishwasher in a local diner. He is, however, ambitious. His ambition, unfortunately, comes with naïveté. After quitting his job and dressing himself like a cowboy, he takes a one-way trip to New York, convinced he will become a successful hustler. Joe's eastward pursuit of an American dream is, of course, counterintuitive. On one level, America's master narrative has dictated that a pursuit of a dream happens westward. John Gast's painting "American Progress" is a prime example of this Manifest Destiny. In the painting, Columbia, or the personification of the U.S., travels west, along with farmers, animals, and locomotives. Joe clearly reverses this narrative, rather ominously.

On his bus ride to New York, his hope rises. From the very beginning, Schlesinger uses sound as a means to show Joe's transition. Fiore summarized,

> Director John Schlesinger depicts some of the gaudy empty values of American society by means of sounds from Joe's plastic companion, his radio. We first hear an advertisement for guns while Joe is still in Texas. After seeing a sign "Jesus Saves" on a shack, we hear a preacher–faith healer on a program called the "Sunshine Hour" state that he received a letter with ten dollars and the two malignant tumors that some woman expectorated during the previous week's prayer meeting. The preacher then advertises a five-dollar home worship kit which his listeners can send for. Next we hear from a New York radio station, a foolish talk show in which women are being interviewed about their tastes in men [272].

For returning viewers of the film, probably his proximity to nuns in the bus may be read as their cry to stop him. But as the music goes, he does not hear the voice of others. As the accompanying tune by Nilsson hints, the signs of imminent hardship may not be reaching Joe's consciousness clearly. He can only hear his own mind and voice. As Stanley Corkin wrote, the beginning scenes of the film are hopeful (620). He also continues that the film "evokes an earlier romance of the West" (621). This sense of nostalgia expressed with harmonica, as discussed later, reminisces the good old days. Joe seems to imagine that the East Coast, where the country started, might be a place with hope for him. The romance, of course, will be short lived. The promised land of this reverse Manifest Destiny leads to New York, an urban space where the sun does not keep shining.

As Corkin argues, *Midnight Cowboy* was one of the first films to depict New York as a locus of urban decay and decline (617). In the past, films produced in the 1930s, particularly gangster films, often depicted the city as a space filled with "violent and loutish behavior" (619). Even as an aspiring hustler, it is not a most inviting environment. This is the second reason why Joe's westward adventure is counterintuitive. New York has a history of being associated with vice. One of the songs featured in the soundtrack of the film, Elephant's Memory's "Jungle Gym at the Zoo," agrees with these critics. The lyrics state that the city is a jungle gym with a lot of fun. But it also hints at loneliness with its fleeting phrase. It is a chaotic place, as well. David Quigley noted that collective violence and working class radicalism were often prevalent in the city. Focusing on the period between 1890 and 1940, George Chauncey also recorded urban lives in New York. As these historians agree, New York is a city coated with hope and elegance; however, underneath lies the harsh reality. Indeed, upon arrival in the city, Joe faces this version of the city, and not its romanticized counterpart, to his dismay.

Nonetheless, Joe remains hopeful, probably because he knows he cannot go back west to give up on his dream, but also because of his naïveté. As Schlesinger stated, this film was about the dualism between fantasy and reality (Riley 104). The reality of New York is harsh. It is also a film about loneliness (Riley 104). Nonetheless, once again, in this process, Nilsson's voice seems to raise Joe's slight optimism. Written by Fred Neil, "Everybody's Talkin'" serves as a cohesive theme for the entire film. Thanks to this successful musical storytelling of this lonely character, the song won a Grammy Award for Best Male Pop Vocal Performance.

"Everybody's Talkin'" as the Theme

Born in Cleveland, Ohio, in 1936, Fred Neil became popular in the mid-1960s with his release of *Tear Down the Walls* with Vince Martin. "Modern Don Juan," "The Other Side of This Life," and his album *Bleecker and Mac-Dougal* are some of his major successful works in his lifetime. No other song, however, made him more popular than "Everybody's Talkin'." Neil later renamed his album *Fred Neil*, which was released in 1966 and included the song, to *Everybody's Talkin'* at its re-release in 1969. After the film's hit song, Neil's successful life continued for a short term. His appearance in the music scene dwindled in the 1970s, though years later he wrote music for The Dolphin Project in 2000. He got increasingly engaged in a project to stop dolphin exploitations in his later life ("Obituary: Fred Neil").

What is intriguing about "Everybody's Talkin'" is the way in which this cover song greatly contributed to the popularity of Harry Nilsson. As Terry Gilliam, film producer, surmised, "['Everybody's Talkin'" is] his most famous song and he didn't write it" (Heyman 50). Originally, other songs, including Nilsson's own, were considered for the theme. Nilsson had his "I Guess the Lord Must Be in New York City" considered for the film (Bronson 307). But John Schlesinger decided to adopt Nilsson's cover of Neil's work, instead. For Neil, "Everybody's Talkin'" was the last major hit of his career; he passed away at age 64 in 2001 ("Fred Neil"). As for Nilsson, he later won Grammy Awards twice and was nominated for his album *Nilsson Schmilsson* later. In 2007 the song was rated as the fifty-first most successful cover song by the *New York Post*, which characterizes his contribution as such: "Nilsson's remake of this blues- and folk-singer's song was only a minor hit until it was featured in *Midnight Cowboy*" (Huhn and Shen). The film allowed for a much wider audience to be exposed to his singing.

This is not to say that the alternative option of "I Guess the Lord Must Be in New York City" would not have depicted the sentiment of the film well. As William J. Schafer wrote, it would have captured Joe's move to the East Coast. Schafer stated that the song reflected the "enduring myth of the naïve country boy emigrating to the heavenly city of our collective dream to discover his future" (755). His prayers were not answered in Texas, as Nilsson sang, "my prayers goin' unanswered." Needless to say, Joe did not find his Lord in the city of New York either, at least in a sense of achieving his dream to become a hustler. But the story to unfold as he finds his companion whom he would accompany to Miami might be a divine sign for Joe that there was more in life than doing well as a hustler.

Schlesinger was convinced that "Everybody's Talkin'" was the song for the film. Unlike *Easy Rider*, another key counterculture film of 1969 that featured songs by various artists, *Midnight Cowboy* heavily relies on music by one artist, Fred Neil. Eddi Fiegel explains the obstacles he faced and was willing to overcome to use the song as the film's main music. The first difficulty was a matter of the copyrights because United Artists, the distribution company, wanted to hold on to the copyrights of all the songs used in the film. It was also possible to have Nilsson write a new song. But Schlesinger was determined. Nilsson agreed to record the song again purely for the film (226).

Talking About Taboos

Along with the buoyant music, the film's treatment of taboo matters—underground urban lives, homosexuality, and sex for pleasure and money—accompanied by tunes by The Groop, Leslie Miller, Elephant's Memory, etc., also contributed to its success. On the one hand, of course portrayals of these topics led the film to receive its X rating and, in some ways, to establish its unique position in film history of having won an Academy Award for Best Picture with the rating (Maslin). It was only after these awards that the rating was lowered to an R. On the other hand, the film's portrayal of Joe Buck and Ratso's lives made it an epitomic countercultural film. Andy Warhol and Pat Hackett wrote in *POPism*, "There were two types of people doing counter-culture-type things—the ones who wanted to be commercial and successful and move right up into the mainstream of society with their stuff, and the ones who wanted to stay where they were, outside society" (250). As Osterweil assessed, Schlesinger took the first option and dealt with "the taboo subject matter of the Underground and made it fit for mainstream consumption" by producing the film (41). This treatment of a taboo subject matter and selling it for mainstream consumption was the key to the film's success and the music helped the audience swallow the pill.

By "rendering the seedy life of an urban hustler fit for mainstream consumption," *Midnight Cowboy*, as stated previously, qualified to win the Oscar for best picture in 1969, despite its X rating (Osterweil 41). A significant phrase here is "mainstream consumption." Although the 1960s is often classified as a decade of counterculture and a decade that reversed many of the traditional social values in the U.S., the mainstream consumers remained conservative, especially in relation to sexuality. *Playboy* might have existed for over ten years. Alfred Kinsey might have revealed the truth—or at least to the extent his taxonomy-based approach could allow him to—of American sexual lives over a decade ago. The filmmaker was willing to include materials which would grant the film the X rating. But the rating board's decision to actually rate the film as such hints that even though consumers were intrigued by the theme of the film as attested to by its successful box office figures, it was not something that American consumers would feel comfortable admitting to consume in their daily lives.

Schlesinger was fully aware of this social and cultural resistance to taboo topics. Sex was not a topic to discuss in a film that aimed to be consumed by the mass public. What is intriguing, however, is the gap between what the rating seems to suggest and what the film actually portrayed. Despite the X rating, the film actually has no "significant violence, profanity or frontal nudity." What the movie offers is "partial nudity, simulated sex and painful metaphors" (Maslin). Maslin's assessment is correct. As she wrote in her film review, Schlesinger's "painful" or probably desperate metaphors included "a shot of creamed corn" to signal an orgasm. This is just one of many examples of "[saying] and [doing] radical things in a conservative format" so that the movie could be "counterculture and have mass commercial success" (Osterweil 41).

Even though the film was radical in the sense that it aimed to bring X-rated content to the mainstream, its music use was far from radical. Although "Everybody's Talkin'" was not a popular track until it was adopted in the film, it was far from risqué music. Its lyrics talk about loneliness and hope. It addresses emotional and psychological inflection. It is not about sexuality or deviance. Similarly, John Barry's score is safe. It is nostalgic. It signifies the "good old days," especially with its harmonica. It is conservative and traditional in this sense.

The movie's conservative images paralleled with the context of homophobia in which the film was consumed. As for New York specifically, it was not a city of liberalism as is the case with today, but it was the city that witnessed the Stonewall riots. Moreover, as Floyd noted, "The New York premiere of *Midnight Cowboy* took place less than a month before the Stonewall riots sparked the gay liberation movement in the United States" (101). As David Carter characterized, the riots were "the motivating force in the transformation of the gay political movement" (1). The social sentiment toward homosexuals was rough, nonetheless. Corkin discusses Richard Nixon's presidential campaign of 1972, only a few years after the film's release. He wrote, "The president and many of his close advisors well understood that combining anti-urbanism and fear—including fear of 'unconventional sexuality'—was good politics" (619).

Because of the conservative view on sexuality, Joe's attempt to be successful as a hustler does not pan out well. Generally he seems to have difficulty finding wealthy women who might be interested. But even when he finds one and asks if she could tell him how to get to the Statue of Liberty, his intention is easily seen through. The prototypical American idealism as symbolized by the statue cannot easily be deceived. If someone ever tries to subvert America's way of life, which, for sure, at the time does not include or welcome homosexuality, the American response to that person would be, "You ought to be ashamed of yourself" as Corkin noted (623). Joe might have assumed while in Texas that men in New York lacked masculinity and women were hungry for sex, but the reality was not as easy.

Sex is also geographically and environmentally contained. Once Joe Buck arrives in New York, it is a city of destitution. The audience does not see families or children on the screen. As Corkin wrote, "There is little definition of a middle class and almost no view of materially productive employment, no central characters are married, nor are there any children" (621). Champlin put it similarly by writing in his review of the film that it is "a two-character story in which nobody else matters much." Harry Nilsson's theme song portrays this sense of loneliness. New York City in this film is a place of class struggle, labor, and cynicism. The life of a hustler, even an aspiring one, is grim. Maslin noted that in New York, Joe never experiences sex "as anything other than an act of anger or humiliation." The idea of sex for entertainment permeates in the film. But it is the case under one condition. Such sex must remain "grimy" and only in the underworld (Howe). *Midnight Cowboy* is not a film about sexuality but about containment of sexuality.

New York in the film is also a lonely place. Champlin's aforementioned depiction of the film as one in which nobody else mattered is just one depiction of loneliness that Joe and Ratso felt without each other. On his way from Texas to New York, as mentioned earlier, Joe's radio was his only companion. Right after he arrives at his hotel, Paul Newman's poster as a cowboy seems to be the only image of a human body in his environment. This sense of isolation is enhanced further with the theme song. The world is happening around Joe, but for some reason, nothing registers in his mind (Fiore 272). As Nilsson sang, Joe or Ratso cannot hear what others are saying or cannot see their faces. This is the loneliness of "a pićaro," or "a type of rogue, who travels and observes, with his partial and necessarily prejudiced view, various social conditions, usually the seamy side of life" (270). Because of his rogueness, he has to "[exist] outside of the mainstream of society" (271). His presence outside of the mainstream is lonely. Barry captures this sentiment well with his score. Segal wrote, "Few pieces of music pierce more fiercely than this brief paragon of melancholy." The music is an expression of "resignation and longing" (31).

Just as sexuality is more confined than liberated, the film makes homosexuality look safe for mass consumption. Joe's homosexual rape in his past haunts him. He also agrees to engage in oral sex in a movie theater in New York. He struggles with his homosexual encounters while there is no sign of heterosexual encounters to happen. None of these homosexual encounters are not enjoyable for Joe. This is just one of many examples of the clash between "old conservatism" and "new permissiveness" that Floyd discusses (100). Even though signs of permissiveness materialized as the film's success at the Oscars showcases, this victory came at the expense of homosexuality, whose image was adjusted for general viewing of the film.

Sexuality becomes safe when it becomes consumable. It is the case with even "deviant" sexuality, like homosexuality in the minds of traditional American idealism. As will be discussed later, Joe's cowboy image is a representation of his compromised sexuality. On one level, his cowboy image reflects his "commodified status" (Floyd 106). The cowboy is no longer a national hero or a symbol of masculine exploration. To make matters worse, it is a complete reverse. Floyd surmises:

> [The] bus ride from semi-rural Texas—where, the film suggests, some possibility of identifying heterosexual masculinity with the cowboy image remains—to Manhattan—where no such possibility remains—leaves this cold war, mass-cultural commodity completely behind and replaces it with a new, urbanized version, appropriated and homosexualized by an increasingly visible gay male culture [111].

This is why "the frontier hero becomes a commodified boytoy" and "Joe is a casualty of a sociocultural and historical disjunction" (Floyd 115).

It is, however, simultaneously true that Joe appears unaware of the disappearing opportunity as a heterosexual hustler. He is more successful as a homosexual worker in the sex industry. Furthermore, when Joe begins to live with Ratso, their relationship starts to have an uncanny homosexual overtone. Schlesinger, however, may disagree how this relationship needs to be interpreted. In an interview, he stated that it "really isn't *per se*. It's about the need of one human being for another" (Riley 108). It can be argued that there is an obvious homosexual undercurrent in the depiction of the two, and many, including Harry Benshoff and Sean Griffin, have done so. If so, does this make Joe an unaware homosexual who is yet to come out? The moviegoers of the 1960s, however, can rest assured. The mid-century counterculture experienced moral panic against homophilia, including the one felt against the Mattachine Society, one of the first homosexual organizations in the U.S. that aimed to protect the rights of homosexuals (Floyd 112). The sense of panic was further strengthened because such "undesired" individuals were often hidden. This was partially why organizations such as the House Committee on Un-American Activities (HUAC) were successful in infusing fear among Americans that their good American values and lifestyles were under threat from an invisible enemy. But as for Joe's homosexuality, it is not hidden. It is revealed and visible. It is only in the eyes of Joe that being dressed like a cowboy is a signifier of one's homosexuality. Standing in front of a movie theater like a cowboy is not the way to be a hustler and to attend a wealthy but sexually deprived female customer. It is a signal that Joe is looking for a male customer, ironically unknown to himself. As Floyd characterized, "Joe quickly [discovered], to his dismay, the cowboy image's largely exclusive appeal to gay men" (102). He cannot stay unaware of his homosexual tendency for long. As Ratso said, "No rich lady with any class at all buys that cowboy crap anymore" (Floyd 102). Not only did he have to come to this realization, but he also had to admit to the fact that the city was a homosexualizing environment.

This emasculating effect of the city is a kind of reverse Manifest Destiny. If American conservative and traditional heteronormativity dictated that masculinity came from sexual prowess and the achievement of American dream, Joe's life in New York is a total opposite. He not only services his homosexual customers, but he cannot perform with his rare female customer. His self-esteem is low to the ground. He can only perform in bed when the aforementioned female customer calls him gay.

Osterweil also argues that the film "eliminated whatever threat [homosexuality] posed to normative sexuality" (40). The threat imposed by homosexuality that some Americans felt as a moral panic was appeased, as stated earlier, by the publicness of homosexual dress and clothing. By putting homosexuality in the public sphere, nothing was kept in the closet. The film nonetheless followed a heteronormative narrative. Osterweil continues:

> Like the melodramatic films that were *Midnight Cowboy*'s true precursors, the illicit object choice must die in order to preserve the dominance of heterosexuality.... [In] *Midnight Cowboy* it is the more effeminate, more diminutive, more expressive and ultimately less complacent protagonist whose pound of flesh is demanded. When Ratso Rizzo dies a bleak, unheralded death of an unspecified, incurable, and invisible disease while riding on a bus in search of a new world and better future with Joe Buck, Schlesinger succeeds in eliminating the threat of queer contamination [40].

In this anti-homosexual scheme, Ratso is eliminated. It is, however, not just a small-figured bedridden con-man that is removed from that world. It is also the threat of homosexuality that dies simultaneously. The relationship between Ratso and Joe has developed in a unique way that suggests that the two are more than just good male friends who found each other in their toughest time. There is clearly a hint of homosexuality. Even a hint, or a slight possibility, is a sufficient threat to society. But it no longer is once Ratso dies on the bus.

Interestingly enough, the film lacks music during the final moments of Ratso's life. His monologue is quiet. When Joe talks to his friend, not realizing Ratso is already dead, there is no music. It was only after the bus driver closes Ratso's eyes that the film's score comes back to accompany Joe's sadness.

Ratso and Joe's trip to Miami is where homosexuality is treated. When Joe tried to make and save money for their trip to Florida, he agreed to meet with an older homosexual customer. But this encounter resulted in violence. Denby depicts the scene well. In his review of the film, he wrote: "With his mind now concentrated on raising enough money to get to Florida and save Ratso's health, Joe allows himself to be picked up by an elderly faggot, whom he beats, robs, and nearly kills—at the poor man's invitation" (21). Joe's homosexual "symptom" is left wild in this scene. As Richard Barrios analyzes, this old homosexual played by Barnard Hughes even deserved such a treatment (348). It is the destiny of an aging homosexual.

As for Joe, his sense of guilt and regret, if anything, is what makes his homosexuality contained. It exists in his closeted self and in a hotel room filled with violence and guilt. Albeit confined, homosexuality is present posing a threat to socially accepted normativities of the time. The bus trip to Florida, however, makes this threat disappear. While at one of the stops that their bus makes, Joe buys himself new clothes and throws away his cowboy costume. This is when Nilsson's theme song comes back on the screen. Joe is no longer in New York where homosexuality and sex as work were confined in its underground. Once Joe is back on the bus, he helps Ratso change his clothes. At one point, Ratso asks, "What are you doing?" to which Joe responds, "I'm zipping your fly. What the hell do you think I'm doing?" He no longer has to worry about flashbacks of homosexual rape. In what Gary Arnold called a "traditional tearjerker," or "melodrama" according to Osterweil (40), the threat is gone. Homosexuality in the 1960s can appear on a Hollywood movie screen as long as the story can exercise control over the taboo topic. A way for the film to do so was through its nostalgic and upbeat music choice that made unsafe sexuality contained and eventually eliminated.

The film's mass-proofing homosexuality for consumption points to conflicting social sentiments of the counterculture. On the one hand, Al Auster and Leonard Quart explain that "as a result of relaxing societal sexual standards and court rulings overturning rigid obscenity laws, the sexual taboos long governing Hollywood began to fall by the wayside. Gone was the twin bed and in to replace it came full-frontal nudity" (5). As discussed elsewhere in this book, the popularity of *Deep Throat* is an example of this changing attitude to sexuality. On the other hand, this "widening of the range or permissible film topics" did not guarantee all forms of sexuality were welcomed. Even though counterculture was a strong social force of the 1960s and early 1970s, there still was a strong undercurrent of American conservatism. Even contemporary American politics reveal, over half a century after the beginning of the counterculture era, that strong resistance to accepting homosexuality persists in various parts of the nation. The relationship between Ratso and Joe hinted at this long-lasting prejudice against homosexuality even in the counterculture period.

This melodramatic ending does not necessarily portray Joe as someone who has gotten wise from the experience in New York. Throughout the film, he is innocent and naïve. Denby summarizes Joe's characteristic well. He writes:

> Herlihy's story is a paradox of innocence—of innocence surviving and health flourishing in the vilest of circumstances and through the vilest of acts. The beautiful

and dumb Joe Buck leaves Houston to make his fortune in New York, where, he believes, hordes of wealthy women have been sexually stranded by the town's population of "tootie-fruities" and will gratefully empty their pocketbooks for his services [20].

He stays the same in New York. This is not simply because Ratso so easily tricks him. But it is because he continues to be "strangely possessed with an earnest desire to make contact and give pleasure," despite the fact that "he suffers from being used, as a prostitute is used, for a variety of unusual purposes [when] his clients are far more corrupt than he, and the city grinds him down" (Denby 20–21).

Conclusion

Midnight Cowboy is a film about a boundary. Through various ideas such as loneliness, homosexuality, reality and fantasy, commercialism, commodification, and others, the film shows the counterculture's intrusion to the mainstream. The chaos is well represented by Nilsson's theme song. Countercultural values push the boundaries and attempt to offer an alternative lifestyle. It starts with the reversed Manifest Destiny, which even the alternative theme song for the film would have accurately pictured as the Lord waiting for Joe in New York. Nilsson's music reflects his loneliness, though, because Manifest Destiny was met with despair, not with success. The city is a jungle gym and is filled with melancholy. The appropriation of a cowboy identity faces not a heroic welcome in New York, but a blatant realization about its gay image. Joe's deviation from the Victorian sexuality is a lead to his underground lifestyle. Attempts to commercialize and commodify sex only take Joe to rejections by upper-class women, acceptance by men, or inability to perform in front of the previously mentioned rare female customer who cures his impotence by calling him "gay."

The film is a testament to the presence of the counterculture. It is a powerful social movement. After all, it was strong enough to push an X-rated film to win an Academy Award for best picture. The film ends with Barry's melancholic theme song while Joe stares out of the bus window holding Ratso's dead body. Ratso is dead. Joe's homosexuality is perceived to be cured as symbolized with his new clothes. Joe is probably ready to get a new lease on life as he gets to Florida. But the boundary line that the story has tried to push against social normativity is once again pushed back. This is particularly why the film's music use is worth attention. As Fiegel wrote, "*Midnight Cowboy* was a link between [Schlesinger's] Sixties' score and what would follow. It gave a nod back in the style direction, but it also looked forward to the more emotive, sweeping scores of the Seventies, Eighties, and Nineties" (231). Barry's tune reminisces about the good old days. Schlesinger suggests that as much as the counterculture pushes the terrain, the traditional mainstream pushes it back. If the film's melodramatic ending with a voyage to where the sun shines is the only hope at the end of the film, it seems to signal traditionalism and conservatism that maintained its strengths through the 1960s.

12. Ambiguous Meaning of Music: Combining Technology and Music in the Dystopian World of *A Clockwork Orange*

Introduction

Based on Anthony Burgess' novel *A Clockwork Orange* (1962), the film by the same title (1971), directed and produced by Stanley Kubrick, features a wide array of music. The list of tunes includes classical works composed by Ludwig van Beethoven and others, futuristic music by Rachel Elkind, synthesizer-produced versions of existing music as produced by Wendy Carlos, and the iconic music from Gene Kelly's musical *Singin' in the Rain*. The film, often characterized with its view on the dystopian future and state control, is also a film rich with musical signatures to invite its audience to the innermost psyche of the film's main character, Alex. Music is a means to not only set up a scene or portray a general tone of a scene, but also to allow viewers to share the experiences of Alex and contemplate the implications of technology and government control in the coming decades. Most significantly, the film challenges its audience to question if the meaning of music is permanently set upon its moment of composition based on the composer's intent and message and audience's interpretation, or if it continues to shift as it survives the test of time. The question is particularly significant especially when it concerns what has become known as classical music. This iconic film of the counterculture period challenged the notion of established interpretations of music and what it is assumed to mean in society. Kubrick suggests that the meaning of music is fluid. In *A Clockwork Orange*, he demonstrates how changing social contexts challenge and reconstruct the meaning of music.

Along with *2001: A Space Odyssey* (1968), *The Shining* (1980), *Full Metal*

Jacket (1987), and *Eyes Wide Shut* (1999), *A Clockwork Orange* is one of the most prominent films of Kubrick's. Featuring Malcolm McDowell, Patrick Magee, Adrienne Corri, and Miriam Karlin, this British film had an estimated budget of $2.2 million and had gross sales of over $25 million in the U.S. alone. For Warner Brothers, the film generated the second highest gross ticket sales at the time, surpassed only by *My Fair Lady*. It was nominated in four categories of the Academy Awards in 1972, and won the Best Foreign Film award at the Venice Film Festival. As recently as in 2012, the film won the Best DVD Collection award given by the Academy of Science Fiction, Fantasy, and Horror Films ("A Clockwork Orange," IMDb).

Despite the success of the film, it was also one of the most contested and controversial films of the era because of its critical view on governmental control and its assumed impact on violence in society. In the U.S., the film initially received the X rating. It was changed to the R rating in 1973, after Kubrick replaced two sexually explicit footages ("Three Films"; "A Clockwork Orange: X and R"; "Clockwork Orange: The X-Rating"). In Britain, the film was accused of inspiring copycat rapes and murders. Primarily for this moral panic, the film was not available much in England, the rest of Europe, or the U.S. The social context at the time explains this sense of panic. It was an unsettling period for Britain. Alexander Walker explains:

> Twelve days after the premiere [of the film], on 24 January, an IRA bomb explode[d] at Aldershot military barracks, killing five civilians, one a woman. Ultra violence [could] now reach into every community in Britain. The film [got] linked even more closely to the overcast political mood of the country. Chase the devils off the screen, goes the argument, and peace will be restored to our doorsteps.

In Britain, at the time, there was a fear of widespread indiscriminate rape and murder. An increasing number of crimes began to be associated with the film as an instigator or an inspiration. A fourteen-year-old male, for example, blamed the film for his murdering of his classmate. A sixteen-year-old boy who had beaten a sixty-year-old man to death argued that he had seen a similar act in the film. A Dutch girl was also raped by a group of men singing "Singin' in the Rain," as the main character of the film did. Even though the defendants were rarely proven to have seen the film or that the film instigated the offences, the public outcry to ban and censor the film expanded rapidly (Gehrke 272; Walker; Beard; "Clockwork in TV Debut" Robey; "Stanley Kubrick's").

Consequently, soon after the completion of the film, it was withdrawn from British distribution. In 2000, Walker explained:

> A critical and box-office hit when it opened in London 28 years ago, this savage black comedy about the right of the state to control individual lives provoked unprecedented national outrage, from the Home Secretary of the day down,

through MPs, judges, city councilors and moralists of all hidden agendas and blatant prejudices. And then, amid the tempest, the film disappeared from the screens with tornado suddenness. Kubrick withdrew it. Since then, *A Clockwork Orange* [*sic*] has remained ... unseen—not even an intended National Film Theatre retrospective screening in 1979 was permitted.

Robey also wrote:

> Fuelled by a rare combination of critical acclaim and ballooning controversy, it had a phenomenal run at the box office for two straight years, before Kubrick himself pulled the film from UK circulation, alarmed and finally defeated by accusations of "copycat" rapes and killings, and no longer able to stomach the thought that his film had become a tool for evil—a template.

The situation changed only after the death of Kubrick. It was released in 2000 on DVD and premiered on Sky TV's *Sky Box Office* in the summer of 2001 ("Clockwork Orange Set"; Beard).

Throughout this highly controversial film, there exists a wide array of musical backgrounds. But the music of the film has been less examined than its other features. For example, Planka asked several significant questions such as, "To what extent is it possible and permissible to manipulate a person's nature without damaging his or her individuality and personality?" "What power is the state permitted to exert over the individual, and how much is it allowed to invade the individual's private sphere in order to protect society?" and "When is a society worth protecting?" (53). On this shortage of musical analysis of the film, Kate McQuiston correctly points out that

> critical writing on *A Clockwork Orange* has tended to focus on ways in which the dialogue and visual elements contribute to perceivers' repulsion. Of course the music, containing Wendy Carlos's synthesized versions of classical pieces as well as orchestral rendered ones, is mentioned, but rarely does the music factor into analysis of the film. Kubrick's deployment of the soundtrack is one of the film's primary mechanisms in dragging the perceiver into the gears of *A Clockwork Orange*. The soundtrack provides much of the power to engage, by shrinking the apparent space between the perceiver and characters, so that the world of the story may invade a perceiver's most vulnerable psychological reaches [106].

As the main character of the film, Alex casually refers to Beethoven as "Ludwig van." His Fifth and Ninth symphonies are consistent pieces that move the story of the film. On some occasions, they are the fuel to Alex's gang activities. In some others, it is the reason for his suffering. Beethoven's Fifth Symphony is once a precursor to the rape of Mr. F. Alexander's wife, played by Adrienne Corri, and another time a precursor to his reencounter with Alex. Rachel Elkind and Wendy Carlos create what Blair Jackson called "a strange, haunting, futuristic quality" for the film's soundtrack (144). "Singin' in the Rain" is the bridge between Alex as a gang member and Alex as a victim of state control but nonetheless a perpetrator in the eyes of many victims and his family members.

Adapting Existing Classical Music

Although *A Clockwork Orange* captured the interest of the public for its portrayals of violence, it also was a notable film for its use of existing music. Claudia Gorbman suggested that Kubrick's "rhythms of narrative, editing, camerawork, and music" began to define Kubrick's cinematographic world (4). Hickman explains that it was thanks to Kubrick that many films of the 1970s started adopting various types of music that substantially predate the films themselves. He wrote, "Following the lead of Kubrick's *2001: A Space Odyssey* and *A Clockwork Orange*, a number of films with adapted scores appeared during the 1970s. Music for these films was borrowed from a wide range of sources. In addition to taking from the nineteenth century classics, filmmakers explored music from the recent past, including avant-garde compositions and classic rock" (319). In *A Clockwork Orange*, Kubrick adapted classic works by Henry Purcell, Gioacchino Rossini, Nikolai Rimsky-Korsakov, and Edward Elgar, to name a few. Kubrick's decision to do so was in line with the trend in the 1960s which "saw a move towards the greater use of pre-existing classical music" (Lapedis 367). Cooke characterizes this use of classical music as "unsettling applications" (444). In addition, the film included more recent musical pieces with a psychedelic tone such as those by a British band, Sunforest. As Gorbman explained, "pre-existing music [played] a range of prominent and distinctive roles" (4).

The film opens with "Music for the Funeral of Queen Mary" by an English composer, Henry Purcell. The film's main character, Alex, is sitting with his friends, Pete, Georgie, and Dim. They stare at the camera, and each has a sip of "milk plus" in the Korova Milk Bar. Purcell's music is rearranged by a synthesizer and has not only the solemnness of the original version but also an amplified sense of eeriness. The creepy atmosphere is furthered by Alex's unfathomable facial expression and the disturbing decor of the bar. The music prepares the audience well for what is to come on the screen, over two hours of dystopian views on the future and disbelief in the role technology would play in society. McQuiston discusses that "the range of Alex's power includes not just ingratiating voice-over narration, but initial eye contact with the spectators, and the ability to vocally and musically inhabit the diegetic and nondiegetic regions so as to collapse the spectator's sense of distance and safety from him" (106–107). As the theme music of the song, Purcell's electric version reflects and shapes the mood of the film.

Purcell's music, the main theme music of the film, comes back throughout the story. For example, as will be discussed shortly, Sunforest's upbeat music is played when Alex is directed to lick the bottom of a boot as a way to prove that he has been cured after undergoing the Ludivico treatment. However, his second test, facing a topless female model without succumbing to his sexual urge, is accompanied by Wendy Nelson's version of the funeral march. In one scene, a camera zooms into the breasts of the model with Alex's hands almost grabbing them. His hands reach just a few inches away from them, when Alex feels nauseated and falls on all fours. Although featuring the same music, this scene is significantly different from the opening scene. As the priest points out soon after, Alex has no choice in this latter scene. The solemn but also eerie music captures the unsettling nature of what has come to Alex's body and mind.

If Purcell's music signified Alex's victimizing behaviors in the first half of the film, it reflects his victimized behaviors in the second half. For example, after being beaten up by a group of homeless men, two police officers come to Alex's rescue. To his dismay, though, the officers are Dim and Billy Boy. Looking up to their faces, Alex reacts, "It's impossible. I don't believe it." The funeral march is heard again. This time, it could very well be Alex's funeral or precursor to it. His face is pushed in a basin filled with rain water until he is almost drowned. The music only ends when Alex, without any sense of direction or sense, finds himself by the sign that reads "home." He is unable to remember where he is, even though the sign was a memorable part of his previous visit that led to his first rape case.

Music by Rossini, an Italian composer of operas, chamber music, and other classical pieces, also appears multiple times in the film. His "The Thieving Magpie" is played a few times in the film. The first time it appears is as four gang members try to rape a female in what appears to be a torn-down casino. Alex and his gang show up to get in a fight with the rapists. The music is merry. It does not match the heinous act of an impending rape or the violence Alex gets involved in. Alex's behavior is not heroic, either, despite the fact that he saves the female character from being raped. Alex and his friends seem to be more interested in physical fights than a rescue attempt.

Rossini's tune continues to the following scene in which Alex drives a stolen car on a country road at a high speed. This recklessness causes multiple accidents. Cars smash into the ditch. In this sequence, Kubrick clearly shows that using classical music as accompaniment of a speeding scene is not a taboo. Once the meaning and interpretation of music is challenged and recreated, classical music can have a characteristic of more popular music. At the end of Alex's reckless driving is a house with a lit sign that reads, "HOME." As the gang members seek a way into the house, the music dies down. This whole sequence, once again, does not match the mood of the music, begging the question of what it means to use existing music in an environment that challenges the preconceived notion about what the music is supposed to signify.

Also as significantly, Rossini's music appears over the scene in which Alex and his gang members walk along the Flat Block Marina, after Alex's leadership is challenged. Alex's voiceover explains his psychology and Rossini's musical inspiration. He says,

> As we walked along the Flat Block Marina, I was calm on the outside but thinking all the time. So now, it was to be Georgie the general saying what we should do and what not to do, and Dim as his mindless bulldog. But suddenly, I viddied that thinking was for the gloopy ones and that the oomny ones used like inspiration and what Bog sends. Well now, it was lovely music that came to my aid. There was a window open with the stereo on and I viddied right at once what to do.

Rossini's jovial overture does not match the violence shown in this scene. Two gang members have been pushed into the water. Georgie's palm is sliced with Alex's knife. This is very different from another famous adaptation of "The Thieving Magpie" in the comical baby changing scene in Sergio Leone's *Once Upon a Time in America* (1984). This gap, just as other scenes in the film do, forces us to question the assumed stability about the meaning of music.

In the first section of the film, groin protectors play a meaningful role. All four gang members wear their protector over their white pants. Their exaggerated sign of masculinity is evident. In this scene by the marina, all four continue to wear exaggerated protectors. However, Alex decides to attack his friends on their groin protectors, denying their masculine assertion of power and control. This equation between the groin protector and masculinity is exactly why, when Alex is arrested and interrogated by the authorities later in the film, his groin protector is nowhere to be seen. His emasculation is evident. Rossini's consecutive drum roll seems to support this assertion of masculinity effectively. An expression of power is a common theme between the overture and Alex's behavior.

The violence of the scene and Rossini's music, however, do not match up. Hughes explains that "whenever the woodwinds and brass turn up on the sound track, one may be fairly sure that something atrocious will appear on the screen." He calls this "the irony of juxtaposition" (186). The only feasible explanation for this paradoxical parallel is that the music exists only in Alex's mind. The primary purpose of music in *A Clockwork Orange*, in the first half of the film at least, is an expression of Alex's feelings. It is, in other words, an extension of his mind. In his mind, the scene in the marina is a celebratory one in which he re-asserts and reconfirms his masculine power. Violence, rape, recklessness, and other behavioral characteristics associated with masculinity are no longer threatened once he makes it clear who the leader is. In the next scene, Alex's gang members reluctantly but clearly acknowledge Alex's leadership by the simple answer of "Right."

"The Thieving Magpie" that started at the marina continues through the somber discussion and recognition of Alex's leadership. Georgie suggests his plan for the next violent act. He says, "It's this health farm, a bit out of the town. Isolated. It's owned by like this very rich ptitsa that lives there with her cats. The place is shut down for a week and she's completely on her own. And it's full up with like gold and silver and like jewels." Following this scheme, Alex and his friends proceed to the second rape scene. The soon-to-be victim lady in a green leotard is seen stretching. Alex tries to go in the house through the front door claiming that he needs to use a phone, the same excuse he used to get in the house for the first rape scene. He is unsuccessful. The Cat Lady calls the police to report that something similar to what she had read in a paper had just happened to her. Clearly, she has heard about the rape of Mrs. Alexander. Alex, nevertheless, finds his way in. The lady picks up a bust of Beethoven to defend herself. Alex, on the other hand, picks up a giant sculpture of a penis. They fight. There is no rape, but as soon as the lady is on the floor, Alex uses the penis statue to hit her in the face, specifically in her mouth, leading to her death. The implicit message is clear. In this entire scene, Rossini's music is consistently heard. The music is only replaced by the siren of the police after Alex is hit with a bottle of milk plus in the face. This is another mismatch between the severity of violence and the music, but a sadistic reflection of Alex's psychology.

A similar usage of Rossini's music as Alex's expression of masculinity manifests when he is involved in an orgy with two females whom he met in a record store. In this scene, the finale of Rossini's "William Tell Overture" is played. Assisted by this fast-paced music, Alex has intercourse with two females repeatedly, sometimes together, and some other times, separately. The act happens in front of a large painting of Beethoven. Even when one of them gets dressed back up as Alex has sex with the other, he returns to the other female and undresses her. This scene, one of the scenes that had to be edited to avoid the X rating and to obtain the R rating, is, once again, a celebration of Alex's sexual prowess as accentuated by Rossini's upbeat piece.

The Overture to *William Tell* is used more than once in this film. Its orchestral version is heard when Alex is told by his parents that although he had returned from the correctional facility, his room had already been rented out. Later in the film, Kubrick adapted the introductory part of the piece. This portion of the music is maybe less known than its finale used in the orgy scene, but it is as powerful. Alex comes home after treatment only to learn that his room is no longer his, and his parents are no longer welcoming him.

They look at him not as son, but more like a monster who has been treated and changed scientifically. Without a place to stay and having no other options, Alex leaves his parents' apartment. This lonesome and depressing scene is underscored by the somber tone of the "William Tell Overture."

Nikolai Rimsky-Korsakov's *Scheherazade* also appears in this film. This opus, based on *One Thousand and One Nights*, or *The Arabian Nights*, starts with its glorious first movement, "The Sea and Sinbad's Ship." The music is heard when Alex reads the Bible after two years in the correction facility, or what he calls "this hell hole and human zoo." He says,

> It was my rabbit to help the prison Charlie with the Sunday service. He was a bolshy great bastard, but he was very fond of myself. Me being very young and now interested in the big book, I read all about the scourging and the crowning with thorns and I could viddy myself helping in and even taking charge of the tolchoking and the nailing in. I didn't so much like the latter part of the book which is more like all preachy talking than fighting and the old in-out. I like the parts where these old yahooties tolchok each other and then drink their Hebrew vino and getting on to the bed with their wife's handmaidens. That kept me going.

The background of this monologue with a visual cue of Alex whipping Jesus is a piece from *Scheherazade*.

Another work by Rimsky-Korsakov replaces "The Sea and Sinbad's Ship." Right after Alex's monologue and whipping in his dream, he is now lying with three women, all of whom are topless. One lady offers him grapes. Another is lying down next to Alex, looking away. The other is gently waving a large leaf to give him a breeze. In this scene, the accompanying music is "The Story of the Kalandar Prince." This is a short scene. But the music effectively portrays a utopian environment in which Alex is calm.

Edward Elgar, an English composer, makes multiple contributions to the film. "Pomp and Circumstance No. One in D Major" for example is played as the minister inspects prison cells, finds Alex's picture and bust of Beethoven (along with pin-ups of topless models), and appears in front of the prisoners making two lines against a high prison wall. The heroic and glorious tune is seemingly appropriate for the rank and responsibility of a government leader. His walk through the prison corridor and entry to the small prison concrete yard celebrates his total control over the prisoners' bodies and minds. The glory of the music, however, is betrayed by an ominous statement by the minister. Walking in front of the prisoners, he states, "The government can't be concerned any longer with outmoded penalogical theories. Soon we may be needing all of our prison space for political offenders. Common criminals like these are best dealt with on a purely curative basis. Kill the criminal reflex, that's all. Full implementation in a year's time. Punishment means nothing to them." Overhearing this statement, Alex responds, "You're absolutely right, sir." A prison guard admonishes him, "Shut your bleeding hole." But a short conversation to follow with the minister leads Alex to be sent to the Ludovico facility for a new experimental curing method.

When Alex is taken out of the prison and sent to the facility with two guards, "Pomp and Circumstance No. 4 in G Major" is played. This creates a conversation with the earlier use of Elgar's D Major. Similar in its motif, G Major is glorious but also more cheerful and promising. It is also an upbeat tune that signals Alex's transition to a prison environment to a freer—at least according to his imagination—clinical environment. This difference is obvious in the prison guard's very controlled behavior to the facility officer's more relaxed attitude. Elgar's music assists Kubrick with the development and transition of his story from the penal system to the clinical system, and from years of imprisonment to a far lesser period of confinement.

Adapting Existing Popular Music

In addition to classical music composers of the pre-twentieth and very early twentieth centuries, *A Clockwork Orange* adapted recordings of more recent works. For example, "Overture of the Sun" from *Sound of Sunforest* is played, as mentioned before, when Alex is forced to lick the bottom of a boot to demonstrate the effectiveness of the Ludovico technique. The song from the only studio-recorded album by Sunforest, a psychedelic folk band of Terry Tucker, Erika Eigen, and Freya Hogue, is upbeat. Just as Rossini's "The Thieving Magpie" did not match the violent scene early in the film, this overture does not match the humiliating and sadistic portrayal of Alex's experience.

This shift in musical representation is significant. Early in the film, the music and cinematographic visual depiction did not match because the abhorrence that audiences would naturally feel toward violence shows on the screen was not shared by Alex. The music was an extension of his psychology. Alex was in control. After he is treated with the Ludovico technique, he is stripped of his personal will or agency. As the minister who appeared in front of him after Elgar's glorious tune said, he had been "dealt with" through science and technology. Alex is no longer in control. His psychology and emotion are gone. Music, therefore, no longer reflects his mind. Instead, it reflects the sense of achievement felt by the scientists and psychologists observing Alex's self-less behaviors with sadistic smiles on their faces. The state is now in control. This is exactly the social environment in which the counterculture gained popularity. Sunforest's music shows this shift in power.

This is probably why Erika Eigen's "I Want to Marry a Lighthouse Keeper" is played when Alex returns home from the Ludovico treatment. The music is hopeful and upbeat. Alex, holding a brown bag in his arm, also seems hopeful about his future. In his mind, he is cured. He is ready to get back to the real world. At the first sight, his hopefulness and the music's tone match well. Soon, Alex notices that something is different. His room does not look the same. In the living room are his parents, as well as a stranger eating toast. The *Daily Telegraph* talks about Alex on its front page. When Alex's perplexed father turns off his radio, Eigen's music is also turned off, signaling that the music was not reflective of Alex's psychology but that of his parents. Despite the fact that their son had committed a murder, their life has improved in the past two years with a renter of Alex's room who considers them almost as his parents. The hopefulness of his parents is not difficult to understand. This is another instance of Alex's inability to control music in the story of the film.

Another one of the most iconic songs in the film that connects Alex to the audience is "Singin' in the Rain." The music was composed by Nacio Herb Brown and the lyrics were written by Arthur Freed. The song, originally performed as early as the late 1920s, became popular when it was adapted to the musical film of the same title in 1952. Gene Kelly's dance in a rainstorm with a folded umbrella is one of the best known scenes of the film. Kelly's jovial dance tune appears in *A Clockwork Orange* multiple times.

In Kubrick's film, however, the song has a very different significance. It carries two symbolic functions. First, it reflects the shift of Alex's status. When Alex sings the song for the first time, it is when he and his gang members break into a house and rape Mrs. Alexander in front of her husband who was crippled by them. In other words, Alex is "ready for rape," not necessarily "ready for love" as Gene Kelly sang in the musical (Ramussen 122). Alex uses his stick to stab the wife and kicks the husband in his abdomen. He has been seeing a probation officer. But he is nonetheless in charge of his conduct. He makes his own choices. He is also in control of his own gang. He chooses to be violent. A major problem in Alex's life at this point is clearly his violent tendencies. It changes later in the film.

The second time the audience hears Alex sing the song, however, Alex does not have the same dominant position. He is in the same house, that of Mr. Alexander. But he had gone through the Ludovico therapy and his personal will and choice had been stripped from him. He bathes in a tub and sings the song in a small bathroom he imagines to be safe, especially after being beaten up by two of his former gang members who had become police officers and running away from them on foot in a rainstorm. Although the scene is significantly calmer and peaceful in this second instance of the song than in the first, the problem in Alex's life at this point is the victimization by the state control over his body and mind and the absence of his personal judgment.

While this first function of the music is comparative to Alex's changing problems, the second function is about consistency. Alex sings the song both times in the Alexander residence. The first time, Mr. Alexander is forced to watch his wife raped without being able to do anything to stop Alex. The second time, his wife has been dead from pneumonia. The writer, however, believes otherwise. He explains to Alex,

> She was very badly raped, ya see. We were attacked by a gang of vicious young hoodlums in this very room you're sitting in now. I was left helpless crippled. Doctors said it was pneumonia, because it happened some months later during a flu epidemic. The doctor told me it was pneumonia, but I knew what it was. Victim of the modern age.

Mr. Alexander, who at first was unaware who Alex was, becomes fully aware of his identity when he overhears Alex sing "Singin' in the Rain" in the bath. The screen shows the writer's distorted face in agony. For him, Alex's different types of suffering make little difference. The song shows the image of Alex as a perpetrator in the eyes of the writer.

Additionally, this sense of threat that he felt as he overheard Alex might also be read as a general threat to society. When he was unaware of who Alex was, the writer once called him a "victim of the modern age," as well. This sense of lost agency and a fear about an increasing amount of state control felt in many modern societies across the Atlantic at the time represent Kubrick's critique of where the world was headed. From this perspective, Alex indeed was a victim of the modern society. He was a victim of the uncertain world in which he sought to find his identity through youthful violence. He was then met with the punitive system that did not actually rehabilitate him. Such a social critique is underscored by the repeated use of "Singin' in the Rain."

Ludwig van and Alex

Although *A Clockwork Orange*'s controversial violence overshadowed the provocativeness that Beethoven's music has in this film, the use of Beethoven's symphonies has invited many critics to make a wide range of comments. The film does not make any direct reference to composers, except for Beethoven. There is no reference even to Bach, whose work Wendy Carlos once worked with. To some, there was clear disconnection between what the music originally portrayed and what the film had it represent. To some others, Kubrick's music choice was effective because of this seeming discord which hid the ambiguity of the music. Regardless of the view, however, it is clear that Beethoven's music functions as various types of cues in this work by

Kubrick. First and foremost, Beethoven is a significant part of Alex's personal identity. Beethoven is more than just his favorite composer. He is seen listening to his music, especially the Ninth Symphony, multiple times in the film. Before the Ludovico treatment, Beethoven's music was what made Alex feel at home. After the treatment, it became a source of agony. This is why the Ninth Symphony is a "double-edged sword" (Rasmussen 113). With the healing process, however, Beethoven returns as a source of pleasure. Throughout the film, Beethoven appears both visibly and audibly. Beethoven's pictures, portraits, bust, and other objects are put in various scenes. His music, especially the Fifth and Ninth symphonies, carry deep provocative meanings in the film.

The symphony works in multiple ways partially because it is a complex composition that is used in Kubrick's complex film. Höyng states that the "film not only abundantly exhibits acoustic and visual representations of Beethoven, and especially of his Ninth Symphony, but also unveils the links of both to the ambiguities, and in some cases, certainties, of violence" (160). The music sometimes reflects Alex's free-willed lifestyle. It is also reflective of his risk-taking youthful behaviors. It can signal an impending violence. Sometimes such violence comes with certainty and some other times, with mere possibility. It is disruptive of Alex's life, as well as that of others. Höyng continues to explain that "Kubrick amplifies how the symphony can at once serve as the paradigm for the dialectics of aggressive acts, while he simultaneously deconstructs an aesthetic icon so beleaguered by its political baggage" (160).

The "Ode to Joy" from Beethoven's Ninth Symphony appears when Alex is back to the Korova. Alex, after committing the rape of Mrs. Alexander, along with his gang members, sits at a table, drinking milk plus. Across from them is a group of customers whose attire does not seem to match the interior of the bar. Totally unaware of the presence of Alex, let alone his affinity to Beethoven, a female customer of the group starts singing the "Ode to Joy." She is with four other male customers who almost look like Alex and his entourage. As Rasmussen explains, "From [Alex's] perspective, the camera zooms in on the opera singer, obliterating the rest of the Korova Milk bar, now part of the wicked world he seeks to escape." Rasmussen's assessment is correct that if Alex met the singer in a different circumstance, "she would rate the same low regard as did Mrs. Alexander" (124). Beethoven, however, saves this lady in the milk bar.

This scene at the Korova is also significant in that it truly shows the importance of Beethoven in Alex's mind. His friend, Dim, for example is not particularly a fan of his music. He even dismisses the composer. Alex is not amused by Dim's statement, and punished Dim by hitting him in the leg with his stick. In Alex's gang, undervaluing Beethoven, the audience now knows, is equivalent to undervaluing Alex. But this small schism that rises over Beethoven is a hint of coming disagreement within the gang which will later lead to the scene at the marina and to the residence of the Cat Lady in front of which Alex is arrested (Rasmussen 124). Denying Beethoven is little different from denying Alex.

In one of the most violent scenes of the film in which Alex and the Cat Lady get in an altercation, Beethoven is not audible, but visible. In this scene, the importance of Beethoven for Alex becomes also evident. The audible accompaniment is "The Thieving Magpie." However, when Alex finds a giant sculpture of a penis and uses it as his weapon, it is an art work that symbolizes the Cat Lady's taste. In the meantime, she grabs a bust of Beethoven to defend herself. The fight between the two characters in this scene is not significant not just because of imminent rape or its eventual consequence of sending Alex to prison. Rather, a major musical theme of the film, Beethoven, asserts himself on the screen as a representation of Alex's personal interests. This fight is an attempt "to prevent their opponent from sullying their own preferred art forms," naturally leading to "an attack on the personality, the personal taste, and the personal preferences of the opponent" (Planka 55; Polan 88). This is not just a fight for survival. It is not an attempt to sexually violate another or to defend oneself from the other, but rather an expression of one's deep interests as manifested through two tangible artistic objects. The object for Alex, of course, is Beethoven.

The Ninth Symphony is clearly one of the best known symphonies in the world, especially its final movement with chorus. Although its second movement, Scherzo, may not be as popular as its concluding movement, it is still a very important ingredient of the film as it tells the life story of Alex's. Scherzo, or "joke" in English, is a common movement in any symphony. It is a fast-paced piece, oftentimes somewhat comical and moves all over the place. The second movement of Beethoven's Ninth is not an exception. When Alex comes home one night and enters his bedroom, the audience may be shocked by the tidiness of the room. It is very different from the chaotic nature of Alex's public life. It is an "ironic Eden" (Rice 70). After removing his fake eyelashes, he reaches for a cassette tape of Beethoven's Ninth Symphony. Although Alex is relaxed in his bed, the music is moving fast and, on one level, keeps reflecting his life outside of the house. But the music also hints, especially for those who are familiar with Beethoven's composition, that the third movement is a slow movement that is serene. Alex's pet snake, four small statues of Jesus, and Beethoven's stern-looking picture all suggests that once Scherzo ends, something calmer might happen. Of course the audience is betrayed with such an expectation because next morning, Alex is not willing to change as he is met by his probation officer. Instead, he is accompanied by Beethoven's Ninth Symphony in the record store as he convinces two girls to come to his apartment for an orgy. In front of Beethoven's stern face, Alex and the girls have an orgy with a version of Rossini's overture in the background.

A key moment arrives in the life of Alex when he is exposed to the "Ode to Joy" during the Ludovico treatment. During his second session, he is forced to see documentaries about Adolf Hitler and the Nazi Party. This association between Hitler and Beethoven could have multiple meanings for Alex, as well as the audience members of the film that who, like Alex, are fond of the German composer. The symphony that assumes a particularly important meaning as we study the relationship between an iconic leader and Beethoven is his Third Symphony. He completed his Third Symphony in 1804, originally dedicated to Napoleon. When Beethoven learned that Napoleon put himself in a position to lead France, he scratched the title of the symphony out of rage and later changed it to *Eroica*. Beethoven, therefore, would not have been keen to the idea that his composition would adorn Hitler and his party's control over Germany. It is possible that Alex made this connection. Or, he might not. Rasmussen also questions, "Alex ... might have dreamed up such a combination on his own. But in the context of Ludovico conditioning, that combination is a threat to his very capacity for creative association" (151).

Suffering from the treatment, Alex screams, "Using Beethoven like that [is wrong]! He did no harm to anyone. Beethoven just wrote music!" The symphony was a "source of joy," but now, for Alex, it is now a means of torture (Höyng 171). Rasmussen is critical of Alex's linking between the use of Beethoven in the treatment process and the idea of sin. He writes,

> It is a hypocritical position for Alex to take. More than anyone else in the film, Alex arbitrarily appropriates music for his own use. It is his personal loss of Beethoven as a source of inspiration that he objects to, not any injustice done to the composer's memory. And as for Beethoven, no composer even "just wrote music." Music is an extension of the composer's will. It is an instrument of power, however abstract [151].

This is to say that Beethoven's Ninth Symphony is not just an expression of Alex's artistic taste, but also a tool. Alex uses the music to his advantage.

Just like the Nazis indeed appropriated the works of Beethoven and Wagner, Alex and the Ludovico therapists appropriate Beethoven's work (Gengaro 123). Once Alex completes the Ludovico treatment and loses his personal agency, however, it is no longer Alex that uses the symphony for personal gains. When Mr. Alexander invites his friends over to have them meet Alex, he explains to Rubinstein that Alex cannot listen to the Ninth without feeling sick. Explaining his condition, however, Alex is unaware that he has been drugged. Soon he passes out onto the plate of spaghetti only to be woken up by the Ninth Symphony played with two large speakers facing upward just a floor below the bedroom where he wakes up. With the door locked, there is nowhere for him to go. Mr. Alexander looks ecstatic. For Mr. Alexander, "Singin' in the Rain" is a symbol of violence. It is the song that Alex and his friends sang as they raped Mrs. Alexander. When the writer overhears the song for the second time, he is reminded of the violence. The same can be said about the Ninth Symphony for Alex. For post–Ludovico therapy Alex, the music symbolizes violence that he experienced at the treatment facility. Just as Mr. Alexander was reminded of the rape, Alex is reminded of his torture as he hears the final movement of the symphony in the attic of the writer's house, and finds suicide to be the only escape route (Mamber 176).

The iconic rhythmical cell of four notes and the motif of the whole Fifth Symphony of Beethoven's is heard twice in the film. It is the doorbell of Mr. and Mrs. Alexander's. The symphony, also known as "the Symphony of Destiny," sounds deceivingly "thin [and] quaint" (Rasmussen 122). Beethoven's biographer Anton Felix Schindler explained that the motif was how destiny would knock on your door. It is very much the case in *A Clockwork Orange*. When the doorbell rings for the first time on Alex's first visit to the house, it is truly destiny knocking on the door for the writer and his wife. Alex explains to Mrs. Alexander that his friend is injured and he needs to use her phone. Looking worried, Mr. Alexander tells his wife that they should help them. As soon as the door chain is released, Alex and his friends pour into the house, turning themselves into the masters of the house and Mr. Alexander a powerless figure. Destiny, or fate, truly arrives with those repeated four notes at the Alexander residence.

Beethoven only makes Alex non-suicidal after the government admits to Alex, albeit for political reasons, that the treatment had done him wrong. Alex says to himself, "I was really cured at last." Alex is finally able to have his affection to Beethoven back on his hospital bed as he is photographed next to the minister. Rasmussen states that "the power of Alex's favorite music is restored to his emotional palette by the government that stole it from him" (171). Schiller's *Ode to Joy*, well known for the chorus in the Ninth Symphony, is reflective of Alex's status at last.

What is noteworthy is that, even after he is cured and his joy is supplemented by "Ode to Joy," Alex is never seen or heard singing along with this iconic music. Although Höyng extensively discusses the meaning of the Schiller's poem (166–169), Beethoven's interpretation of it, and Schiller's view of the world in his essay, it is still the sound that makes Alex ill and signals his recovery. Kubrick seems to challenge his audience how to interpret aural messages. The ambiguity of texts, including poems, is rather clear. The filmmaker challenges his audience to contradict established ideas and questions if the same can be said about music.

Silence as Alex's Psychology

Although music reflects Alex's psychology in most of the film, its absence is also meaningful in this work by Kubrick. Particularly in the first half of the film, music and Alex are inseparable. Pezzotta explains that "not only do Alex's performance and the montage follow the rhythm of the music, but also the protagonist's thoughts and actions are moved by music itself" (91). If music is a way for Alex to reach out to his audience and share his psychology, the lack of music is a reflection of lost agency on his part in many parts of the film. When the audience hears only the conversation between characters without any music, it is often when Alex has lost control and does not own the situation.

For example, immediately after the orgy Alex is walking down the stairs only to be greeted by his three gang members on the ground floor of his apartment. Georgie says that there is a "new way" in the relationship. This is when his leadership is put to challenge, preceding the scene at the marina. This is a great difference from just a few scenes ago in which Alex's orgy was accompanied by the tune from *William Tell*. The entire scene is silent. There is no emotion expressed via music. Pete looks scared. Georgie looks ambitious. Alex's facial expression is blank. The musical cue is absent between Rossini's overture and "The Thieving Magpie" played in the succeeding scene at the marina.

Similarly, after Alex's arrest, he is interrogated at a police station. As mentioned earlier, he has by then lost his groin protector, a symbol of his masculinity and power. He attempts to fight back and resist the authority by burping into the face of an officer or by holding onto his own groin. The power hierarchy is, however, clear. He is soon quieted by a group of officers. Furthermore, soon after, he learns that he is no longer just an addict but also a murderer. His probation officer tells him that he has just made it back from the hospital where the lady hit in the face with a penis-shaped statue has died.

Once Alex is taken to the prison, there still is no music. He is told to empty his pockets. Standing behind a line on the floor, he tosses his item onto the table. A prison officer tells him to pick it up and place it onto the table gently. He obliges. The officer tells him to strip down and conducts a cavity check. No music is heard. Alex is simply a number on the prison roster. There is no music; there is no agency for Alex.

This parallel between the presence and the absence of music is similar to the overall scheme of the film that Julian Rice discusses. Rice states that the premise of the film is that "the nation-state is the enemy of nonconformity, self-realization, and the single one's transfiguration," and that "moral progress may just be emasculation" (53). In other words, once someone loses impulses, he is not moral. Overcoming impulses is a way to be moral. In this scheme, music-less Alex is an individual without individuality. Kubrick's social critique particularly on the role of the state over individuals is visible through not only the ways in which music is used, but also the ways in which music is sometimes not used in the film.

Using Synthesizers and Wendy Carlo's Contribution

Although music by classical composers and contemporary psychedelic musicians characterize the film and effectively portray psychology and the condition of Alex, the film's use of electronic synthesizers also distinguished *A Clockwork Orange* from other films of the period. For example, Purcell's "Music for the Funeral of Queen Mary" has a very distinct texture as the film's main theme, compared to its original version used for Queen Mary's procession, composed over 300 years ago. Phillip calls this version of the march the "nasty-ized" version (308). Wendy Carlos was a vital figure in the use of synthesizers in the film to offer different textures to existing music.

Wendy Carlos was born as Walter Carlos in 1939. In an interview with *Playboy*, she stated, "I was about five or six.... I remember being convinced I was a little girl, much preferring long hair and girls' clothes, and not knowing why my parents didn't see it clearly" (Bell 82). In 1972, she underwent a sex reassignment surgery to become Wendy Carlos. She received education in classical music and physics at Brown University for her dual undergraduate degree and Columbia University for her master's degree. In 1968, she made "an enormously popular recording" of "Switched-on Bach" and sold over a million copies. Ammer explains that that this recording made synthesizers popular (235). With "Switched-on Bach," Carlos won three Grammy Awards in 1969, making herself an established composer and a synthesizer player before working with Kubrick for *A Clockwork Orange* ("Blood, Sweat and Tears").

Carlos's formal introduction to electric music production stems back to the mid–1960s when she was in New York. Working at the Columbia-Princeton Electronic Music Center, she explained, "I thought what ought to be done was obvious, to use the new technology for appealing music you could really listen to" (Jackson 44). She was also aware that many of the people who worked with electronic music were not trained musicians. She stated, "The typical electronic music setup of the '60s was a cluttered lab bench and a technician wearing a lab coat. It was hard to make music—melody, rhythm, orchestration, harmony, counterpoint—with these setups. Many of these technicians were not trained musicians, so we heard funky sound effects" (Jackson 144).

A change happened in the mid-twentieth century with the development of Robert Moog's synthesizer. Carlos remembers that he "combined many of these devices into a cabinet with a touch-sensitive keyboard.... A composer or a pianist who knew something about electronics and the properties of sound could create real music" (Jackson 144). Although this synthesizer by the American physicist was nothing elaborate or complex, as Wierzbicki, Platte, and Roust discuss, it was nonetheless different from what had been available in the U.S. since the late 1920s and enabled musically trained talents like Carlos to produce quality music, eventually leading her to compose a Grammy winner in 1968. For the film, Carlos "respected the pitches and rhythms of the original scores but colored the materials with sonorities that before this time were scarcely imaginable" and helped the synthesizer's debut on the big screen (231–232).

A key figure in the collaboration between Kubrick and Carlos was Rachel Elkind, Carlos' producer. Jackson explains,

> Carlos had loved the Burgess book and was a fan of Kubrick's work, and fantasized aloud that she'd love to get some of her music into the film; she thought it would fit well. When word filtered back to New York that principal filming had been completed, Elkind managed to get a tape of their version of the choral movement, as well as a stunning original composition by Carlos called "Timesteps," into the hands of the director. Kubrick was bowled over by what he heard and summoned Carlos and Elkind to England. He agreed to use both pieces in the film and also arranged to have the team synthesize some other classical themes he was planning to use in the film and to create some background cues from scratch [144].

Carlos writes extensively about Elkind on her personal website, reflecting the strong tie that these figures had over their music careers. Carlos explains that her website could "set the record straight" because there was "a notable contribution that's often bypassed." She continues that it was "one that was important during the inception of [her] music from about 1967 until 1980 or so. There was a 'silent partner' for all of these projects, who was seldom credited properly" (Carlos).

Carlos's "Timesteps" is her way of turning Burgess' literary work into music. Both Carlos and Kubrick discovered the book around the same time. For Carlos, the discovery of the novel came about the same time as about when she was composing "Timesteps" (Appleton 98). She "was so struck by what she perceived as parallels between the mood of the book and her new work" (144). Carlos realized that her work was "an autonomous composition with an uncanny affinity for *Clockwork*" (Phillips 144). As Jackson also wrote, Carlos and Elkind sent Kubrick a tape of the new song, as well as an electric rendition of a part of Beethoven's Ninth Symphony. Eventually, they were invited to his home for a meeting. The outcome of the meeting was not just having "Timesteps" adopted in the film. Kubrick explained to them that he had decided to use numerous classical music pieces including works by Purcell and Rossini and that he was "depending on [Carlos and Elkind] to convert these into futuristic electronic timbres" (145).

"Timesteps" is futuristic but also somewhat eerie music. It is heard as Alex undergoes his first Ludovico treatment. He sits in a chair with his eyes forced open. This is a therapy in which Alex is exposed to various movies and documentaries that are designed to create aversion to violence. He takes drugs to prepare for the treatment. A clinical assistant sits next to him to keep his eyeballs lubricated. At first, he seems to enjoy the film. But soon, he begins to feel sick. The first film is about physical violence. The second film depicts violent rape. He says, "I began to feel really sick." But he could not close his eyes. They were forced open. He continues, "Even if I tried to move my glassballs about, I still could not get out of the line of fire of this picture." Alex, once a perpetrator, is now victimized. "Help me out," he pleads. But the doctors ignore him. Dr. Brodsky says,

> Very soon now the drug will cause the subject to experience a deadlike paralysis together with deep feelings of terror and helplessness. One of our earlier test subjects described it as being like death. A sense of stifling and drowning. And it is during this period that we have found the subject will make his most rewarding associations between his catastrophic experience and involvement with the violence he sees.

The futuristic tune accompanies throughout Alex's suffering. The music may hint at what is to come in the future. The future has both hope and uncertainty. "Timesteps" also has a sense of hope that comes from its futuristic musical features, while it also contains a sense of the unknown detectable in the eeriness of the music.

Carlos' musical talent becomes even more evident when her music is compared to its other variations. For example, the main music of *A Clockwork Orange*, "Music for the Funeral of Queen Mary" was also used in *The Young Poisoner's Handbook* (1995). Produced about twenty years after Kubrick's work, with Benjamin Ross as the director and Sam Taylor as the producer, the film plays this iconic music at its closing scene. The music is appropriate with its solemnness. But its texture is completely different in Carlos' version. The solemnness is far less present. Rather, it matches closely with the psychedelic nature of music by Terry Tucker, a member of Sunforest. This rendition of the funeral march is noncommittal. It can be interpreted in many different ways: a solemn tune or a representation of a dream. As Ian MacDonald characterized the culture of the mid-twentieth century and especially LSD, music "could turn its [audience] into anything from florally embellished peaceniks to gun-brandishing urban guerrillas" (17).

Conclusion

When existing music is used in a film, significant questions arise about the very nature of the original music. Does the film change what the music stands for? Does it enhance or denigrate the music? Is this fair to the composer? Should filmmakers be limited with their options of using music? These questions are even more complicated when the original music is considered a classical masterpiece. The same is true when the music is altered to carry a new texture. In *A Clockwork Orange*, both of these complicating factors are at play. On the one hand, Kubrick adopted music by Rossini, Beethoven, and many other renowned composers. On the other hand, Wendy Carlos used synthesizers to reinvent existing music and to give it new flavor. These decisions were provocative. Kate McQuiston discusses this "stable identity" that music may or may not have. She writes, "When a new rendition or context seems to go against the spirit (if not the letter) of the work, hackles go up. Music's ontological slipperiness ... is precisely what allows old works to live on through reinvention in new forms, and it is a large part of the logic behind the persistent production of recordings and performances of the same work again and again by different artists" (146). Understanding this nature of music, McQuiston is sympathetic to Kubrick and supports his decision to use classical music, despite its provocativeness. Explaining that Beethoven's Ninth Symphony was "performed both on Hitler's annual birthday celebrations and at the memorial concert of 2000 in Mauthausen, Austria's main concentration camp," Höyng argues that audiences of music "can (mis)understand this music's meaning and brings to the fore of the symphony's paradoxical nature" (160). McQuiston continues that this 1971 film "directly addresses and reframes our previous music experiences and with great specificity bears upon our subsequent musical experiences" (147).

When Kubrick adapted various existing music, this cinematographic choice could have easily been considered as a selfish appropriation of classical works for his own interest. It is true that if a meaning of the music was stable, Kubrick took the music out of its original context and planted it in a completely different environment beyond the reach of its composer. This perspective explains Edward Rothstein's view expressed in the *New York Times*. He wrote, "We object to the psychologists' forced associations of Beethoven with violence and nausea. Our old love for the music as noble and transcendent is meant to kick in." However, if music, just like any other system of meaning creation, is inherently context dependent and if its meaning is constantly constructed and changed, then Kubrick's choice is just another example of underscoring the fluid nature of meaning.

The meaning of music was challenged particularly with the use of the synthesizer. Wendy Carlos' contribution in this regard is immense. The use of classical music like that of Beethoven in itself made the film even more controversial. Furthermore, the use of technology in music production also encouraged the question about the meaning of music, especially when technology allows composers and musical experts to offer completely different texture to the tune.

In the meantime, Kubrick simultaneously challenged his audience to consider what technology would mean in society. As Leonard Steinhorn discussed, this is the period when citizens of advanced nations continued to "embrace technology and progress," while they also "rejected what technology came to represent." He continues, "to Boomers, technology symbolized an increasingly mass-produced, bureaucratized, and depersonalized America, and it was that, not the actual technology, that Boomers disdained" (77). The condition was the same in Europe. Viewers of *A Clockwork Orange* today can easily see the sense of disapproval in the film about what technology and progress had come to signify.

The ultimate question of the film is that of ownership. "Who owns the music?" "Who owns the agency of an individual?" "Who owns the control of society?" Repeatedly, Kubrick shows that the power resides with individuals. Even Beethoven cannot escape the test of time. Schiller's poem can be read and understood only within the social context specific to a culture. A state's attempt to control an individual and strip his agency is met with criticism. Technology and social advancements thanks to science may be appealing, but they can also be threatening. It is not only via obvious visual and aural cues such as the portrayals of illegal substances or an inclusion of a psychedelic tune, but also via more tacit messages that the film offers, that demonstrate it truly is a film to challenge, or counter, the existing culture.

13. Understanding Country Ways: A Talk with Country Joe McDonald About Counterculture Film

Country Joe McDonald understands that he will always be inherently connected to the sights and sounds of the 1960s and early 1970s, and to the counterculture. McDonald lived and played in various groups in Berkeley, California, in the mid–1960s. Berkeley was home to the Free Speech Movement at the time, a movement that would play a significant role in the developing counterculture. In 1965, the same year he penned the "I Feel Like I'm Fixin' to Die Rag," Country Joe and the Fish released their first recordings. Ultimately, the group would find great success internationally, making a significant impact, even among several personnel changes throughout the years.

The group signed up with Vanguard Records and in 1966 released *Electric Music for the Mind and Body* in 1967. The album has been considered by many to be one of the first and most influential psychedelic albums of the time. The band would go on to release a total of six studio albums (one, a reunion album in 1977), live albums, compilations, and singles. During that time the group held a prominent place within the San Francisco music scene, becoming regulars at the Fillmore and Avalon ballrooms.

Their inclusion in the D.A. Pennebaker film *Monterey Pop* further cemented their central role as a group of and for a new generation of music listeners and film viewers, including those that identified themselves as part of the counterculture of the late 1960s and early 1970s. It was Country Joe's appearance in the film *Woodstock*, though, that would make him a household name for the baby-boomer generation and beyond. Asked to go on stage to fill in during a dead space between performances, McDonald encouraged a crowd of several hundred thousand to participate in reciting a version of the

"Fish Cheer" and then into a sing-along performance of the "I Feel Like I'm Fixin' to Die Rag." Audiences around the world were welcomed to do the same thing when bouncing ball lyrics were added to this part of the *Woodstock* film.

Mike Evans and Paul Kingsbury's *Woodstock: Three Days That Rocked the World* cites that Country Joe and the Fish were "arguably the most appropriate to the countercultural thrust of the event, having been central to the politico-protest movement on the West Coast since the mid–1960s" (190). McDonald, because of this impromptu acoustic set, would be pushed much further into that spotlight thanks to the cameras turned on him. McDonald and that performance became an icon, or "Greek chorus" (Rima) of anti-war sentiment and the counterculture, whatever that meant, to the audiences finding identity within or understanding from outside. However the performance, the artist, the sentiment, or the film itself, or the validity of that moment functioning as a historical and cultural marker are viewed, the text exists as a common referent that is easily accessible.

As the interview will detail, McDonald saw a great deal of worth and direction coming from Woodstock, thanks to its widespread success and presence in American and international culture. In *USA Today* he reflected, "I think Woodstock is very important, but I'm personally surprised by the response it's getting. The change of generations took place at Woodstock—politics, culture, art, technology, lifestyle, everything—and it's still extremely controversial. Woodstock is the American dream manifested in a new chapter" (Dieringer).

McDonald and the Fish were featured in numerous other films following, including *Gas-s-s-s* (1970), *Zacharia* (1971), and *More American Graffiti* (1979). The music of McDonald and the Fish has been also featured as soundtrack music, in addition to the above, in such films as *Hamburger Hill* (1987), *Steal This Movie* (2000), *Purple Haze* (1982), and numerous television programs that have all contributed to McDonald's iconic stature within the counterculture, within American history, and within American popular culture.

McDonald has continued to write, record, and tour over the last several decades, releasing several albums, DVDs. His latest album, *Time Flies By*, was released in 2012 on his *Rag Baby* label. He also currently runs countryjoe.com. He has also been active in several organizations such as the Vietnam Veterans Against the War, Swords to Plowshares, and the Vietnam Veterans of America.

McDonald agreed to sit down and talk with us in 2013 about his musical career and its relation to film. In the following interview, McDonald discusses his roles as a musician and as a featured actor in several of these films. The following is an edited version of that discussion.

Did the presence of cameras affect your performance in Monterey Pop and Woodstock? Was that something that you had been used to in the Haight-Ashbury scene and elsewhere, or did the cameras add something new in terms of just the way that you approached the performance or the way that people viewed the performance?

No, personally for me it didn't affect it at all. I was not familiar with cameras really for either Monterey or Woodstock. I don't think I even knew they were filming at Woodstock.

In terms of overall experiences was there anything that was remarkably different or similar between being featured in both of them?

I don't think for me. I mean of course, Pennebaker's film was a smaller scale. It was really small. Both filmmakers were documentary filmmakers; they weren't music filmmakers. What needs to be understood is that, I don't think, there had been a film about music before. There wasn't a performance film of this nature. So there was nothing to compare it to and there was no prototype. But, Monterey sort of got lost in the mix but Woodstock became pretty much the primer, the prototype, for how you would do a live concert film.

Being that they were prototypes, were you happy with the results?

I was very happy with Woodstock. I think it's an excellent film, a groundbreaker. The Pennebaker film was okay. It was really just a kind of a traditional documentary focused on musical performances. And our particular performance is a mystery to me. Still, I don't understand how that particular music got played the way it did, in terms of the editing. I think it's live, I don't know; it was a confusing experience. Not on stage but afterwards.

So it's possible that editing might have tripped up the live experience that you recall?

No, no, not that. The bass, there was an effect unit on the bass players' amplifier before we played and our bass player used it and we, it just happened that that fuzz-tone sound; it wasn't anything that we planned. And for some reason on "Section 43," the composition we played at Monterey, there is no harmonica and I don't understand how that happened because it has always been played with a harmonica. And the harmonica is just absent in it. I don't know if Pennebaker edited it out or we didn't play it; I have no idea really.

So it sounds like there really isn't any kind of control coming from the bands themselves, in terms of asking for specific songs to be featured or anything of that nature. It's the filmmaker's prerogative?

Oh, absolutely. I think in both films there was approval or disapproval or acceptance or non-acceptance of being filmed. I think in Big Brother's case they refused to be filmed the first day and then they performed the second day in Monterey, being filmed, because they realized I think that it was important. For some groups, Monterey was very important. But for Country Joe and the Fish, it wasn't.

Is there any kind of difference that you saw in terms of being a subject of the film? How did that maybe change between '67 and '69 with those two projects?

Well, the films are reflective of the performances and the band at Monterey was more psychedelic than the band at Woodstock. But the band, I mean that's not a portrayal, that's just what was ... and that's what it was. There was no manipulation. Some of the stuff, I mean like widely used effects, and visual effects were used on Woodstock. The effects used with bands like The Who, the stop motion and the split screen and that stuff was important and created an image. But The Who was theatrical anyway even at Monterey where they were breaking their instruments and stuff. But on the larger screen it communicated more of a ... it was more than just a documentary, Woodstock was. It projected an image. It's sort of hit and miss. I think in both films there were certain things a filmmaker couldn't do but only with the footage that they had. You know, they couldn't make something seem like it happened, if it hadn't actually happened.

It definitely seems as if, with Woodstock, the bands were one of the attractions but the audience seemed to have much more of a focus on it. With the split screens and seeing the audience sing along with the "'Fixin' to Die Rag,'" there was much more attention being paid to folks that were out there and appreciating it...

Yeah, I think you're right but although in Monterey there is audience footage, but the two events are not the same at all. Woodstock was a phenomenon. Monterey was a concert and it was unique in that it showed the world the new Aquarian age, the hippie, psychedelic generation. But Woodstock showed a nation; it was huge in many, many, many ways.

In terms of your perspectives, why do you think these films maintain a place for themselves? Why do you think they remain relevant?

Well, they are touched on for social and political change in America and the world also. The world that is depicted in Monterey is completely different than the world that existed before Monterey Pop. People didn't dress that way, they didn't act that way, and music didn't sound that way. And by the time of Woodstock, well Woodstock was not a financial success. But as far as the documentary was concerned, it was a huge success. But it didn't make happen anything on its own, but it gave momentum and validation to what was happening within the country and globally: perhaps with middle class countries, in every aspect.

And the homework had been done by the ... well, the bands knew how to perform with the new electronic equipment, but more importantly, probably, is the sound engineer was a genius and knew how to do their job. And the staging and the filming all came together for a moment to communicate a brand new mindset which has remained the protocol and the standard for everything that came afterwards. I mean the first election of Barack Obama, when he gave his acceptance speech with his family in Chicago, I believe it was, all the staging and the sound and everything was just like Woodstock, except for the video cams which now project images on screens, that wasn't possible. Woodstock left everything behind. It was like a brand new day and it was so ... the public and the world were ready for it. Not the entire world, but I mean that world that embraced modernity.

And I believe every aspect, social, political, artistic, musical was changed forever. It seemed like it was changing at Monterey, but by the end of Woodstock, it was changed. It would never, never be the same, never. And the gestalt, the combination of audience and all the different kinds and genres of music launched a brand new world for the youth of America and for the world.... The 1960s music, that culture, took everything to the extreme as it existed then. The amplifier.... I like the metaphor of turning the volume now up to ten, which literally was done and you can see that with certain groups' performances. But there was also represented the traditional stuff in the form of Ravi Shankar and Joan Baez, but historically, today, looking back on it, I don't think too many young people today know anything about Ravi Shankar or Joan Baez.

That particular sound is what I am talking about: that sound and that performance style. The in your face, wild as hell, "fuck you, we're doing our own thing and we're not part of what the old world has," where it is now the way that people live. And it's kind of amazing, and it's been quite a number of years, that exposure to those two events, and probably the films of those events, are today still outlawed in many countries in the world. You can get a prison sentence in many countries, even Russia as recently as with Pussy Riot, you know, doing that with music. In a way, rock and roll was against the law. I'm sure the showing of Woodstock and the movie is against the law in South Africa and Greece. I believe my performance and Hendrix's performance were cut out of the film because it was considered just too shocking and demoralizing.

So there were different versions for some international theaters?
   Yes.

It's hard to picture the film without those two things.
   Yes, it is. It's kind of defaming the film. The amazing thing about both of those films is that every part of the film is radical. And I say it in a social-

political sense. But just dressing that way, just acting that way, was really radical. So an amazing change took place and I think that only in America can something happen like that. I don't know. But, in those two years, an amazing change took place in America and it was like the invention of the fork, really. Before the fork came around, people probably didn't think they needed a fork, but as soon as forks showed up, people said, "I want it, I'll take a dozen of those." Because eating with a spoon and a knife was awkward and when Woodstock happened, I think, not the old people of the world, but the young people of the world who were bored and dissatisfied in the middle class countries where they could see and hear about it said, "Yeah, I'm going to do that," exactly like that.

And then it was, I don't know, maybe ten years later that we had the new generation of musicians who had grown up on the music of *Monterey Pop* and *Woodstock* and they could play everything, just like that. And that wasn't what they played. They invented their own music, but that was their "school" that they went to, they went to that "school": the school of Monterey and Woodstock. They went to that school and then you have heavy metal, thrash, punk and the second wave explosion that happened, which shocked the world also. This is very different than Elvis Presley and James Dean. Those phenomena tended to be egocentric … not that Woodstock and Monterey weren't egocentric. But it did have a basis in a new community. A new social-political-global community, including particularly England and then it eventually expands all over the whole planet. Today, that kind of behavior and that kind of music is the standard for every free nation on the planet.

So in terms of that lasting effect and also the radicalism you talked about, do you think that both films have accurately represented and defined the counterculture for following generations?

Yes, I think so. It was such a huge thing that it is hard to simplify it. And historians love to simplify things, you know? To talk about the Beatnik culture, you can say okay, they invented a literary style of poetry, a fashion style in a way of dressing, and perhaps drugs a little bit. But when you get into Woodstock, that generation collectively affected every single aspect of modern life as we know it today. I think you can trace every single thing that we have today back to Woodstock and Monterey. And that includes, because it was so radical, that the status quo was destroyed. We're not going to dress that way, we're not going to make amplifiers that way anymore, we're not going to make music that way, we're not going to take drugs that way, we're not going to talk that way, we're not going to walk that way, we're going to believe new things. No, it wasn't that we're going to believe new things, we *are* believing, we are dressing a new way, we're acting a new way, we're thinking a new way, we're going a new way. This is our brand new world. Here it is, right here. You can see hints of it in Monterey, and then at Woodstock, there it was. And we would travel around the world playing our music and we would go somewhere and the audience was sort of like pre–Monterey or Monterey, and after Woodstock, we would go somewhere in 1971 and '72 and the audience would be just like Woodstock.

So it seems as if the cameras being there insured that these would become the works that they are. If the cameras hadn't been there do you think that these events would have lasted in public memory?

Oh no, I don't think so. But it's not just the cameras being there, because like I said, those camera people did have an experience and history. They were documenting political filmmaking. I don't know about Pennebaker's people but the *Woodstock* people did. And it does not have the feel of a PBS documentary on poverty in the Appalachians or something. But they took those techniques and they created the gestalt that is *Woodstock*. It could have turned into something else. I mean they could have had the footage to do so.

There were incredible, unbelievable problems in putting the *Woodstock* film together because they did not have soundboards and they didn't sync up the sound and the visuals. The sound editor who went on to receive ... she received lots of awards and things from Hollywood. A lot of those people did afterwards, and they have been in the business. They went really an extra mile and they did things in depicting the event that went beyond realism. It was not a documentary in the old school way. *Monterey* was, but *Woodstock* wasn't anymore.

It had cross-editing, the stop-frame, the freeze-frame, the matting as they call it where you see three images on the screen. And the screen was big, you know. And *Monterey Pop* was not on a big screen [it was originally, a television special]. But *Woodstock* was on the big Hollywood screen. And it was a bigger ... it was more music, longer, bigger and by today's standards, I think it still stands up. *Monterey* doesn't stand up but *Monterey* paved the way for *Woodstock* for sure. And I don't think it could have happened anywhere except in America. And it was in many ways a mistake. You know, the size of the audience, the success of it, the bands, and the company allowing, I mean it's unbelievable that the "fuck" cheer got allowed to be put in that film. There were a lot of things that just sneaked right on by that might be problematic today.

So going into the events themselves there wasn't much awareness that this could be something that would be historic. Did you have any idea you would be performing to such a massive audience?

No. Because as far as I'm concerned, I went there [Woodstock] on Thursday because I was aware that there were going to be lots of bands and I wanted to see lots of bands. But the massiveness happened by accident. Five to ten times more people came than they were ready for. The miracle is that the staging and the sound system and everything allowed it to be appreciated and reach the audience.

There's the genius in it, you know. I don't think anybody came to be part of history except maybe some management of bands said it's important for you to be there because it's going to be a big deal. But for me, it was just an exciting, fun event that I wanted to be at. And I wanted to see what the other bands were performing and I had no idea that it would be historic in any way. Because we weren't thinking about the future; we were only thinking about the present. I mean when you're twenty years old or something you're not thinking about making history.

The other phenomenon that was with *Woodstock* that wasn't with *Monterey* was that it had a soundtrack album, which allowed people to hear the sound in their home. There were not a lot of home visual recorders in everybody's house. Nowadays people can, you know, see visuals anywhere on their handheld devices, or tablets, their computers, they go to theaters. People had to wait to see *Woodstock* in a theater and they had to go to the theater to see it. I don't know if VHS home video came up, but I don't even know if it existed then. So what did come out the gate right away was the soundtrack album. Three albums which gave you the entire spectrum of this new cultural, musical phenomenon there, and all those songs not only expressed different styles, introducing electric music to the world ... but they also expressed a lot of different attitudes and excitement which had not been shared before by a generation.

And it was completely, completely detached from the status quo. Richard Nixon is in the White House; I'm sure people hated it. The older generation hated it. They hated it. Really, for real. Hated it. But they could not stop it. It was impossible and people were not listening to this music on the kind of stereo hi-fi systems that we have today. They were listening to it on old things. It was amazing. And it went all around the world, giving us today, Beyoncé, singing at the presidential inauguration, giving us a black family in the White House, giving us gay marriage, legalized marijuana.

Colors, there were no colors back then. None of the colors, literally I mean the chemical composition of colors was invented around the 1960s. We went from black and white all the way up to the pixels that we have now. What is it, like a million, two million, five million pixel combinations of color? Back then, in the '50s people wore t-shirts with nothing on them, white t-shirts, you know. And now it's standard, just taken for granted.

Everything that Woodstock and Monterey had, everything is taken for granted now, and are still despised and hated in traditional cultures, orthodox cultures. The lifestyle, the sound, the attitude is still alive and moving. I don't think it can be stopped. And the amazing thing is that it was transportable. It was transportable by word of mouth, but it was something you had to experience. And half a million people experienced it, along with the people at Monterey. They wanted it and experienced it and then the soundtrack album came out, which is kind of considered old-fashioned now, but it traveled around the world and it's still available and you can easily get it many ways.

You can get music now by just downloading it on your devices. But it wasn't always the case. You had to go to a store and there wasn't a place in the store that sold this kind of music. It's hard to believe but there wasn't. It was the creation of a new genre, a new product, a new genre. And the film, especially when it came out and you could take it home and show it on a device, you know it was transportable. And I heard that when the Iranian revolution came and the Shah was overthrown and the Ayatollah got put in, that revolution was brought about by tape cassettes. In that his voice was transported across borders and miles by tape cassettes. So in a way, that similar sort of thing happened. That technology did not exist before that. Nobody wants to go back to mono sound. Nobody wants to go back to Doris Day music.

And as you said, you see it as being taken for granted.

It's taken for granted that you are going to show up and you're going to be dressed wild and crazy, you're going to perform loud music through electricity, and you're going to be doing your own thing. And if you do your thing too crazily, they'll arrest you. But also, it started that phenomenon of having a free space which existed before Monterey and Woodstock but not for the same group of people. I mean there had been, going back 200 years, they would have revivals and church religious things where people would gather: maybe 50,000, 100,000 people for dramatic events. And they'd camp out and they'd have speeches and music and stuff. A lot of what we did was illegal, like recreational drugs and that sort of thing, but when it was discovered that you could take over a space, a physical space, in the case of Monterey and the Monterey fairgrounds, and the case of Woodstock in the town of Bethel and Max Yasgur's farm, and it would be a safe space for you and your people to do their thing.

And this language makes sense today, but it didn't back then. Then, the people who were there would take the experience and the altered consciousness and go off and do it again. It's considered quite common now to have gatherings like this that go on. Although, multi-day events were banned in lots of states and became very problematic because people realized that young people could have sex and they could use drugs and it was morally and legally problematic. But they didn't stop it because it still happens all over. It happens all over the world in the middle class countries I've performed in. Many, many Woodstock- and Monterey Pop–like events all over the western world.... And they are always the same. Because they were the first, and that's always exciting.

You have also been featured in several other narrative films, including Gas-s-s-s *and* Zacharia. *Starting with* Gas-s-s-s, *how did the film and the music come together? How was the creative process managed?*

Oh, well, that was nothing. It was Roger Corman's last film [for AIP] I believe and obviously he just wanted to do something to cash in on the youth culture, because he wasn't a hippie or anything like that. And the music, I mean, I remember management got us in the film. They must have just said, "Do you want to be in the film?" And management said there's this money and then we did it, you know? But we were just there and they asked me that day, right there, they said, we need a song about, I don't know ... they might have given me a title or something: "The World That We All Live In," and I wrote it in ten minutes. We went through it once and then we performed it for the film. That was it! And then I have a scripted part in there where I got to say something about, I don't know, whatever it is, and it was just wacky, goofy stuff.

I don't know who was involved in the writing of the film. I think I have a book and I don't know that I got off the Internet.... I don't know if the book existed and Corman decided to make it into a film or whether the film existed and then made into a book. [The book by Burt Hirschfeld was based upon the screenplay by George Armitage]. And then when for some crazy reason I don't understand, the people who performed the music in the film were not on the soundtrack album! And Barry Melton from Country Joe and the Fish was involved in the production of the soundtrack album. But the soundtrack album is completely different from the ... they probably got into a licensing beef or something. It remains an esoteric sort of film to this day. It was Corman's last. But he made those campy "B" films or whatever you call them. *Zachariah* was really quite different in that the theater company was involved.

The Firesign Theater?

Yeah ... the story and the script was part of the new generation, you know. That was Zachariah's quest for truth or something. In the same way they threw in a lot of random shit. And we just did what we were told and I wrote a couple songs pretty much on the spur of the moment as I remember, and rehearsed them, and did it. ... *Gas-s-s-s* was not rehearsed, not much of a production, but *Zachariah* was more of a production. George Englund was more of a producer and director than Corman, as far as money was concerned … spending money on it. But both films just disappeared. They were ridiculous. They probably disappeared because they weren't sincere endeavors by integral and organic parts of the new generation. They were just commercial movie-business people wanting to cash in in some way and make a few bucks off of this new hippie thing. And maybe they did.

And that's not a bad thing, but it's radically different than at Monterey and Woodstock, which was very organic and commerciality was not a motivator for those. But it had entertainment value. I saw *Gas-s-s-s* within the last ten years at a museum. They showed it and they had me say a few words about it. It's really a stupid film. And the young college kids, I think they agreed with me that it was stupid! I mean it was hard to relate to. It's like they threw in everything, you know, Native Americans, motorcycles, stings, drive-in theater. Who even knows what a drive-in theater is nowadays?

And a Hells Angels–like group playing golf, right?

Yeah, it was an outsider's attempt to make something for the insider. As they hadn't a clue, it obviously failed.

Was Zachariah *a little bit more involved because of the connection to the Firesign Theater?*

Well, Firesign wasn't there on the set when we were there. We were there a couple of weeks. So there wasn't a lot of that involvement there. And George Englund, the director, wasn't a young guy from the new generation, so he just approached it like just making another film. And Firesign Theater wasn't … they weren't really a part of, I don't know. Agitprop and that sort of thing were around but I don't, in my mind, include them in the Aquarian age explosion that I was talking about. Although they did incorporate many aspects of the mindset of the Aquarian age, I never think of them as being part of it … the Love Generation for some reason. And I'm not sure why. I mean they were making pretty old-fashioned philosophical statements in *Zachariah* which is Zachariah's quest for the truth. Well Zachariah is based on a biblical character, I believe, which is pretty old school.

There wasn't a lot of that going on. It didn't have political teeth to it or social either in some ways. I mean they do smoke a joint at one point and somebody gets called a "fag" at one point. But it was a casual attempt, that's what Hollywood does, the entertainment industry does. And the entertainment industry was trying to figure out how it could get on this new bandwagon. I don't know that they ever did really figure it out.

Were you and the band comfortable with your names being featured so prominently with Gas-s-s-s *and* Zachariah?

Oh, I don't even remember that we were aware of it being featured prominently. I mean sure, we're egomaniacs, but why would we care? It's free publicity.

So even if the film is tainted, your name was out there.

Yeah, right. Yeah, that's good.

Any idea why your voices weren't included in the Gas-s-s-s *soundtrack album, though Barry Melton's [lead guitarist for the Fish] work in terms of scoring the picture was included?*

It was very confusing. I don't know the year of *Zachariah* but I think the group was breaking up and Barry went off and did his own thing. I remember at one point I got the album and listened to it and thought, "What the hell!?! I'm not on the album? What the hell happened here?" Actually, as I remember it, the soundtrack album sounded like *Hair* in a way. It was kind of a Broadway production. [The album featured Robert Corff on vocals. Corff was the star of both *Hair* and *Gas-s-s-s*.] But the movie itself wasn't like that. We played rock and roll in the movie. I don't know, confusing.

Did you see the role of music changing within film in the late 1960s and early 1970s?

No, not at all. I did have hope that it would change and that you would see rock and roll soundtracks. What you do see jumping right to today is rock and roll playing an incredible role in television drama, but not in movies. And it's really kind of a locked shop there. Like Randy Newman's father worked in film soundtrack music, you know. For Hollywood, the music that is put into films is put on at the very last minute. It's not an integral part of the film. I think there have been some films that have, like the *The Graduate* incorporated Simon and Garfunkel. But Simon and Garfunkel is not The Who nor is Santana, or Country Joe and the Fish. Hollywood really didn't know what to do with electric rock and roll as soundtrack. I remember getting really excited thinking, "Wow, we're going to get a lot of opportunities to employ rock and roll, electric music, this new 1960s & 1970s music to film," but that never happened. Randy Newman did go on but the symphonic music and basic themes stuck; *2001* came out and employed several hundred year old music. Symphonic sounds, a Strauss waltz, Erik Satie's music became something of the point.

Keeping in mind how mainstream Hollywood theater operates, it makes *Woodstock* and *Monterey Pop* even more remarkable because they didn't find that place in the regular theaters for a while. But that has never been a follow-through, I mean Metallica had a quite successful documentary and The Who had their *Tommy* film, and *Hair, Jesus Christ Superstar*, and occasionally, Broadway shows have been transferred onto film. But when you go to a theater and it really is an exception to hear rock and roll as the soundtrack part of a Hollywood movie in the last fifty years.

And I don't know why, but I would venture a guess that it is economic. Because as I said, and I have had some experience in licensing, because people will say, we are going to use your song in the film and the licensing aspect of it happens in the last 10 percent of the film. It's the editing, the acting, all of that, and that's the important part. And then they think of what kind of music and sound they are going to put to it. Like I said, television and the small screen uses rock 'n' roll a lot, all the time, to create tension and that sort of thing. In *Hamburger Hill*, they used "Fixin' to Die Rag" but that was the acoustic version, not the electric version.

And then there is the union, too. I think has something to do with it. In Hollywood, the union rates for a symphony orchestra.... It's still surprising to me that you go to a really modern film and you essentially hear the same kind of scoring that you would have heard behind the film in Charlie Chaplin's time. The fidelity of it has changed, but it really is still not very creative. But it still works. They still build that tension. They also have used electronic music. They kind of just jumped twenty years ahead and Hollywood used a lot of electronic stuff in films for building tension and that sort of thing. But electronic music existed at the turn of the last century. That's not new. So as far as Hollywood films are concerned, addressing this issue of 1960s and 1970s electric rock and roll, I think rock and roll is still radical.

So a film like Easy Rider *at the time would have been an exception to the rule even with this new generation of filmmakers?*

Oh yeah, because *Easy Rider* demanded, because of the subject matter, demanded that it have '60s rock and roll sound to it. It wouldn't have made any sense, you know. But that's a specific film with a specific message for a specific audience. And *The Graduate* also.... Aside from that I can't think of any. I mean, if you have a rock band and you set out to make music providing sound for film, you're not going to make any money.

I just thought of Harold and Maude *as well, and obviously that seems to be along the same lines as* The Graduate *where it's not obviously Country Joe and the Fish or Hendrix being featured.*

But *Harold and Maude* was never a mainstream film, I don't think. It's an art film and I think I may have seen it but I don't know what the music was to it.

It was Cat Stevens primarily.

Well, Cat Stevens is really pop rock. What I think about is straight-ahead Santana, The Who, loud, in your face rock and roll. And that is what has never made it, maybe because it detracts from the action on the big screen. And it doesn't detract from the action in the small screen, television, for some reason. When you watch *CSI* or modern TV dramas ...though in melodramas, they don't use rock and roll. It's a whole separate world unto itself, the movie soundtracks.

In terms of both good and bad associations, did your experiences with film and being featured in film somewhat mirror some of your peers at the time? Were there musicians that were not really happy with the presence of cameras?

Well, it's always awkward being filmed, I think. For live musicians, we're not used to that. But in the end, you had anticipation that it would affect your career or affect your music in some way, and it never did. That's the odd thing. You know these appearances in these documentaries and whatever, we didn't alter or act in any way and it didn't increase our audience in any way, whereas, *Woodstock* and *Monterey* did. Nothing else, as far as I know, did.

It's hard to imagine, say Janis Joplin being framed within the media without that performance of "Ball and Chain" that makes its way into Monterey Pop. *But, from what you're saying here, it's not as if this necessarily was a make or break thing for folks, at least going into it.*

No, no, it's an exception when that happens, when you have Janis' best performance, yes, that really was very important to her career, and Whitney Houston singing that song in *The Bodyguard*, that was very important to her career. But generally speaking, I think that it's live performances for performing musicians in rock 'n' roll that makes or breaks you. Not your appearances in a film. You're able to think that because it's easy, but the reality is, really, for live performers and probably everybody, you have to go out there and you have to do one-night stands. You have to build your audience and your audience is live, it's not in theaters, so it's a whole different animal. I have had that experience with working with actors and they would say they're shocked always that there are no retakes, there is no editing. This controversy over Beyoncé lip syncing.... It's one mindset, a superstar kind of mindset, but for the average live performer they have to go out there and savor the mistakes and see what's going to happen. It's that excitement. The excitement of we're going to see what's going to happen that creates the adventure. That certainly was a part of Woodstock and Monterey. We're going to see what happens here.

So the filming of music being played live, like it was in those documentaries, was something that was generally welcomed by bands then?

I don't think we had much.... I don't think bands really cared about that. Management might have cared as far as money was concerned. But I don't think the bands gave a shit. When we were performing, I mean … I was surprised when Mike Wadleigh took me down to L.A. and showed me the footage, because I didn't even realize they were filming. Although, when you see the cameras on stage, how could you ignore that? But when you're performing live, you're just concentrating on doing your performance and on the audience. You're not concentrating on the cameras. And for rock and roll bands, I think that's what they're doing. We're concentrating on the performance and the audience; we're not playing to a camera. But there are people who do play to cameras, like Whitney and Beyoncé. There are people who can do both of those things, but I think that's an exception to the rule. You could play to a camera and you could play live. It's kind of multi-tasking and a gift that some people have, but it's not in the average person. You know to us it means, you're making an extra hundred bucks because they're filming. Really. That's all it means. You can't wait. It takes so long for a film to come out anyway. You can't wait around for a film to make you famous. You'll starve to death.

McDonald's interview highlighted several key insights that stress the usability of film and music to various audiences, including to the participants themselves. As a subject of documentary film and as a narrative character in feature films, McDonald's experiences certainly point to the fact that the process of incorporating and using music within film was not and in many cases still isn't necessarily an extensively choreographed operation, by any means. Yet, as a finished product at the time and in retrospect, music fulfills a central role and becomes a necessary ingredient in a complex mixture of influence and voice.

Additionally, issues connected to genre and conventions exist on multiple levels when we talk about the interaction of film and music. For instance, the boundaries established by McDonald in qualifying film and music into certain realms like: pop, rock, electric rock, classical scores, etc., intersect with concepts of film, like mainstream films, art films, redemptive, and expendable works. These concepts, as dictated by studio interest, artist interest, and audience interest help to position each film's importance and inclusion or exclusion as a piece of countercultural … culture.

As a totality, both music and film were important expressions and molders of the counterculture's identity and since, the legacy of the movement and those that identify or identified with it. Whatever way those films fell into the public's mind, they all have become part of a canon of works in popular culture that are a part of history's narrative of time, the movement, and the lasting influence of a wealth of voices and perspectives that made up the counterculture. McDonald, as a key figure of the time and as a figure with feet in both mediums, alerts us to the fact that the narrative and meaning of the counterculture and the time period is still in flux. Thanks to the music and the films made at this time (and since) generations to come will have the same capability to discuss, debate, and make sense of a time so rich partially because of its ability to be documented or captured as events unfolded at eye level.

14. Bringing the 1960s to Life: An Interview with Director Robert Greenwald

In the digital age, a great deal of potential power comes from bringing history to the big screen. Dominant narratives and associations find their way into the public mindset and their conceptions of history that are brought forth by films interpreting and documenting history. Naturally, this may be for good or for ill: pulling in people to stories of the past that they may have never been exposed to before, or bastardizing history in the eyes of those that have lived through or studied the events portrayed on screen. As baby boomers continue to age, there is a natural want to discern, determine, or interrogate what their own lives and historical paths have meant. One pathway that allows for this reflection is through films looking at the times and at targets like the counterculture.

The counterculture of the 1960s and early 1970s is far from immune to such treatments. Films like *Fear and Loathing in Las Vegas* (1998) or even *Spinal Tap* (1984) take aim in the context of their own time periods at portraying and making sense of the lineage and legacy of this time and a major movement within it. From earnest to humorous, the possibilities to frame and interpret or reinterpret historical events for the general public falls upon Hollywood in a way that many academics would welcome, but are not likely to get in terms of exposure.

So how does one begin to portray something like the counterculture in a fixed amount of time for an audience that seeks to be entertained as well? Robert Greenwald took on this task of creating the sights and sounds of the counterculture for the general public via a treatment of the controversial life and legacy of Abbie Hoffman. Greenwald, an Emmy and Golden Globe nominee as well as a Peabody and Robert Wood Johnson Award winner, directed and produced *Steal This Movie* in 2000. A political and social activist, Hoffman's media-savvy Yippie Party became a testament to rebellion and meaning for some and a representation of style over substance for others.

Part of the challenge of making the film, in addition to taking on a disputed figure in a disputed time, was to recreate the zeitgeist. Along with costuming, set design, etc., an important foundational part of creating the film was to offer music that would communicate the ethos of the times, as well as to represent within the film the role that music, like other forms of popular culture, played in the creation, maintenance, and dissolution of the 1960s counterculture in America.

To better understand and to provide some juxtaposition to the perspectives of someone on the other side of the lens with the last chapter's focus on County Joe McDonald, we sat down with Greenwald in the hopes of understanding how music factors into the creation of films. As many chapters have shown, the process of collecting and incorporating music can sometimes be a haphazard one. Yet, as we have also seen, this incorporation becomes a main artery in the circulatory system of a finished filmic work. The following interview obviously does not represent a comprehensive view of all directors or all films (much like the discussion with one musician within a body of work that has come to filmically define the counterculture). Still, such conversations remove the veil from the production process and offer additional concrete footholds in determining the life of popular culture products in everyday life, especially in constructing historical narratives and identities for the mass public.

To begin, I'm wondering, as the producer and director of the film Steal This Movie, *what role do you see music playing in the finished product?*

Well, to state the obvious, music and the '60s had a very close, intimate and important marriage. So, at the beginning of the conception of the film, I was always playing '60s music, listening to it, dreaming to it and didn't know the specifics early on because there are the realities of budget and creativity, but I was very committed to using it as an additional element in the storytelling.

As you were coming into the creative process of putting this together did you have at least some inklings or hopes for songs that you might be able to feature, even knowing the legalities that might need to be pursued?

Yes, I don't remember, you know it was quite a few years ago, I don't remember which were the "dream" hopefuls or the "must-haves" or the "I'll die" ones. But, there is such an extraordinary selection of music from that period and then as we worked on it further, we had Evyen Klean, the music supervisor, had Steve Earle, who played a big role in the album, had Danny

Goldberg, who was the producer of the album; there were lots of different people with good and creative ideas.

And that follows up a little bit to the next question; in terms of the filmmaking process, what is the relationship like between the folks you mentioned, Evyen, Mader [the film's scorer] and others in constructing the musical sound of the film? Did the process entail you going back and forth with each other or did you ultimately have a vision you tried to communicate?

No, I think it wasn't an either-or situation, in fact, it was both. I had some specific ideas of, as I was saying before, communicating non-verbally, if you will, through music, using the image, using that stock footage that we found back then and integrating it into footage from that we filmed ... using music to tie all that footage together. So that was the key part of what I was thinking. We worked very closely with Mader in trying to find a sound that had a resonance for today and yet also moved the narrative line along, deepening some of the emotional responses, and deepening some of the tension, and then with Evyen, Steve and Danny, we scoured for existing music and found ways that Steve was able to create quite a great soundtrack, bringing in artists, bringing in favors. I remember a session in Los Angeles where Ringo [Starr] came to play. And so, there were lots of strong ideas. Ultimately, it's the job of the director to inspire or pick and choose or a combination of both.

I hadn't been aware of the role that Earle played in addition to, of course, being featured in the soundtrack. Was this a personal relationship or was he interested in the project because of the subject matter?

Danny Goldberg really gets the credit. Danny's an old friend, acquaintance. I had not wanted to impose on him and then, I don't remember exactly, but he heard about it, we talked, and he said that he would be happy to take on the soundtrack, take on the album, and then he brought Steve in. Steve has extraordinary connections in the music community, was able to use them and reach out to people, and the fact it was about Abbie, the fact it was political, the fact it had something to say, was a significant added inducement.

Does the process, in regards to going back and forth here, create a challenge in terms of how the soundtrack versus the score is being created? Or is there hope to have all interested parties involved in all aspects to get the continuity?

Well, there were separate skill sets. It's one skill set to write original music. It's another skill set to find existing songs or to redo them, as Steve was able to do with several pieces in the film. My constant job working with each of them and with the editor was weaving it together so that the music score bled seamlessly into the existing track which then bled back into the score. We tried to tie it together so that the music didn't stop, to have an oldie but goodie, but it was integrated and driving the storyline.

This is just a quick aside out of curiosity. As a director, is it possible to propel a film forward with the soundtrack by itself or is the score just a very necessary part to the process?

Probably by itself I wouldn't have done it, but tied into images, tied into storytelling, tied into characters you love and care about and are involved with, it's an essential part of the process. But if you removed all of those, I don't think the scoring in and of itself would do it.

Did you have any kind of frame of mind as to how you wanted to portray the 1960s, how to bring about the ethos of the era and Hoffman's interaction with it? Especially say for film-goers that might not have been born at the time, what was the ultimate kind of ambience that you wanted to create?

Well it was a layered-textured one that we, both story-wise and element-wise, had the characters, had the music, we had sound effects, we had visuals and bring them all together trying to replicate some of the energy and drive of that period was a challenge throughout.

According to an article I read in the New York Times *that's dated 2004, "How to Make a Guerrilla Documentary," it was stated in there that Abbie Hoffman was a friend. Is that correct?*

I knew him. I guess you would say a friend. Given that he was hiding in the underground, he was not somebody that I could be in constant touch with, but I knew Abbie when he was in the underground. He would reach out to me with different disguises and aliases. I met him in fact when he was underground at a restaurant in Los Angeles a couple of times. I was able to try to be helpful to him in certain ways, and then when he surfaced, when he was above ground, I was in contact with him a little more frequently. I also lived in Venice, California, very close to his former wife, Anita, who is portrayed in the film, and their son, America.

Did that personal knowledge of Abbie, and of course of his family, did that bring to mind any kind of connections that you thought would be important to make? Was there anything especially that Abbie would have enjoyed seeing in the film or hearing in the film?

I don't think so. It made the personal connection another element in raising the bar for the film, in terms of the integrity, in terms of the politics, in terms of the accuracy of the portrayal while also trying to keep it dramatic. But I don't associate my connection with Abbie or Anita with any particular musical choices.

Why did you choose to incorporate contemporary musicians like Steve Earle and Ani DiFranco, musicians that could easily be labeled as political activists, along with being musicians themselves ... versus having the original selections within the film?

Well, there were a couple reasons. The fact that they were activists obviously was a big plus in terms of their caring, compassion, their connection to the material. And then from a practical point of view, if you take an existing piece of music, you can have a brilliant music editor, you can cut it out, you can slice it and dice it. But it's a world of difference when you can have somebody doing a version for you both from a simple technical point of view, can you extend this down, can you slow this up, can you drop out here, can you come back. And then, in terms of giving the music a kind of more contemporary feel, you know, Ani and Steve and others were able to do that and, I think, contribute very handsomely to the film and its impact, and the fact that people continue to see it, I continue to get emails about it.

Was the participation of Ani DiFranco, Bonnie Raitt, etc., due to the Steve Earle connections that you mentioned earlier or was that a different process to obtain those artists?

Well Ani was, and Danny Goldberg used to manage her so he was also very helpful, but Ani was, I don't remember how that came about. I just remember she had at the time a manager, I think in Buffalo, who I kept calling and calling and calling until we were able to get through. And then she was in Los Angeles and met her and she went out and did it.

There are so many different images and sounds and associations that filmmakers, along with many other creators of popular culture products, will utilize to symbolize the 1960s: whether it's Jimi Hendrix burning his guitar at Monterey or visions of people marching upon Washington. With the music that was incorporated, was there any kind of concern on your part about how much some of this music had been utilized before to symbolize the 1960s? That there might be any kind of potential triteness coming out or did these pieces seem to fit very well?

Well, that was part of the value of having some of the pieces redone, like "War," which I thought was given a terrific new energy and vitality. You can't worry too much when you're in this insane job being a director; you know where you can never get out of bed in the morning. Everything's been done by somebody in some place, sometimes better, sometimes worse. So you kind of plow ahead. I just knew that the music was really important, so I made a series of decisions to utilize it as much as possible.

Did you consult any other films just to kind of get a bearing of how music had been utilized with portrayals of the 1960s or was it more of an organic process that was instilled within you throughout?

It was pretty organic. I mean there again I said there is music or there are films that would jump up. I don't remember which ones I screened. I actually did a lot more screening for the integration of the stock footage, you know the stuff that was already shot and then the stuff I shot so that could work together very closely. That took a lot of time and energy, and then as I say, music and sound effects helps weave it all even closer. But I don't remember any particular film that I said "this is the one that's the guideline."

I'm wondering, what role do you see as a director in film playing in managing public memory, of the counterculture especially? Can the incorporation of music be either a helpful thing or a hindrance in some regards? How does film help maintain what the public believes and thinks of the 1960s?

Well you know memory is an interesting, strange beast. There was just a series in the *New York Review of Books* about memory and how an individual had written an autobiography and there were certain things in it and his brother called him up and said, "You know that's not true." And he said, "No, it must be. I'm sure of it." And his brother proved to him that something he believed for all these years was factually inaccurate, it never happened or happened in a different way. So, I think memory is a series of impressions. I think it's a changing universe that varies as we age, as we get further away from the experience. I think that film and cultural references are actually quite critical, in terms of what I call emotional memory, which is much more important than any list of facts. And, to that sense, images, music combined with images, sound effects with images are very, very important in giving people an emotional feeling, "oh yes, I remember how I felt back then."

I think you mentioned before that you can't take everything too close to heart or be overly concerned about things as you're in the process of filmmaking. However, is it somewhat concerning or encouraging that your text might become almost a kind of form of historical memory for those following these events?

You know when you say I'm making a movie, I can't remember, there is that great quote and I'm going to paraphrase it badly but it's something about you start like a stagecoach ride I think was the metaphor somehow and you're going to change the world and then by the end of the movie you just want to get to your destination. So, there's lots of highs and lows with the process and often one varies from incredible grandiosity about changing the universe to just hoping and keeping your fingers crossed you'll get through the next day shooting. And we certainly had all of those variations. I do think the film had a huge impact on me personally and led to ultimately a series of decisions which led me to begin the work I've been doing for the past seven, eight, nine years. I'm doing documentary-political stuff. And I think Abbie's spirit and passion and integrity that I tried to absorb when I was directing the movie stayed with me.

This is a question that hearkens back to prior film experience. Did the filmmakers of the late 1960s, early 1970s influence you in terms of standards that were set that you think were not only important perhaps for you as a director but for the industry?

Well those were brilliant directors, brilliant films so, and it's never linear, it's not like you see one film and then decide, well that's the least of it, I'm going to use that camera angle or that lens or something like that. I just think in general they were breaking down conventional ways of storytelling, opening up the process. But it becomes impressionistic in the way that it impacts other creators and I think it's probably the same with me.

Again, not being a student of this history but being a consumer of it, I find the connections more ephemeral. And in ways I often don't know: you know I'll suddenly be sitting, thinking about a scene for the next documentary and an image from the movie will jump up or suddenly I'll remember, oh wait, somebody brought a song in in the middle of a fight scene or something. It just breaks down the rules, but it's more for me, more general than abstract. It's generally not literal.

In terms of being a producer and director of the film, how does the process of taking care of the legality work, is this something in which you need to approach the artist as well as the publishers, or do the publishers ultimately have the say? Can artists who are very much interested make sure that they are part of the film if they want to be?

Well, nobody can make sure they are part of the film. That is the decision of the director, depending on the film. But, if I remember correctly, it's been awhile, there were two rights you need to secure. The publishing rights and then there is performance rights. Artists sometimes control both, sometimes they control neither. It depends on the artist, the manager, the deals they've had.

Is this legality something that you feel ever limits you as a filmmaker?

Oh, sure. A huge limit. There are songs that you can never get an answer about, some of the songs that are obscenely expensive and with the documentary universe there is something that's called fair use, where you are allowed to use certain clips if they are essential to telling the story. It doesn't exist with music as far as I know. And you've got to go to the record companies, the artists, the managers, and the publishers.

Thanks for your insight. Finally, is it true that this is the second most stolen DVD in history?

(laughing) I hope so. I'm hoping for first. I read that it's *Clerks*. I think that took the first one.

Greenwald's interview gives us a glimpse into the production of a film. Though far from a comprehensive view of how music is incorporated and utilized in film, one can start to gauge the functionality of music and the legality and business of bringing music into film, as well as the ways audiences are able to use it as they decode and take in what is in front of them on the screen. Sometimes ornately orchestrated, sometimes haphazard, and sometimes even the primary focus of film itself, music lives a rich, engrained life in cinema. Music plays a role in shaping the very conception of a time and the films that become representations of it. When it comes to establishing the legacy of a historical time, music provides a shorthand that helps us accept or at least situate ourselves into the sounds as well as the vision of our past. Hearing, in so many ways, is identity, as well as context in how we make sense of the world around us and the worlds we picture before or after us. The director's vision, legal issues, happenstance, use values of audiences, etc., all influence the incorporation and use of film music. The sound, much like the vision, creates a lasting influence when it comes to the life of the film, and even the subject matter or historical time or event taken on.

With all of those contingencies, many filmmakers are happy to negotiate the sometimes long and bureaucratic process of obtaining the right music for a film. Music, whether the focus of the camera's eye itself or as ancillary part to the whole, proves itself often to be a key in the construction, remembrance, and continued use of films as historical texts. Its ability to "influence emotions (Gavin 2006, Bruner 1990), increase cognitive activity (Chebat et al., 2001; Sacks 2008), [and] improve memory (Balch and Lewis 1996)" (Gerlich, Browning, and Westermann 61) demands attention not only as a text of cultural creation, but also as texts of potential historical, social, and political importance. The path taken by Greenwald does show the ways in which there is a sort of humbling practicality of incorporating music into film, but it also showcases the fact that pursuing it is of the utmost importance in shaping the reception and usability of the film by audiences. In framing the counterculture in the 1960s through today it is possible for such "ephemera" to maintain a cheapening role in "today's nostalgia economy" (Vognar), or to be a key signifier in the construction of memory and meaning (with many positions filled in between). Whether ornately orchestrated or captured ever-so-frequently to random events, its place in film is anchored into the completed structure that can for good or ill shape our collective notions of times, places, and events in our history.

Coda

A soundtrack/score is an indispensable part of a movie. On an emotional level, it allows the audience to sympathize with film characters to share their pain, joy, sorrow, happiness, and many other feelings. Music also may drive a story. It can slow or quicken the tempo of the film. This is why a horror movie would not scare its audience when it is shown silently. Robynn Stilwell and Phil Powrie were correct in arguing that "music underlines, emphasizes, inflects, *underscores* the deepest levels of film, structural and emotional [emphasis original]" (xix). From the business perspective, it is a significant part of the profit-generation scheme of the entertainment industry, especially as it observes more and more consolidations of various media corporations. It is, therefore, no surprise that a parent company benefits both from the box office sales and the soundtrack/score sales, not to mention merchandizing, downloading or streaming and DVD sales.

In this book, we have explored the meaning of such an essential part of the cinematic experience. As Self problematized, "Film conveys information through five means: images, written language, spoken language, music, and sound effects. Although three of these tracks are aural, scholarship and reviews have tended to address film primarily as a visual medium" (141). Our work here is partly a response to Self's assessment about the centrality of sound in a film and also an attempt to encourage more studies on how a movie sounds. Our particular focus on the counterculture period enabled us to observe how music and society interacted with each other through cinematic cultural productions during a time when many social norms and expectations were challenged. Social instabilities, Woodstock, sexual revolution, racial politics, and the anti-war movement were just a few examples of issues pertinent to the period and to the themes that movies and its music commented on. Furthermore, movies during the counterculture era played a significant social role in history. Peter Biskind notes that the late 1960s and early 1970s were the time when "film culture permeated American life in a way that it never had before and never has since" (17). Elaine Bapis also adds that "filmmakers found new commercial value for a grittier America between 1965 and 1975" (11). It is our hope as authors that the book illuminated some of the ways in which film music captured the sentiment of the era and framed it for generations.

Of course, a book alone cannot explore all the complexities through which counterculture film soundtracks navigated. But a combination of stories told by movies discussed here can help us understand how small pieces helped make up the overall counterculture. Film music may be forgotten in many instances from academic analyses to conversations after a casual viewing of a film. Acting, camera work, and especially technology-heavy visual effects seem to capture the mind of contemporary moviegoers and soundtracks/scores are oftentimes afterthoughts. But in reality, music reflected countercultural sentiments, underscored counterculture values, and has kept counterculture memories alive to this day. As Donald Costello mentioned, counterculture films "[dealt] with values of the past, of the present, and of the future." They bring both the reality and the fantasy of social and cultural moods (193). Music, simply, was an indispensable part of this cultural memory and value production.

Works Cited

Adinolfi, Francesco. *Mondo Exotica: Sounds, Visions, Obsessions of the Cocktail Generation*. Trans. Karen Pinkus and Jason Vivrette. Durham: Duke University Press, 2008. Print.

Adler, Lou. "Flash Back to the Real Pop Mart." *Los Angeles Times*, 6 July 1997: 9, 60. Print.

All You Need Is Sushi. "Long Live Harold and Maude." *Harold & Maude, Original Soundtrack Recording*. Amazon.com Inc. Web. 10 June 2014.

Allen, Michael. "'I Just Want to Be a Cosmic Cowboy': Hippies, Cowboy Code, and the Culture of a Counterculture." *Western Historical Quarterly* 36 (Autumn 2005): 275–299. JSTOR. Web. 4 June 2014.

Altman, Rick. "Cinema and Popular Song: The Lost Tradition." *Soundtrack Available: Essays on Film and Popular Music*. Ed. Pamela Robertson Wojcik, and Arthur Knight. Durham, NC: Duke University Press, 2001. 19–30. Print.

"Alumni of Distinction." New York Military Academy. 2013. Web. 29 May 2013.

Ammer, Christine. *Unsung: A History of Women in American Music*. Portland, OR: Amadeus Press, 2001. Print.

Appleton, Jon. "Clockwork Orange by Wendy Carlos: Sonic Seasonings by Wendy Carlos." *Computer Music Journal* 24.1 (Spring 2000): 97–98. Print.

Aronowitz, Stanley. *The Death and Rebirth of American Radicalism*. New York: Routledge, 1996. Print.

Auster, Al, and Leonard Quart. "American Cinema of the Sixties." *Cineaste* 13.2 (1984): 4–12. JSTOR. Web. 5 June 2014.

Baker, Glenn A. *Monkeemania: The True Story of the Monkees*. New York: Plexus, 1986.

Bapis, Elaine M. *Camera and Action: American Film as Agent of Social Change, 1965–1975*. Jefferson, NC: McFarland, 2008. Print.

_____. "*Easy Rider* (1969): Landscaping the Modern Western." *The Landscape of Hollywood Westerns: Ecocriticism in an American Film Genre*. Ed. Deborah A. Carmichael. Salt Lake City: University of Utah Press, 2006. 157–181. Print.

Barrios, Richard. *Screened Out: Playing Gay in Hollywood Film from Edison to Stonewall*. New York: Routledge, 2003. Print.

Barron, Lee, and Ian Inglis. "'We're Not in Kansas Any More': Music, Myth and Narrative Structure of *The Dark Side of the Moon*." *Speak to Me: The Legacy of Pink Floyd's Dark Side of the Moon*. Ed. Russell Reising. Burlington, VT: Ashgate, 2005. Print.

Bart, Peter. *BOFFO! How I Learned to Love the Blockbuster and Fear the Bomb*. New York: Miramax Books, 2006. Print.

Bates, Stephen. "Findings." *The Wilson Quarterly* 34.1 (Winter 2010): 12–15. Print.

Beard, Matthew. "Kubrick's Ultra-Violence Finally Makes It on TV." *The Independent*, 18 June 2001: 7. Print.

Bell, Arthur. "Playboy Interview: Wendy/Walter Carlos." *Playboy* 26.5 (May 1979). Print.

Benford, Robert D., and David A. Snow. "Framing Processes and Social Movements." *Annual Review of Sociology* 26.1 (2000): 611–639. Print.

Bennett, Andy. *Remembering Woodstock*. Burlington, VT: Ashgate, 2004. Print.

Benshoff, Harry, and Sean Griffin. *Queer Im-*

ages: *A History of Gay and Lesbian Film in America*. Lanham, MD: Rowman & Littlefield, 2006. Print.

"The Big Idea." Montereyinternationalpopfestival.com. The Monterey International Pop Festival Foundation. 2012. Web. 13 May 2013.

Biskind, Peter. *Easy Riders, Raging Bulls: How the Sex-Drug-and-Rock 'N' Roll Generation Saved Hollywood*. New York: Simon and Schuster, 1999. Print.

"Blood, Sweat and Tears Beat Out Beatles, Cash." *Beaver Country Times*, 13 March 1970: 21. Print.

Blumenthal, Ralph. "Porno Chic: 'Hard-core' Grows Fashionable and Very Profitable." *The New York Times*, 21 January 1973. Web. 7 January 2014.

Bogle, Donald. *Toms, Coons, Mulattoes, Mammies, & Bucks: An Interpretive History of Blacks in American Films*. New York: Continuum, 2006. Print.

_____. *Blacks in American Films and Television: An Illustrated Encyclopedia*. New York: Freeside, 1988. Print.

Booth, Stanley. *Dance with the Devil: The Rolling Stones and Their Times*. New York: Random House, 1984. Print.

Bowman, Rob. *Soulsville U.S.A.: The Story of Stax Records*. New York: Schrimer Trade, 1997. Print.

Briggs, Joe Bob. "Who Dat Man?: *Shaft* and the Blaxploitation Genre." *Cineaste* 28.2 (Spring 2003): 24–29. JSTOR. Web. 9 June 2014.

Bronson, Fred. *The Billboard Book of Number 1 Hits: The Inside Story Behind Every Number One Single on Billboard's Hot 100 from 1955 to Present*. New York: Billboard Books, 2003. Print.

Burlingame, Jon. *Sound and Vision: 60 Years of Motion Picture Soundtracks*. New York: Billboard Books, 2000. Print.

Burnham, Emily. "Classic Silver Screen Revels at the Grand." McClatchy: Tribune Information Services, 22 November 2010. ProQuest. Web. 14 March 2014.

Byrge, Duane. "'Monterey Pop' Feature Kicks Off First Annual Film Fest." *Hollywood Reporter*, 10 February 1987. Monterey Pop Clippings File. Margaret Herrick Library. The Academy of Motion Picture Arts and Sciences.

Calavita, Marco. "'MTV Aesthetics' at the Movies: Interrogating a Film Criticism Fallacy." *Journal of Film and Video* 59.3 (Fall 2007). ProQuest. Web. 21 May 2014.

Canby, Vincent. "Easy Rider (1969)." *The New York Times*. n.d. Web. 21 May 2014.

Carlos, Wendy. "Rachel Elkind-Tourre." Wendy Carlos. n.d. Web. August 26, 2013.

Carson, Tom. "DVD to Own 'The Complete Monterey Pop Festival.'" *GQ: Gentlemen's Quarterly* 76.7 (July 2006): 74.

Carter, David. *Stonewall: The Riots That Sparked the Gay Revolution*. New York: St. Martin's Press, 2004. Print.

Champlin, Charles. "'Midnight Cowboy' Rides Manhattan's Lower Depths: Ride of the 'Midnight Cowboy.'" *Los Angeles Times*, 27 July 1969: P1. Print.

_____. "'Monterey Pop' at Fine Arts Theater." *Los Angeles Times*, 2 May 1969: E9.

"Charles Fox." Allmusic. n.d. Web. 17 February 2009.

"Charles Fox Biography." American International Artists, 2006. Web. 17 February 2009.

Chauncey, George. *Gay New York: Gender, Urban Culture, and the Making of the Gay Male World, 1890–1940*. New York: Basic Books, 1994. Print.

Chion, Michel. *Film, A Sound Art*. Trans. Claudia Gorbman. New York: Columbia University Press, 2009. Print.

Christgau, Robert. "Found Weekend." *Village Voice*. Robertchristgau.com. 14 January 1997. Web. 9 September. 2013.

Christiansen, Rupert. "Must-have movies Harold and Maude (1971) Directed by Hal Ashby: The Classics That Every Film-lover Will Want to Own." *The Daily Telegraph*. 12 May 2006: 30. Print.

Chudacoff, Howard P. *The Age of the Bachelor: Creating an American Subculture*. Princeton, NJ: Princeton University Press, 1999. Print.

"Clockwork in TV Debut." *The Mirror*, 18 June 2001: 17. Print.

"A Clockwork Orange." IMDb.com. n.d. Web. 19 August 2013.

"Clockwork Orange Set for First British TV Screening." *The Herald*, 18 June 2001: 28. Print.

"Clockwork Orange: The X-Rating." Malcolm McDowell.net. n.d. Web. 19 August 2013.

"A Clockwork Orange: X and R." *Kubrick Film Ratings Comparisons*. Angelfire. n.d. Web. 19 August 2013. Print.

Collier, Barnard. "Tired Fans Begin Exodus." *New York Times*, 18 August 1969: A1 Print.

Cooke, Mervyn. *A History of Film Music*. New York: Cambridge University Press, 2008. Print.

Corkin, Stanley. "Sex and the City in Decline: Midnight Cowboy (1969) and Klute (1971)." *Journal of Urban History* 36.5 (2010): 617–633. Print.

Corman, Roger. *How I Made a Hundred Movies in Hollywood and Never Lost a Dime*. New York: Random House, 1990. Print.

Costello, Donald P. "From Counterculture to Anticulture." *The Review of Politics* 34.4 (October 1972): 187–193. JSTOR. Web. 24 February 2014.

Cotner, David. "Janis, Anyone?" *L.A. Weekly*. 17 June 2012. *Monterey Pop* Clippings File. Margaret Herrick Library. The Academy of Motion Picture Arts and Sciences.

"The Counterculture of the 1960s." *CliffNotes*. Houghton Mifflin Harcourt. n.d. Web. 30 May 2014.

"Counterculture of the 1960s." Wikipedia. n.d. Web. 30 May 2014.

"Cover Story: Samuel L. Jackson Brings Back Role of 'Shaft' in New Film." *Jet*, 12 June 2000: 98. ProQuest. Web. 29 July 2014.

Dahl, Bill. "Steppenwolf." Allmusic. n.d. Web. 30 May 2014.

D'Amico, Francesca. "The Revolution Will Not Be Televised, But It Will Be Recorded: Soul, Funk, and the Black Urban Experience, 1968–1979." *The Global Sixties in Sound and Vision: Media Counterculture, Revolt*. Ed. Timothy Scott Brown, and Andrew Lison. New York: Palgrave McMillan, 2014. Print.

Davis, Stephen. *Old Gods Almost Dead: The 40-Year Odyssey of the Rolling Stones*. New York: Broadway Books, 2001. Print.

Dawson, Nick. *Being Hal Ashby: Life of a Hollywood Rebel*. Lexington: University Press of Kentucky, 2009. Print.

Decker, Christof. "'Irony Is a Cheap Shot': Robert Altman, Luis Bunuel, and the Maneuvers of Comic Deconstruction." *Amerikastaudien* 52.1 (2007): 63–79. Print.

"Deep Throat." *Fused Magazine*. n.d. Web. 24 January 2014.

"Deep Throat." IMDb.com. n.d. Web. 7 January 2014.

DeMain, Bill. *In Their Own Words: Songwriters Talk About the Creative Process*. Westport, CT: Praeger, 2004. Print.

Demers, Joanna. "Sampling the 1970s in Hip-Hop." *Popular Music* 22.1 (January 2003): 41–56. JSTOR. Web. 9 June 2014.

Denby, David. "*Midnight Cowboy* by John Schlesinger; Jerome Hellman." *Film Quarterly* 23.1 (Autumn 1969): 20–22. Print.

Dieringer, Maura. "Catching Up with Woodstock Stars." *USA Today*. 13 August 2009: P6d. Print.

di Franco, Philip. *The Movie World of Roger Corman*. New York: Chelsea House, 1979. Print.

Dolenz, Micky. *I'm a Believer: My Life of Monkees, Music, and Madness*. New York: Hyperion, 1993. Print.

"The Drawbacks of Reality." *Time* 7 March 1969. Print.

Dusty Groove America. Dustygroove.com. N.p. n.d. Web. 19 September 2007.

"Easy Rider: Awards." IMDb.com. n.d. Web. 21 May 2014.

"Easy Rider." IMDb.com. n.d. Web. 21 May 2014.

Elley, Derek. "PFA at the BAM." *Films & Filming*. September 1974. *Gas-s-s-s* Clippings File. Margaret Herrick Library. The Academy of Motion Picture Arts and Sciences.

Evans, Mark. *Soundtrack: The Music of the Movies*. New York: Hopkinson and Blake, 1975. Print.

Evans, Mike, and Paul Kingsbury. *Woodstock: Three Days That Rocked the World*. New York: Sterling, 2009. Print.

Fiegel, Eddi. *John Barry: A Sixties Theme*. London: Faber & Faber, 2012. Print.

Finn, Ed, and T. Bone. *The Monkees Scrapbook*. San Francisco: Last Gasp, 1986.

Fiore, Robert L. "The Picaresque Tradition in *Midnight Cowboy*." *Literature/Film Quarterly* 3.3 (1975): 270–276. Print.

Fisher, Hannah. "American War and Military Operations Casualties: Lists and Statistics." The Navy Department Library. U.S. Navy. 13 July 2005. Web. 31 May 2013.

Floyd, Kevin. "Closing the (Heterosexual Frontier): 'Midnight Cowboy' as National Allegory." *Science & Society* 65.1 (Spring 2001): 99–130. Print.

"Fonda Auctions 'Easy Rider' Memorabilia." *USA Today*, 10 October 2007. Web. 21 May 2014.

Fonda, Jane. *My Life So Far.* New York: Random House, 2005. Print.

"Foundation." Montereyinternationalpopfestival.com. The Monterey International Pop Festival Foundation. 2012. Web. 13 May 2013.

Fox, Charles. *Killing Me Softly: My Life in Music.* Lanham, MD: Scarecrow Press, 2010. Print

"Fred Neil, Folk Singer and Composer, 64." *The New York Times,* 11 July 2001: B9. Print.

French, Philip. "Review: Film Appreciation Robert Altman 1925-2006." *The Observer,* 26 November 2006: 12. Print.

Frith, Simon. *Sound Effects: Youth, Leisure and the Politics of Rock 'n' Roll.* New York: Pantheon, 1981. Print.

Gallo, Phil. "'Harold and Maude': Soundtrack Becomes an Instant Collector's Item." *Variety.* 2 June 2008. Web. 20 September 2010.

Garrison, Joshua. "The Teenage Terror in the Schools: Adult Fantasies, American Youth, and Classroom Scare Films During the Cold War." *American Educational History Journal* 36:1 (2009): 3–21. Print.

Gas-s-s-s. Pressbook. American International Pictures, 1970. Print.

Gehrke, Pat J. "Deviant Subject in Foucault and *A Clockwork Orange*: Congruent Critiques of Criminological Constructions of Subjectivity." *Critical Studies in Media Communication* 18.3 (September 2001): 270-284. Print.

Gengaro, Christine Lee. *Listening to Stanley Kubrick: The Music in His Films.* Lanham, MD: Scarecrow Press, 2013. Print.

George, Nelson. *Hip Hop America.* New York: Penguin Books, 2005. Print.

Gerlich, R. Nicholas, Leigh Browning, and Lori Westermanni. "I've Got the Music in Me: A Study of Peak Musical Memory Age and the Implications for Future Advertising." *Journal of College Teaching and Learning* 7.2 (February 2010): 61–69. Print.

Gilliatt, Penelope. "The Current Cinema." *The New Yorker,* 22 March 1969. *Monterey Pop* Clippings File. Margaret Herrick Library. The Academy of Motion Picture Arts and Sciences.

Gimme Shelter. Dir. Albert Maysles, David Maysels, and Charlotte Zwerin. Perf. Mick Jagger, Charlie Watts, Keith Richards, Mick Taylor, Bill Wyman. Maysles Films, 1970.

Gitlin, Todd. *The Whole World Is Watching: Mass Media in the Making and Unmaking of the New Left.* Berkeley: University of California Press, 1980. Print.

Gleason, Ralph J. "Aquarius Wept." Esquire.com. August 1970. Web. 7 January. 2013.

Glitz, Michael. "Harold Loves Maude." *The Advocate.* 1 February 2005: 55. Print.

Goldblatt, Burt. *Newport Jazz Festival: The Illustrated History.* New York: Dial Press, 1977. Print.

Goldman, Vivien. *The Black Chord.* New York: Universe, 1999. Print.

Goldsmith, Melissa Ursula Dawn. "Lounge Caravan: A Selective Discography." *Notes* 61.4 (June 2005): 1060–1083. Print.

Gorbman, Claudia. "Ears Wide Open: Kubrick's Music." *Changing Tunes: The Use of Pre-existing Music in Film.* Eds. Phil Powrie and Robynn Stilwell. Burlington, VT: Ashgate, 2006. Print.

Gordon, Robert. *Respect Yourself: Stax Records and the Soul Explosion.* New York: Bloomsbury, 2013. Print.

Gorman, John. "The Counter Culture in Crisis." *Soundings: An Interdisciplinary Journal* 55.4 (Winter, 1972): 390–407. JSTOR. Web. 5 June 2014.

Grace, Kevin Michael. "Happiness Implosion: Seven Cult Films Chronicle the Collapse of '60s Idealism." *The American Conservative* 10.7 (July 2011): 35–38. ProQuest. Web. 5 June 2014.

Graham, Bill, and Robert Greenfield. *Bill Graham Presents: My Life Inside Rock and Out.* New York: Delta, 1992. Print.

Greenwald, Marilyn. *Cleveland Amory: Media Curmudgeon and Animal Rights Crusader.* Hanover: University Press of New England, 2009.

Gross, Robert L. "Heavy Metal Music: A New Subculture in American Society." *The Journal of Popular Culture* 24.1 (Summer 1990): 119–130. ProQuest. Web. 30 May 2014.

Guerrero, Ed. *Framing Blackness: The African American Image in Film.* Philadelphia: Temple University Press, 1993. Print.

Hall, Mitchell K. "The Vietnam Era Antiwar Movement." *OAH Magazine of History* 18.5 (October, 2004): 13–17. Print.

Harding, Louette. "Jane Fonda's Emotional Workout." *Mail on Sunday.* 26 February 2006: 26. Print.

Helfrich, Ronald. "'What Can a Hippie Contribute to Our Community?'': Culture Wars, Moral Panics, and the Woodstock Festival." *New York History* 91.3 (Summer 2010): 221–244. JSTOR. Web. 4 June 2014.

Hewitt, Kenneth. "Place Annihilation: Area Bombing and the Fate of Urban Places." *Annals of the Association of American Geographers* 73.2 (June 1983): 257–284. Print.

Heyman, Stephen. "Wild About Harry." *New York Times Magazine* (Fall 2010): 50. Print.

Hickman, Roger. *Reel Music: Exploring 100 Years of Film Music*. New York: Norton, 2006. Print.

Hilzik, Michael. "'Deep Throat' Numbers Just Don't Add Up." *The Los Angeles Times*, n.p. 24 February 2005. Web. January 7, 2014.

Holson, Laura M. "The Long View on 'Deep Throat.'" *The New York Times*, 5 September 2004. Web. March 8, 2014.

Hopkins, Jerry, Jim Marshall, and Baron Wolman. *Festival! The Book of American Music Celebrations*. New York: Macmillan, 1970. Print.

Hotchner, A.E. *Blown Away: The Rolling Stones and the Death of the Sixties*. New York: Simon and Schuster, 1990. Print.

Howe, Desson. "'Midnight Cowboy' Rides Again." *The Washington Post*, 15 April 1994: D6. Print.

Howell, Peter. "Truth Was Just a Shout Away." *The Toronto Star*, 8 December 2006: E01. Print.

Höyng, Peter. "Ambiguities of Violence in Beethoven's Ninth through the Eyes of Stanley Kubrick's *A Clockwork Orange*." *The German Quarterly* 84.2 (Spring 2011): 159–176. Print.

Hubbert, Julie. "'Whatever Happened to Great Movie Music?': Cinema Verite and Hollywood Film Music of the Early 1970s." *American Music* 21.2 (Summer 2003): 180–213. JSTOR. Web. 24 February 2014.

Hughes, Robert. "The Décor of Tomorrow's Hell." *Perspectives on Stanley Kubrick*. Ed. Mario Falsetto. New York: Hall, 1996: 185–186. Print.

Huhn, Mary, and Maxine Shen. "They've Got It Covered: The 100 Best Cover Songs of All Time." *New York Post*, 18 July 2007. Web. 15 February 2013.

"Interview: Johnny Mandel (Part 1)." JazzWax. N.p. 20 October 2008. Web. 29 May 2013.

"Interview: Johnny Mandel (Part 2)." JazzWax. N.p. 21 October 2008. Web. 29 May 2013.

"Interview: Johnny Mandel (Part 3)." JazzWax. N.p. 22 October 2008. Web. 29 May 2013.

"Interview: Johnny Mandel (Part 5)." JazzWax. N.p. 24 October 2008. Web. 29 May 2013.

Islam, Yusuf. "Interview." *Harold and Maude: The Criterion Collection*. Dir. Hal Ashby.

Issitt, Micah L. *Hippies: A Guide to an American Subculture*. Santa Barbara, CA: Greenwood Press, 2009. Print.

Jackson, Blair. "Wendy Carlos' 'March from "A Clockwork Orange."'" *Mix* 26.5 (April 2002): 144. Print.

Jacobs, Diane. *Hollywood Renaissance*. New York: Delta, 1980. Print.

Johnson, William. "*M*A*S*H*." *Film Quarterly* 23.3 (Spring 1970): 38–41. Print.

Jordaan Mason. "Re: Harold and Maude Sountrack [sic] No Where [sic] to Be Found." *MUBI*. N.d. Web. 30 November 2012.

Kael, Pauline. "The Current Cinema: Beyond Pirandello." *The New Yorker*, 19 December 1970. 112. Print.

Keech, Andrew. "Barbarella" Liner Notes. *Barbarella: Original Soundtrack Recording*. Sound Track Classics, 2004. Print.

Kelman, Steven. *Natural Enemies: Youth and the Clash of Generations*. Ed. Alexander Klein. Philadelphia: Lippincott, 1969. 36–40. Print.

Kitts, Thomas M. "Documenting, Creating, and Interpreting Moments of Definition: *Monterey Pop*, *Woodstock*, and *Gimme Shelter*." *The Journal of Popular Culture* 42.4 (August 2009): 715–732. Print.

Kiuchi, Yuya. *Struggles for Equal Voice: The History of African American Media Democracy*. Albany, NY: SUNY Press, 2012.

Klein, Alexander. *Natural Enemies: Youth and the Clash of Generations*. Philadelphia: Lippincott, 1969. Print.

Kornbluth, Jesse. "Where Will 'Easy Rider' End Up?" *The New York Times*, 25 October 1970. ProQuest. Web. 5 June 2014.

Kubernik, Harvey, and Kenneth Kubernik. *A Perfect Haze: The Illustrated History of the Monterey Pop Festival*. Solana Beach, CA: Santa Monica Press, 2011. Print.

Lacher, Irene. "The Sunday Conversation: Lou Adler on Monterey Pop." *Los Angeles Times*, 10 June 2012. Web. 24 April 2013.

Lapedis, Hilary. "Popping the Question: The Function and Effect of Popular Music in Cinema." *Popular Music* 18.3 (Oct. 1999): 367–379. Print.

Larsen, Peter. *Film Music*. London, Reaktion Books, 2005. Print.

Lee, Martin A., and Bruce Shlain. *Acid Dreams: The Complete Social History of LSD: The CIA, the Sixties, and Beyond*. New York: Grove Press, 1992. Print.

Lefcowitz, Eric. *Monkee Business: The Revolutionary Made-for-TV Band*. Port Washington, NY: Retrofuture, 2011. Print.

———. *The Monkees Tale*. Berkely, CA: Last Gasp, 1985. Print.

"Legendary Soul Singer Isaac Hayes Passes." *The Sacramento Observer*, 1 August 2008. ProQuest. Web. 28 July 2014.

Legge, Charles. "Making of a *MASH* Hit." *Daily Mail*, 24 November 2011: 68. *Regional Business News*. Web. 31 May 2013.

Leonard, Tom. "Abused by the Porn Industry and Her Feminist Saviours: How *Deep Throat* Star Linda Lovelace's Tragic Life Was a Very Modern Morality Tale." *Daily Mail*, 26 March 2012. Web. January 24, 2014.

Lewis, Grover. "Day of the Angels: Let It Bleed!" blogs.villagevoice.com. The Village Voice. 23 August. 2010 (Originally published in print 11 December 1969). Web. 7 January 2013.

"Liner Notes." *Gas-s-s-s: Music from the Soundtrack*. (Rerelease). Reel Time, n.d. CD.

MacDonald, Ian. *Revolution in the Head: The Beatles' Records and the Sixties*. New York: Holt, 1994. Print.

Macquarrie, J.W. "The Teenager: A By-Product of Industrialism." *Theoria* 31 (1968): 15–25. Print.

Mamber, Stephen. "*A Clockwork Orange.*" *Perspectives on Stanley Kubrick*. Ed. Mario Falsetto. New York: Hall, 1996: 171–186. Print.

Marcus, Greil. *Woodstock*. San Francisco. Straight Arrow Publishers, 1969.

Market, John. "Sing a Song of Drug Use-Abuse: Four Decades of Drug Lyrics in Popular Music from the Sixties through the Nineties." *Sociological Inquiry* 71.2 (April 2001): 194–220. ProQuest. Web. 30 May 2014.

"MASH." IMDb.com. n.d. Web. 19 May 2013.

Maslin, Janet. "The Sad Tale of a Hustler Is Reissued." *The New York Times*, 20 February 1994. Print.

McLeland, Susan. "Barbarella Goes Radical: Hanoi Jane and the American Popular Press." *Headline Hollywood: A Century of Film Scandal*. Eds. Adrienne L McLean and David A. Cook. New Brunswick, NJ: Rutgers University Press, 1995. Print.

McQuiston, Kate. "The Stanley Kubrick Experience: Music, Nuclear Bombs, Disorientation, and You." *Music, Sound and Filmmakers: Sonic Style in Cinema*. Ed. James Wierzbicki. New York: Routledge, 2012. 138–150. Print.

———. "Value, Violence, and Music Recognized: *A Clockwork Orange* as Musicology." *Stanley Kubrick: Essays on His Films and Legacy*. Ed. Gary D. Rhodes. Jefferson, NC: McFarland, 2008. 105–122. Print.

Medovoi, Leerom. "Mapping the Rebel Image: Postmodernism and the Masculinist Politics of Rock in the U.S.A." *Cultural Critique* 20 (Winter 1991-1992): 153–188. JSTOR. Web. 5 June 2014.

Millar, Lindsey. "To-Do List." *Arkansas Times*, 23 August 23 2007. ProQuest. Web. 14 March 2014.

Monterey Pop Promotional Materials. n.d. *Monterey Pop* Clippings File. Margaret Herrick Library. The Academy of Motion Picture Arts and Sciences.

"Monterey Pop." *Hollywood Reporter*, 25 November 2002. *Monterey Pop* Clippings File. Margaret Herrick Library. The Academy of Motion Picture Arts and Sciences.

"More Wrong Than Right." Time.com, 25 July 1969. Web. 22 August 2006.

Munroe, Dale. "'Pop' Offers 'Now' Music, Lacks Spirit." *LA Herald-Examiner*, 5 May 1969. *Monterey Pop* Clippings File. Margaret Herrick Library. The Academy of Motion Picture Arts and Sciences.

Murrells, Joseph. *The Book of Golden Discs*. London: Barries and Jenkis, 1978. Print.

Neal, Larry. "The Black Arts Movement." National Humanities Center Resource Tool Box. National Humanities Center. n.d. Web. 28 July 2014.

New York Magazine, 5 April 1971. *Gas-s-s-s* Clippings File. Margaret Herrick Library. The Academy of Motion Picture Arts and Sciences.

"Non-News Story of the Year Award." *Rolling Stone*, 1 February 1969: 18. Print.

Norman, Philip. *The Stones*. London: Sidgwick & Jackson, 1993. Print.

"Obituary of Robert Altman Director of

M*A*S*H, Short Cuts, the Player and Gosford Park." *The Daily Telegraph*, 22 November 2006: 25. Print.

"Obituary: Fred Neil." *Variety*, 383.10 (2001): 39. Print.

O'Neal, Sean. "R.I.P. Don Kirshner, Legendary Music Publisher and Host of Don Kirshner's Rock Concert." AVClub.com, 18 January 2011. Web. 12 April 2014.

"One Sheet: Sudden Impact Monterey Pop (1968)." *The Big Picture Magazine*, n.d. 22. Print.

Osterweil, Ara. "Ang Lee's Lonesome Cowboys." *Film Quarterly* 60.3 (2007): 38–42. Print.

Pasley, Dan. "'Pop' Goes Rockumentary." *Boston After Dark*, 30 April 1969. Monterey Pop Clippings File. Margaret Herrick Library. The Academy of Motion Picture Arts and Sciences.

Patterson, Tony. "Harold and Maude." Ew.com, 20 May 2003. Web. 12 October 2010.

Pezzotta, Elisa. *Stanley Kubrick: Adapting the Sublime*. Jackson: University Press of Mississippi, 2013: Print.

"PFA at the BAM." *Pacific Film Archive*. 31 Aug. 2000. Gas-s-s-s Clippings File. Margaret Herrick Library. The Academy of Motion Picture Arts and Sciences.

Phillips, Paul. *A Clockwork Counterpoint: The Music and Literature of Anthony Burgess*. New York: Manchester University Press, 2010. Print.

Planer, Lindsay. "The Monkees-Head Review." Allmusic.com, n.d. Web. 14 Feb. 2013.

Planka, Sabine. "Erotic, Silent, Dead: The Concept of Women in the Films of Stanley Kubrick." *Film International* 58–59 (2012): 52–67. Print.

Polan, Dana. "The Early Films: *Killer's Kiss* to *Lolita*." *Perspectives on Stanley Kubrick*. Ed. Mario Falsetto. New York: Hall, 1996: 87–99. Print.

"Pop Music: The Most? Or Just a Mess?" *Saturday Evening Post*, 15 July 1967. Print.

Powrie, Phil, and Robynn Stilwell. "Introduction." *Changing Tunes: The Use of Preexisting Music in Film*. Ed. Phil Powrie and Robynn Stilwell. Burlington, VT: Ashgate, 2006.

Price, Brian, and Drake Stutesman. "Babette Mangolte Interview." *Framework* 45.1 (Spring 2004): 34–57. JSTOR. Web. 24 February 2014.

Quigley, David. *Second Founding: New York City, Reconstruction, and the Making of American Democracy*. New York: Hill and Wang, 2004. Print.

Quigley, Rachel. "Win Tickets to See an Ageless Classic Movie." *Belfast Telegraph*, 2 September 2009: 12. LexisNexis. Web. 3 November 2009.

Ramaeker, Paul B. "'You Think They Call Us Plastic Now...': The Monkees and *Head*." *Soundtrack Available: Essays on Film and Popular Music*. Eds. Pamela Robertson Wojcik and Arther Knight. Durham, NC: Duke University Press, 2001. 74–102. Print.

Rasmussen, Randy. *Stanley Kubrick: Seven Films Analyzed*. Jefferson, NC: McFarland, 2001. Print.

Reay, Barry. "Promiscuous Intimacies: Rethinking the History of American Casual Sex." *Journal of Historical Sociology* 27.1 (March 2014): 1–24. ProQuest. Web. 2 June 2014.

Reiss, Ira L., and Albert Ellis. "Sexual Promiscuity in America." *Annals of the American Academy of Political and Social Science* 378 (1968): 58–67. Print.

"Reviews of New R&B Records," *The Billboard* 68 (24 November 1956): 48. Web. 22 February 2014.

Reyes, Damaso. "'Easy Rider' Roars Back into Theaters." *New York Amsterdam News*, 30 April–6 May 2009: 18. ProQuest. Web. 14 March 2014.

Rice, Julian. *Kubrick's Hope: Discovering Optimism from 2001 to Eyes Wide Shut*. Lanham, MD: Scarecrow Press, 2008. Print.

Riley, Michael M. "I Both Hate and Love What I Do: An Interview with John Schlesinger." *Literature/Film Quarterly* 6.2 (Spring 1978): 104–115. Print.

Rima, Ralff. "The Hum: Woodstock Icon Country Joe McDonald Remains Part of a Generation's Moral Conscience." *Taos News*, 4 June 2009: TE-16–1. Print.

Robe. "Gas-s-s-s." *Variety*, 24 Aug. 1970. Gas-s-s-s Clippings File. Margaret Herrick Library. The Academy of Motion Picture Arts and Sciences.

Robey, Tim. "The Look That Shook the Nation: Forty Years on, Stanley Kubrick's 'A Clockwork Orange' Still Has the Power to Shock, Says Tim Robey." *The Daily Telegraph*, 27 December 2011: 22. Print.

Robinson, John P., Robert Pilskaln, and Paul Hirsch. "Protest Rock and Drugs." *Journal of Communication* 26.4 (October 1976): 125–136. ProQuest. Web. 30 May 2014.

Rodman, Ronald. "The Popular Song as Leitmotif in 1990s Film." *Changing Tunes: The Use of Pre-existing Music in Film*. Ed. Phil Powrie and Robynn Stilwell. Burlington, VT: Ashgate, 2006. 119–136. Print.

Rothstein, Edward. "Connections: Kubrick and Beethoven, a Marriage Made in Hell." *The New York Times*, 15 March 1999. Web. September 15. 2013.

Russell, Ethan A., and Gerard Van der Leun. *Let It Bleed: The Rolling Stones, Altamont, and the End of the Sixties*. New York: Springboard Press, 2009. Print.

Russell, Tony. "Mickey Baker Obituary: Versatile American Guitarist Who Had a Million-Selling Hit with Love Is Strange." *The Guardian*, 2 December 2012. Web. 27 February 2014.

Savage, John. *Teenage: The Creation of Youth Culture*. New York: Viking, 2007. Print.

Schafer, William J. "Beyond Bubblegum: Randy Newman and Harry Nilsson." *American Quarterly* 22.3 (Autumn 1970): 742–760. Print.

Scharres, Barbara. "From Out of the Blue: The Return of Dennis Hopper." *Journal of University Film and Video Application* 35.2 (Spring 1983): 25–33. JSTOR. Web. 4 June 2014.

Schickel, Richard. "When Cinema Shouldn't Be Verite." *Life*, 7 February 1969. *Monterey Pop* Clippings File. Margaret Herrick Library. The Academy of Motion Picture Arts and Sciences.

Schiller Institute. "An Early Setting of Schiller's 'Ode to Joy.'" The Schiller Institute. 2005. Web. 22 February 2014.

Segal, Dave. "Start Your Sobbin': Let's Tear It for the Sad Songs That Get Us Through Tough Times." *The Stranger*, 4 December 2008: 31. Print.

Self, Robert T. "The Sounds of *MASH*." *Close Viewings: An Anthology of New Film Criticism*. Ed. Peter Lehman. Tallahassee: Florida State University Press, 1990. 141–157. Print.

Shumway, David R. "Rock 'n' Roll Sound Tracks and the Production of Nostalgia." *Cinema Journal* 38.2 (Winter 1999): 36–51. JSTOR. Web. 24 February 2014.

Sinclair, Craig. "Audition: Making Sense of/in the Cinema." *The Velvet Light Trap* 51 (2003): 17–28. Print.

"Soundtrack Hits Million $ Mark." *Sacramento Observer*, 2 September 1971: D2. ProQuest. Web. 9 June 2014.

Special Correspondent. "Bethel Pilgrims Smoke 'Grass' and Some Take LSD to 'Groove.'" *New York Times*, 18 August 1969. Print.

Spock, Benjamin. "Rebellion in Adolescence." *Natural Enemies: Youth and the Clash of Generations*. Ed. Alexander Klein. Philadelphia: Lippincott, 1969. 301–307. Print.

Stafford, Jeff. "Head (1968)." Tcm.com, n.d. Web. 14 February 2012.

Stahl, Matthew. "Authentic Boy Bands on TV? Performers and Impresarios in *The Monkees* and *Making the Band*." *Popular Music* 21.3 (2002): 307–329.

"Stanley Kubrick's *A Clockwork Orange*." *Culture Shock*. PBS. n.d. Web. 19 August 2013.

Steinhorn, Leonard. *The Greater Generation: In Defense of the Baby Boom Legacy*. New York: St. Martin's Press, 2006. Print.

"Sylvia Robinson, 75, 'Mother of Hip-Hop.'" *The Philadelphia Tribune*, n.p. 30 September 2011. Web. 27 February 2014.

Taylor, Phillip. "First Amendment Rocks Memphis." *First Amendment*, n.p. 15 October 1999. Web. 30 May 2014.

Taylor, Timothy. *Strange Sounds: Music, Technology, & Culture*. New York: Routledge, 2001. Print.

"Thanksgiving Turkeys: Two of the Worst Films of All Times!" *Gas-s-s-s* Clippings File. Margaret Herrick Library. The Academy of Motion Picture Arts and Sciences.

Thompson, Dave. *Hearts of Darkness: James Taylor, Jackson Browne, Cat Stevens, and the Unlikely Rise of the Singer-Songwriter*. Milwaukee: Backbeat Books, 2012. Print.

Thompson, Hunter S. *Fear and Loathing in Las Vegas: A Savage Journey to the Heart of the American Dream*. New York: Random House, 1998. Print.

"Three Films Ahead of Their Times." *USA Today*, 23 February 2010: 7B. Print.

Thurman, Chuck. "Paradise Regained." Montereycountyweekly.com, 14 June 2001. Web. 13 May 2013.

Tincknell, Estella. "The Soundtrack Movie, Nostalgia and Consumption." *Film's Musical Moments*. Eds. Ian Conrich, and Estella

Tincknell. Edinburgh: Edinburgh University Press, 2006: 132–145. Print.

Tolzmann, Don Heinrich. "John Kay & Steppenwolf: A German-American Success Story." *German Life* 13.5 (February-March 2007): 10–11. Web. 21 May 2014.

Turan, Kenneth, and Stephen F. Zito. *Sinema: American Pornographic Films and the People Who Make Them*. New York: Praeger, 1974.

Unterberger, Richie. "Bob Crewe Biography." Allmusic.com, 3 March 2008.

_____. *Turn! Turn! Turn!: The '60s Folk-Rock Revolution*. San Francisco: Backbeat Books, 2002.

Variety Staff. "Barbarella." Variety.com, 1 January 1968. Web. 19 September 2007.

Vogels, Jonathan B. *The Direct Cinema of David and Albert Maysles*. Carbondale: Southern Illinois University Press, 2005. Print.

Vognar, Chris. "Time to Get Real, Man, About Summer of Love." *Dallas Morning News*, 5 August 2007: n. p. Ebscohost. Web. 26 September 2013.

Walker, Alexander. "The Wining Road to Clockwork Orange." *The Evening Standard*, 1 March 2000: 32. Print.

Warhol, Andy, and Pat Hackett. *POPism: The Warhol 1960s*. New York: Harcourt Brace Jovanovich, 1980. Print.

Weber, Bruce. "Joel J. Tyler, Judge Who Pronounced 'Deep Throat' Obscene, Dies at 90." *The New York Times*, 12 January 2012. Web. 24 January 2014.

_____. "Mickey Baker, Guitarist, Is Dead at 87." *The New York Times*, 29 November 2012. Web. 27 February 2014.

"We Have the Harold and Maude Soundtrack LP." Lightintheattic.net. 22 January 2008. Web. 30 September 2010.

Wesson, Donald R. "Psychedelic Drugs, Hippie Counterculture, Speed and Phenobarbital Treatment of Sedative-hypnotic Dependence: A Journey to the Haight Ashbury in the Sixties." *Journal of Psychoactive Drugs* 43.2 (April-June 2011): 153–164. PubMed.gov, Web. 30 May 2014.

Whiteley, Sheila. The *Space Between the Notes*. New York: Routledge, 1992. Print.

Wierzbicki, James. *Film Music: A History*. New York: Taylor & Francis, 2009. Print.

_____, Nathan Platte, and Colin Roust. *The Routledge Film Music Sourcebook*. New York: Routledge, 2012. Print.

World Health Organization. "Annex Table 2: Deaths by Cause, Sex and Mortality Stratum in WHO Regions, Estimates for 2002." *The World Health Report 2004*. World Health Organization. 1 November 2008. Web. 31 May 2013.

Young, Michael E. "Peter Fonda Auctioning Off His 'Easy Rider' Memorabilia." *Chicago Tribune*, 26 September 2007. ProQuest. Web. 21 May 2014.

Index

Academy Award 72, 83, 111, 116, 134, 137, 143, 146; *see also* Academy of Motion Picture Arts and Sciences
Academy of Motion Picture Arts and Sciences 51, 111, 112; *see also* Academy Award
Adler, Lou 9–12, 14–15, 17–18
adolescence 14, 80, 97; *see also* teenager; youth
African American 5, 98, 107–117
AIDS 62
Akatsuki, Teruko 91–93
alcohol 22, 25, 40, 89, 98
Alice's Restaurant 50
Altamont 11, 18, 20–29, 30–33
Altman, Michael 86–94 passim
Altman, Robert 83–94 passim
anti-war movement 44, 77, 84, 88, 90, 167, 190
Arabian Nights see *One Thousand and One Nights*
Armitage, George 104, 175
"As We Go Along" 42
Ashby, Hal 47–53, 55
Atkins, Chet 36

baby-boom 10, 13, 20, 37, 51, 96–98, 102, 106, 166, 182
bachelor 58–70 passim
Balin, Marty 30
Barbarella 3, 58–70
Barger, Sonny 25
Barry, John 134, 138–139
BB King 26
The Beatles 35–36, 40
Beethoven, Ludwig van 5–6, 79, 122–123, 126, 131, 145, 147, 151–152, 155–159, 163–165
Belli, Melvin 24
Berry, Chuck 26
Big Brother and the Holding Company 11, 15, 36, 39
"Big Girls Don't Cry" 59
biker 22–23, 28, 30, 72

Black Panthers 12
Black Power 111–113, 116
Blackboard Jungle 97
blaxploitation 109, 112–114, 116
Bleecker and MacDougal 135
The Bob Crewe Generation 59
Bogdanovich, Peter 95, 100
Bond, James 79, 121–123, 126, 131, 134
"Born to Be Wild" 76, 78, 79
Boyce, Tommy 36
Britain 12, 26, 35, 146, 148
Brown, Jim 110
Brown, Nacio Herb 154
A Bucket of Blood 100
Buckley, Tim 39
Burgess, Anthony 145, 162
"By the Time I Get to Phoenix" 109
The Byrds 73, 75–76, 81

"Can You Dig It" 42
Carlos, Walter see Carlos, Wendy
Carlos, Wendy 145, 147, 155, 161–165
Chicago Renaissance 108
cinéma vérité 26–27
"Circle Sky" 42
civil rights 5, 109, 111–113
classical music 6, 79, 145, 148–149, 153, 161, 163–165
A Clockwork Orange 6, 79, 122, 123, 145–165
"Combination of the Two" 11
conservatism 72, 102, 137–139, 141–142, 144
Coppola, Francis Ford 95, 99
Corff, Robert 95, 101–102, 177
Corman, Roger 95, 99–103, 105, 175–176
Corri, Adrienne 146–147, 152
Cosby, Bill 114
Country Joe and the Fish 36, 95, 101–104, 166–167, 169, 175, 177, 178
Country Joe McDonald 6, 101, 104, 105, 166
Crawdaddy 36, 39
"Creeque Alley" 12
Crewe, Bob 59
Crowe, Cameron 55

203

Damiano, Gerard 118, 121, 131–132
Dark Side of the Moon 65
Dean, James 171
Deep Throat 5, 79, 118–132, 142
Destiny's Child 117
Diamond, Neil 36
DiFranco, Ani 186
Disney 74, 128–129
"Ditty Diego Chant" 41
Dr. Dre 117
Dolenz, Micky 36, 38–42, 44
"Don't Be Shy" 49, 53, 55
"Don't Chase Me Around" 102
Don't Look Back 26
drug 3, 5, 22–32 passim, 37–47 passim, 62–63, 71–78 passim, 91, 98, 159, 163, 171, 174–175
Dylan, Bob 36, 81
dystopia 6, 9, 27, 145, 148

Earle, Steve 183–184, 186
Easy Rider 4, 48, 71–82, 136, 178
Edmonton, Jerry 76
Eigen, Erika 153–154
Electric Music for the Mind and Body 166
Elephant's Memory 135, 137
Elgar, Edward 148, 152–153
Elkind, Rachel 145, 147, 162–163
"Ellie's Love Theme" 111
Escape from New York 110
Everybody's Talkin' 136
"Everybody's Talkin'" 5, 133, 135–136, 138
Eyes Wide Shut 146

Family Guy 87, 118
Fear and Loathing in Las Vegas 7, 22, 182
Federal Bureau of Investigation 118
feminism 66, 119
Firesign Theater 175–176
Flying Burrito Brothers 30
Fonda, Jane 63, 65–66
Fonda, Peter 71–72, 80–81, 95
Forest, Jean-Claude 59
Fox, Charles 59
Frankie Valli and the Four Seasons 59
Fred Neil 136
Freed, Arthur 154
Freeman, Joel 107
Full Metal Jacket 145–146

gangs 23, 39, 108, 112, 135, 147, 149–151, 154–157, 160
Garcia, Jerry 30
Gas-s-s-s 4–6, 95–102, 104–106, 167, 175–177
Gast, John 134
Gaudio, Bob 59
gender 2, 4, 77
Gerard, Jerry *see* Damiano, Gerard
Giftos, Elaine 95, 101
Gilliam, Terry 136

Gimme Shelter 2, 3, 8, 9, 18, 20–33 passim
Gitlin, Todd 32
Goffin, Gerry 36, 40
"Goin' Up to the Country" 27
Goldberg, Danny 184, 186
Golden Globe 83, 111, 134, 182
"Got to Get Movin'" 102
Gould, Elliott 83
The Graduate 177–178
Graham, Bill 14
Grammy Award 84, 111, 134–136, 161–162
The Grateful Dead 14–15, 28, 30, 36, 77, 101
Greenwald, Robert 6, 36, 182–189

The Haight-Ashbury 14, 168
"Hail to the Chief" 90
Hamburger Hill 167–168
A Hard Day's Night 35, 37, 44
Harlihy, James Leo 133
Harold and Maude 2–3, 47–57, 178
Hart, Bobby 36
Hayes, Isaac 5, 107–117
Head 3, 34–35, 40, 42–46
Headquarters 39
heavy metal 4, 76–78, 171
Hellman, Jerome 133
Hell's Angels 11–12, 20
Help 37
Hendrix, Jimi 11–12, 39, 73, 75–76, 170, 178, 180, 186
heteronormativity 133, 141
Higgins, Colin 48
Hoffman, Abbie 182, 185
Hoffman, Dustin 133
Hogue, Freya 153
homosexuality 89, 137–143
Hooker, Richard 83
Hopper, Dennis 8, 71, 72, 74, 80, 95
Hot Buttered Soul 109

"I Feel Like I'm Fixin' to Die Rag" 166–167
"I Guess the Lord Must Be in New York City" 136
"I Love All of the Love in You" 66
"I Want to Marry a Lighthouse Keeper" 153
"I'd Like to Teach You All to Screw" 130
"If 6 Was 9" 76
"If You Want to Sing Out, Sing Out" 49, 50–55, 57
I'm Gonna Git You Sucka 110
Islam, Yusuf 48–49, 51, 53, 55, 56

Jackson, Samuel L. 107
Jagger, Mick 20–32 passim
Jefferson Airplane 30, 36, 77
The Jimi Hendrix Experience 11
Joplin, Janis 12, 77, 179
Joy of Cooking 95, 102
"Jungle Gym at the Zoo" 135

Karlin, Miriam 146
Karpen, Julius 15
Kay, John 76–78
Kelly, Gene 145, 154
Kennedy, John F. 7, 22, 98
Kent State University 98
Kerouac, Jack 75
King, Carol 36
King, Martin Luther, Jr. 111
Kinsey, Alfred 137
Kirshner, Don 36, 38–39
Klean, Evyen 183
Korean War 4, 83–84, 88, 91–93
Kubrick, Stanley 145–165 passim

Lanzarone, Ben 59
Lardner, Ring 83
Leacock, Richard 17
Leary, Tomothy 3, 39, 43
Leone, Sergio 150
Lesh, Phil 30
"A Little Bit Me, a Little Bit You" 39
"Love Is Strange" 125, 127, 130
"Love, Love, Love Drags Me Down" 66
Lovelace, Linda 118–126 passim
LSD 18, 23, 37, 43–44, 62, 68, 77, 164; see also drug

Magee, Patrick 146
"Magic Carpet Ride" 76
Magne, Michel 59
The Mamas and the Papas 9, 11–12
Mandel, Johnny 84–88, 92
Manifest Destiny 134–145, 141, 143
marijuana 11, 25, 37, 40, 77, 80, 173
Martin, Vince 135
masculinity 61, 114, 138, 140–141, 150–151, 160
M*A*S*H 4, 83–94 passim, 128
The Mattachine Society 140
Mayfield, Curtin 116
McDaniel, Hattie 111, 116
McDowell, Malcolm 146
McJohn, Goldy 76
McKenzie, Scott 9, 11, 15
McLuhan, Marshall 98, 102
The Meese Commission 119
melodrama 141–142, 144, 179
Melton, Barry 95, 101–102, 105, 175, 177
mescaline 23, 25, 37
MGM movie studio 107–108
Miami 133, 136, 141
Mickey & Sylvia 125
Midnight Cowboy 5, 75, 133–144 passim
"Minami no Koiuta" 92
"Modern Don Juan" 135
Mona Bone Jakon 48, 55
Monarch, Michael 76
Monck, Chip 25, 27
Monkees 3, 34–46

Monterey Pop 2–3, 7–19 passim, 22, 25–26, 30, 39, 166–179 passim
Monterey Purple 17–18
moral panic 96–98, 100, 105, 113, 132, 140–141, 146
More American Graffiti 167
Moreve, Rushton 76
Morrison, Jim 77
"Move Over" 76
"Music for the Funeral of Queen Mary" 148, 161, 163
"Music to Watch Girls By" 59, 69
"My Blue Heaven" 92–93
My Fair Lady 146

Napoleon 158
Neil, Fred 135–136
Nelson, Wendy 149
Nesmith, Michael 35–36, 38, 40, 42–43
New Hollywood 1, 47–48, 52, 57, 95, 99
Newport Folk Festival 16
Nicholson, Jack 40, 43, 45, 71–72, 95
Nilsson, Harry 5, 40, 133–136, 139, 142, 143
Nixon, Richard 84, 138, 173
nostalgia 74, 80, 117, 135, 189

Ochs, Phil 36
Once Upon a Time in America 150
One Flew Over the Cuckoo's Nest 22
One Thousand and One Nights 152
orgy 124, 151, 158, 160
Oscar 5, 83–84, 111, 133, 137, 139; see also Academy Award
"The Other Side of This Life" 30, 135
"Overture of the Sun" 153

Pariser, Alan 9
Parks, Gordon 107–112, 115
Peebles, Melvin Van 113
Pennebaker, Donn Alan 10, 11, 13–17, 26, 166, 168
Peraino, Louis 118
Perry, Lou *see* Peraino, Louis
Phillips, John 9, 10, 14
Pitts, Charles Skip 110
Playboy 60–61, 70, 87, 89, 137, 161
Poitier, Sidney 111–112, 114, 116
"Pomp and Circumstance" 152–153
porn groove 121, 127, 129, 131
pornography 5, 118–132 passim
"Porpoise Song" 41
Preminger, Ingo 83
Presley, Elvis 171
psychedelic 3–4, 15, 37, 41, 43–44, 58–69 passim, 77, 105, 148, 153, 161, 165, 166, 169
Purcell, Henry 148–149, 161, 163
Purple Haze 167
"The Pusher" 76–78
Pussy Riot 170

R&B 111, 117, 125
race 2, 5, 13, 98, 109, 111–114, 116, 117, 190
racism *see* race
Rafelson, Bob 35, 40, 43, 45
Rebel Without a Cause 97
rebellion 2, 3, 5, 10, 12, 22, 28–31, 34, 37, 39, 45, 47, 96–106, 112, 183
Redding, Otis 11, 13
Reems, Harry 118, 124
Reid, Terry 26
Richard, Keith 27, 31
Rimsky-Korsakov, Nikolai 148, 152
"Rock Me" 76
rock music 5, 12–18 passim, 21, 29, 32, 35–36, 38, 47, 51, 71–81 passim, 97–98, 102–103, 127, 148, 167, 170, 177–180
Rolling Stone 10, 23, 36, 45
Rolling Stones 20–21, 28–30, 32
Rosenbach, Mel 85
Ross, Benjamin 163
Rossini 148–151, 153, 158, 163, 164
Roundtree, Richard 107, 109–110, 112, 114

St. Jacques, Raymond 110
"San Francisco: Be Sure to Wear Flowers in Your Hair" 9, 11, 15
satire 40, 84, 89–90
Scheherazade 152
Schiller 122, 159, 165
Schlesinger, John 133–138, 140–141, 143–144
Schneider, Bert 35, 38–40, 42
Schneider, Ronald 27, 45
"The Sea and Sinbad's Ship" 152
Sears Point 24
"Section 43" 168
sex 2–5, 28–30, 47–48, 58–70, 77, 83, 89–93, 112–118 passim, 120–132 passim, 133, 137–143, 146, 149, 151, 157, 161, 175, 190
Shaft 5, 107–117
Shankar, Ravi 170
Shapiro, Ben 9
Sharp, Dolly 8, 118, 122
"She Hangs Out" 39
"Sherry" 59
The Shining 145
Simon & Garfunkel 12, 177
Singin' in the Rain 145
"Singin' in the Rain" 146–147, 154–155, 159
Singleton, John 117
"Six Days on the Road" 30
"Ski Ride" 66
Slick, Grace 30
Snoop Dog 117
"Soulsville" 111
Sound of Sunforest 153
South Korea 83, 88, 91–93
South Park 116
Southern, Terry 71–72
Spinal Tap 182
Stanley, Augustus Owsley 17–18

Steal This Movie 167, 182–183
Steppenwolf 2, 73, 76–81
Stevens, Cat 2–3, 48–56, 178
The Stones 25–26, 28–31
"The Story of the Kalandar Prince" 152
"Street Fighting Man" 29
The Street Racers 23
"Suicide Is Painless" 4, 86–93
Summer of Love 8–9, 11, 13–14, 17
Sunforest 148–149, 153, 164
Super Fly 113
Sutherland, Donald 83
Sweet Sweetback's Baadasssss Song 113
"Sweetback's Theme" 114
synthesizer 145, 147–148, 161–162, 164–165

Taylor, Mick 27
Taylor, Sam 163
Tea for the Tillerman 48, 55
Tear Down the Walls 135
technology 60–62, 68–69, 145, 148, 153, 161, 165, 167, 174, 191
Teenage Doll 100
teenager 35, 44, 86–87, 96–97, 99–100, 103; *see also* adolescence; youth
television 1, 10, 16, 34–41, 44, 46, 59, 83, 86–87, 98–99, 113, 118, 130, 167–179 passim
"Theme from *Shaft*" 109–111, 114–115, 117
"The Thieving Magpie" 149, 150–151, 153, 157, 160
"This Is the Beginning" 102
Three Tough Guys 110
Time Flies By 167
"Timesteps" 162–163
Tokyo 83, 92
"Tokyo Shoe Shine Boy" 91–93
Tork, Peter 36, 38–40, 45
Townshend, Pete 12, 14
The Trip 95, 100, 105
Truck Turner 110
Tucker, Terry 153, 164
Turner, Tina 26
2001: A Space Odyssey 145, 148

utopia 2, 5, 7–16, 19, 20, 23, 26–27, 30, 33, 51, 66, 102–103, 152

Vadim, Roger 65
Vandor, David 119
Venice Film Festival 146
Vietnam 41–42, 44, 72, 77, 84, 88, 90–91, 93–94, 98, 167
Vietnam War *see* Vietnam; war
violence 6, 11–12, 20–32 passim, 40, 72–73, 98, 101, 115, 135, 137, 141–142, 146–165 passim
Voight, John 133

Wadleigh, Mike 180
"Walk Like a Man" 59

"Walk On By" 109
War 3, 4; culture war 14, 42, 44, 58, 60–62, 67, 71, 80, 84, 88–94, 96–98, 100, 103, 105, 108, 140, 167, 186; *see also* anti-war movement; Korean War; Vietnam
Warner Brothers 146
"Wasn't Born to Follow" 76
Watts, Charlie 25, 28
"Where Do the Children Play?" 53
The Wild Angels 95, 101
Wild in the Streets 105
"William Tell Overture" 151–152
Williams, Cindy 95, 102
The Wizard of Oz 65
Woodstock 2, 8–9, 16–18, 22–32 passim, 166–167, 172–173, 177, 179

Woodstock Festival 2–3, 6, 8–13, 16–19, 23–32 passim, 80, 101–102, 167–179 passim, 190
"World That We All Dreamed Of" 101, 103
Wyman, Rill 26

Young, Terence 122–123
The Young Poisoner's Handbook 163
youth 5, 22, 38, 62, 75, 80, 96–106, 116, 125, 155–156, 170, 175; *see also* adolescence; teenager
Yusuf Islam *see* Stevens, Cat

Zabriskie Point 50
Zachariah 175–177
Zappa, Frank 39

www.ingramcontent.com/pod-product-compliance
Ingram Content Group UK Ltd.
Pitfield, Milton Keynes, MK11 3LW, UK
UKHW042001140426
5217IPUK00015B/920